THE STRANGE HISTORY OF SAMUEL PEPYS'S DIARY

During the 1660s, Samuel Pepys kept a secret diary full of intimate details and political scandal. Had the contents been revealed, they could have destroyed his marriage, ended his career, and seen him arrested. This engaging book explores the creation of the most famous journal in the English language, how it came to be published in 1825, and the many remarkable roles it has played in British culture since then. Kate Loveman – one of the few people who can read Pepys's shorthand – unlocks the riddles of the diary, investigating why he chose to preserve such private matters for later generations. She also casts fresh light on the women and sexual relationships in Pepys's life and on Black Britons living in or near his household. Exploring the many inventive uses to which the diary has been put, Loveman shows how Pepys's history became part of the history of the nation.

KATE LOVEMAN is Professor of Early Modern Literature and Culture at the University of Leicester and an internationally recognized expert on Pepys and Restoration literature. She is the author of *Reading Fictions, 1660–1740: Deception in English Literary and Political Culture*, *Samuel Pepys and his Books: Reading, Newsgathering, and Sociability, 1660–1703*, and the editor of *The Diary of Samuel Pepys* for Everyman.

THE STRANGE HISTORY
OF SAMUEL PEPYS'S DIARY

KATE LOVEMAN

Shaftesbury Road, Cambridge CB2 8EA, United Kingdom

One Liberty Plaza, 20th Floor, New York, NY 10006, USA

477 Williamstown Road, Port Melbourne, VIC 3207, Australia

314–321, 3rd Floor, Plot 3, Splendor Forum, Jasola District Centre,
New Delhi – 110025, India

103 Penang Road, #05–06/07, Visioncrest Commercial, Singapore 238467

Cambridge University Press is part of Cambridge University Press & Assessment,
a department of the University of Cambridge.

We share the University's mission to contribute to society through the pursuit of
education, learning and research at the highest international levels of excellence.

www.cambridge.org
Information on this title: www.cambridge.org/9781009554114

DOI: 10.1017/9781009554107

© Kate Loveman 2025

This publication is in copyright. Subject to statutory exception and to the provisions
of relevant collective licensing agreements, no reproduction of any part may take
place without the written permission of Cambridge University Press & Assessment.

When citing this work, please include a reference to the DOI 10.1017/9781009554107

First published 2025

Printed in the United Kingdom by CPI Group Ltd, Croydon CR0 4YY

A catalogue record for this publication is available from the British Library

A Cataloging-in-Publication data record for this book is available from the Library of Congress

ISBN 978-1-009-55411-4 Hardback

Cambridge University Press & Assessment has no responsibility for the persistence
or accuracy of URLs for external or third-party internet websites referred to in this
publication and does not guarantee that any content on such websites is, or will remain,
accurate or appropriate.

For my friends

Contents

List of Figures	page viii
Conventions	x
Chronology	xi
List of Abbreviations	xiii
Introduction	1
1 Writing the Diary	15
2 Shorthand and Secrecy	32
3 Saving the Diary	48
4 First Publication	64
5 Victorian Pepys	84
6 War and the Diary	108
7 'Every Last Obscenity': Complete and Online	131
8 Reading against the Grain	151
Afterword	177
Acknowledgements	184
Notes	186
Select Bibliography	223
Index	233

Figures

1.1	Samuel Pepys's diary volumes. PL 1836–41. By permission of the Pepys Library, Magdalene College, Cambridge.	page 22
2.1	'The places of the Vowels', from Thomas Shelton's *Tachygraphy* (London, 1660), detail from p. 4. Reproduced by kind permission of the Syndics of Cambridge University Library.	36
2.2	Diary of Samuel Pepys, 2 September 1666. PL 1839. By permission of the Pepys Library, Magdalene College, Cambridge.	38
2.3	Diary of Samuel Pepys, 23 April 1661. PL 1836. By permission of the Pepys Library, Magdalene College, Cambridge.	43
2.4	Diary of Samuel Pepys, 25 October 1668. PL 1841. By permission of the Pepys Library, Magdalene College, Cambridge.	45
3.1	Pepys's Library at 14 Buckingham Street, York Buildings, by Sutton Nicholls (c.1693), view facing away from the Thames. By permission of the Pepys Library, Magdalene College, Cambridge.	57
5.1	Samuel Pepys, by John Hayls (1666), oil on canvas. NPG 211 © National Portrait Gallery, London.	95
5.2	Pepys and Nell Gwynne, by Augustus Leopold Egg (1851), oil on canvas. 33½ x 43½ inches. Collection of the New Mexico Museum of Art. Gift of Lewis Gruber, 1962 (228.23P). Photo by Kevin Beltran.	96
5.3	Elizabeth, Wife of Samuel Pepys, Esq, by James Thomson (1825), after John Hayls (1666), detail, stipple engraving. Published in Braybrooke's *Memoirs of Samuel Pepys*, I. Reproduced by kind permission of the Syndics of Cambridge University Library.	97

5.4	The Wife's Portrait – Pepy's [*sic*] Diary, by Samuel S. Smith (1866), detail, after Alfred Elmore (1852), engraving. Photo by Kate Loveman.	98
5.5	'Comic Lives of the English Kings and Queens, no. 33, Charles II', *Boys of England*, 20, 6 October 1876, p. 304. General Research Division, The New York Public Library.	103
6.1	Johnnie Walker, Historical Spirit Series no. 14, *The Sphere*, vol. 91, 7 October 1922, p. i. Reproduced by kind permission of the Syndics of Cambridge University Library.	109
6.2	*Radio Times*, 28 February 1958. Courtesy of *Radio Times*.	126
8.1	Diary of Samuel Pepys, 5 and 6 April 1669. PL 1841. By permission of the Pepys Library, Magdalene College, Cambridge.	169
8.2	Diary of Samuel Pepys, 14 February 1661. PL 1836. By permission of the Pepys Library, Magdalene College, Cambridge.	171

Conventions

Diary text: The version of Pepys's diary most often quoted in this book is Robert Latham and William Matthews's complete transcription, which was first published between 1970 and 1983. This is the most reliable text of the diary in print. Except for a few cases (which are noted), I have used the Latham and Matthews edition that was published in 2000, as this incorporates some corrections. Where needed, I have added translations of Pepys's foreign languages in square brackets. The edition is referred to in my endnotes as 'LM Diary' (see the List of Abbreviations). It is cited by giving the volume number (in Roman numerals), followed by the page number, and the date of the entry.

In places, I have used my own transcriptions of Pepys's diary. Pepys mostly wrote it in shorthand. **Bold** text in these transcriptions means Pepys wrote the word in longhand. In the endnotes, these new transcriptions are cited in the format 'PL 1836, Diary, 1 Jan. 1660'. This is a reference to the shelf-mark of one of the six diary volumes in the Pepys Library (PL 1836 to PL 1841). Pepys did not add page numbers to his manuscript, so the date is the most accurate way of locating a passage.

Transcriptions: In my transcriptions from manuscripts, contractions are silently expanded. Superscripts are lowered. Thorn (y) is given as 'th'. The transcription of u/v and i/j follows modern usage. Angle-brackets < > signal additions by the source's writer. Square brackets are my additions.

Currency: Before British coinage was decimalized in 1971, one pound (often abbreviated as 1*l*) was worth twenty shillings (20*s*) and a shilling contained twelve pence (12*d*).

Dates: In seventeenth-century England, the new year officially began on 25 March (though there were celebrations on 1 January). In the dates in this book, days and months follow the 'Old Style' Julian calendar, but the year is taken as starting on 1 January.

Chronology

Events and Editions

1633	Samuel Pepys born 23 February.
1639	Start of the Wars of the Three Kingdoms. The next fourteen years see civil war in England, Scotland, and Ireland.
1649	Charles I is tried and executed at Westminster by the army-controlled parliament. Pepys is at the execution.
1651–4	Pepys attends Magdalene College, Cambridge.
1653–8	Oliver Cromwell rules as Protector. Pepys works as a government clerk in the later years of Cromwell's regime.
1655	Pepys marries Elizabeth St Michel.
1658	Pepys survives an operation for bladder stones.
1660	1 January, Pepys starts his diary.
	Restoration of Charles II. In May Pepys sails with the fleet to fetch Charles II from the Hague.
	June, Pepys becomes Clerk of the Acts to the Navy Board.
1661	23 April, Coronation of Charles II.
	24 April, hungover.
1665	22 February, start of the Second Anglo-Dutch War.
	Summer and autumn, the plague is rife in London.
1666	2–6 September, the Great Fire of London.
1667	10–13 June, Dutch attack on Chatham; invasion scare.
	31 July, Second Anglo-Dutch War ends.
1669	31 May, Pepys ends his diary due to failing eyesight.
	10 November, Elizabeth Pepys dies.
1673	Pepys appointed Secretary to the Admiralty.
1679	Arrested for treason, resigns his post as Secretary.
1684	Returns to office as King's Secretary for the Affairs of the Admiralty.
	Becomes President of the Royal Society.

1685	Charles II dies. James, duke of York becomes James II.
1688–9	'The Glorious Revolution': James II is forced from the throne; William and Mary are appointed joint monarchs by parliament.
1689	Pepys arrested for treasonous (Jacobite) plotting.
1690	Arrested again. Pepys has his *Memoires [...] of the Royal Navy of England* printed.
1703	26 May, Pepys dies. His library (with his diary) is left to his nephew John Jackson, along with instructions on its future.
1722	John Jackson dies.
1724	Ann Jackson donates Pepys's library to Magdalene College, Cambridge.
1825	First publication of the diary: *Memoirs of Samuel Pepys*, edited by Lord Braybrooke and transcribed by John Smith; a selection with correspondence.
1828	Second edition of the *Memoirs*, by Braybrooke.
1848–9	'Third' (and expanded) edition: *Diary and Correspondence of Samuel Pepys*, edited by Braybrooke.
1854	'Fourth' edition: *Diary and Correspondence of Samuel Pepys* (with new notes), edited by Braybrooke.
1875–9	Expanded text, *Diary and Correspondence of Samuel Pepys*, edited by Rev. Mynors Bright.
1893–9	*The Diary of Samuel Pepys*, edited by Henry B. Wheatley, publishes 'the whole of the Diary' except what 'cannot possibly be printed'.
1914–18	First World War.
1933	Tercentenary of Pepys's birth.
1939–45	Second World War.
1970–83	*The Diary of Samuel Pepys: A New and Complete Transcription*, edited by Robert Latham and William Matthews, prints what cannot possibly be printed.
2003	Tercentenary of Pepys's death. Pepysdiary.com begins publishing a diary entry daily online.

Abbreviations

Appendix Classica	*Catalogue of the Pepys Library at Magdalene College Cambridge, VII, Facsimile of Pepys's Catalogue, Part ii: 'Appendix Classica'*, ed. by David McKitterick (Cambridge: Brewer, 1991)
BL	British Library, London
Bodl.	Bodleian Libraries, University of Oxford
Braybrooke 1825	*Memoirs of Samuel Pepys, Esq. F.R.S., Secretary to the Admiralty in the Reigns of Charles II and James II. Comprising his Diary from 1659 to 1669, Deciphered by the Rev. John Smith [...] and A Selection from his Private Correspondence, edited by Richard, Lord Braybrooke*, 2 vols (London: Henry Colburn, 1825)
Braybrooke 1848	*Diary and Correspondence of Samuel Pepys F.R.S., Secretary to the Admiralty in the Reigns of Charles II and James II. With a Life and Notes by Richard Lord Braybrooke, The Third Edition, Considerably Enlarged*, 5 vols (London: Henry Colburn, 1848–9)
Braybrooke 1854	*Diary and Correspondence of Samuel Pepys, F.R.S. [...]. The Diary Deciphered by Rev. J. Smith [...] with A Life and Notes by Richard Lord Braybrooke, the Fourth Edition, Revised and Corrected*, 4 vols (London: for Henry Colburn by Hurst and Blackett, 1854)
Bright	*Diary and Correspondence of Samuel Pepys, Esq., F.R.S. From his MS. Cypher in the Pepysian Library, with a Life and Notes by Richard Lord Braybrooke. Deciphered, with Additional Notes, by*

	Rev. Mynors Bright, 6 vols (London: Bickers and Son, 1875–9)
DSP	The Diary of Samuel Pepys, BBC drama series, 1958
LM Diary	The Diary of Samuel Pepys, A New and Complete Transcription, edited by Robert Latham and William Matthews, 11 vols (first published London: G. Bell and Sons/Bell & Hyman, 1970–83; republished London: HarperCollins; University of California Press: Berkeley, 2000)
Magdalene	Magdalene College, Cambridge, archives
PL	Pepys Library, Magdalene College, Cambridge
PL 1836–41, Diary	Pepys's diary manuscript (shelf-marks in the Pepys Library)
TNA	The National Archives, Kew, London
UCLA	University of California Los Angeles, Charles E. Young Research Library
Wheatley	The Diary of Samuel Pepys M.A. F.R.S., Clerk of the Acts and Secretary to the Admiralty. Transcribed from the Shorthand Manuscript in the Pepysian Library Magdalene College Cambridge by Rev. Mynors Bright [...] with Lord Braybrooke's Notes, Edited with Additions by Henry B. Wheatley, 9 vols (London: Bell & Sons; Cambridge: Deighton Bell, 1893–9)

Introduction

In the 1660s Samuel Pepys kept a secret diary whose contents, had they become known, would have destroyed his marriage, ended his career, and quite possibly seen him arrested.[1] Today this is the most famous diary in the English language. Pepys's journal vividly describes momentous events, such as the plague of 1665 and the Great Fire of London, alongside small moments – quarrels with his wife or jokes with servants. Since it was first published in 1825, it has variously been called an 'incomparable masterpiece', 'an historical and literary work of an outstanding character', 'trifling', 'tedious', 'very amusing', 'too gross to print', and 'obscene'. Those divided judgements come just from the people (the editors, the publishers, and the lawyers) who were tasked with getting this extremely bizarre, frequently filthy text into print.[2] For most of the last two hundred years, significant sections of the diary were deemed unpublishable, thanks to Pepys's habits of describing court scandals, his sex life, and his bowel movements. Since nothing could be more intriguing than a secret diary too shocking to print, this censorship only increased the public's fascination.

If there is one verdict that most readers of the diary across the centuries could likely agree on, it is that it is 'strange'. In 1841, Leigh Hunt set out puzzles about Pepys's intentions that have continued to perplex readers. It was, Hunt wrote, 'strange' that for almost ten years Pepys had made the time, despite hectic work and socializing, to describe each day. Given the diary's damaging contents, it was even 'stranger' that Pepys was prepared to risk its discovery during his life and *then* chose to leave it to his old college, Magdalene in Cambridge. That decision meant it might 'be dug up at any future day, to the wonder, the amusement, and not very probable respect, of the coming generations'.[3] If the diary's creation is strange, and its preservation stranger, what generations have chosen to do with it since its first publication is no less strange. The diary has become recognized as a vital source on Restoration history and has served to make the past present in unexpected ways. Over two hundred years, Pepys's diary has inspired parodies, historical novels, TV drama, interpretive dance, and whisky adverts.

Perhaps the strangest thing about Pepys's journal is that, despite its fame and wide appeal, almost no one has actually read it. This is not just a case of the diary's being better known by reputation than by reading, or because parts of it have traditionally been censored. Pepys's diary is in six manuscript volumes, kept on the shelves of the library named after him at Magdalene College. He wrote it in shorthand – a system of symbols that masked its contents. As a result, very few people have ever directly read the diary. Even most of the diary's editors, in a very literal sense, did not understand what Pepys wrote: they relied on others to transcribe the shorthand. This matters, because when we read a longhand text of the diary in print or online, it is in certain respects closer to a translation of Pepys's writing than a simple transcription. Without closer attention to the shorthand and its implications, important clues about Pepys's intentions and his meanings have been missed.

To trace the history of Pepys's diary, we need to look at why he wrote, how he wrote, and why the diary became famous. Its publishing history is, to say the least, an unusual one, featuring battles with the shorthand, efforts to cast a highly 'indelicate' diary as highly respectable history, and stratagems to circumvent the laws against obscene publications. Even the writer's name is a puzzle. 'Peeps' is now taken to be the historically correct pronunciation but, until the early twentieth century, to most readers he was 'Peps'.[4] From the first, readers of Pepys's diary (or parts of it) have been led to reflect on which experiences are historically significant, who gets to write history, and who should be able to read that history. They have also been drawn to consider their own relationship to the past and to the future. Meanwhile, Pepys – a naval administrator, gossip, clotheshorse, and routinely unfaithful husband – has come to stand as both the personification of the Restoration period and, when needed, as a manifestation of an enduring national character. How he was cast in these dual roles tells us as much about British society over the last two hundred years as it does about his diary; his strange history has become, in more ways than one, British history.[5]

Beginnings

Since the first selection of Pepys's diary was published in 1825, certain themes and passages have become famous or, indeed, infamous. The diary runs to around one and a quarter million words, so reading all of it is no small task. It has always owed a large part of its popularity to the fact that entries can be extracted and enjoyed without knowledge of the whole.

These well-known episodes have, typically, shaped the diary's reputation and dominated tellings of Pepys's life. We therefore need to give them, and Pepys's biography, some attention.

When Pepys began his diary, on 1 January 1660, he was twenty-six, working as a government clerk, and worrying if he could keep his job during the current round of political turmoil. He had few resources to fall back on if he did not. Although he had some influential relatives, his immediate family were not wealthy. His father, John, was a tailor and his mother, Margaret Kight, was a victualler's daughter who had come to the capital from Gloucestershire to work as a servant.[6] Pepys had grown up in parliamentarian London during the civil wars. He was nine when the English Civil War began in 1642 and fifteen when Charles I's forces were finally defeated by the parliamentary army in 1648. Showing an early talent for being on the scene, he was at Whitehall to witness and to celebrate the execution of Charles in January 1649.[7] Soon after, he won a scholarship to Cambridge. By virtue of his education at Magdalene, he could now claim to be a gentleman and a cut above his parents. In 1655, when he was twenty-two, he fell in love with and married Elizabeth St Michel, the fifteen-year-old daughter of an impoverished French gentleman (exactly which of their families was the most disreputable was one of the subjects they subsequently fought over).[8] The new couple badly needed money. At this time, Britain was notionally a republic, though power resided with the Lord Protector Oliver Cromwell as head of state and with army leaders. Fortunately, Pepys had a relative who was flourishing in this new modelled nation: Sir Edward Mountagu, the son of his great aunt. Mountagu held high offices in Cromwell's government and navy, and he found work for Pepys in his household. Pepys also took up a government post as a minor clerk in the Exchequer. While starting his married life and his career, he was also dealing with excruciating pain from bladder stones – a condition that became life-threatening. In 1658, he endured an extremely risky operation to remove the stones. His survival gave him a new relish for life and a sincere thankfulness for a narrow escape, which he would commemorate each year.

A few months after Pepys's operation, Oliver Cromwell's death triggered a period of political chaos. For more than a year, various factions in the army, navy and parliament struggled not just for control of the state, but to determine which system of government would prevail: a republic? a protectorate? a monarchy? Pepys succeeded in holding on to his Exchequer post during these many changes of regime. Yet, as he began his diary, he feared his luck would not last. Again, Mountagu proved a valuable patron. Unknown to Pepys, he had been secretly liaising with Charles Stuart, son of the executed king. It was Mountagu's role in aiding Charles II's Restoration that transformed Pepys's prospects and made him an eyewitness to the major events of the Restoration. When parliament, seeking to restore stability, voted to invite Charles II to take the throne, Mountagu was involved in the machinations. He sailed to collect the new king from the Hague in May 1660. Pepys was at his side as his secretary, recording his impressions of Charles. 'The King seems to be a very sober man', he noted.[9] This was the start of Pepys's long relationship with Charles II and with Charles's brother, James duke of York, who would later become James II.

Scandal

Charles II enthroned proved to be a considerably less sober man than Charles Stuart auditioning for the crown. Pepys was present at the lavish celebrations for Charles's coronation in April 1661, rising at 4 am to bag a good seat and going to bed almost twenty-four hours later, more drunk than at any time in his life ('if ever I was foxed it was now').[10] The Restoration brought splendour, pleasures, and a moral laxity that Pepys enjoyed and deplored. His diary is a principal source of scandal on Charles's infamously scandalous court. In 1663, for example, Pepys sedulously recorded how Sir Charles Sedley had appeared naked on a tavern balcony in Covent Garden, 'acting all the postures of lust and buggery that could be imagined'. After abusing the bible, Sedley boasted of a powder that 'should make all the cunts in town run after him'. He concluded by dowsing his prick in wine, downing the wine, and then, loyally, drinking the king's health. Sedley's subsequent trial for 'debauchery', incidentally, was later used to establish the legal grounds for preventing the publication of obscene texts – such as Pepys's diary.[11] The year 1663 proved a particularly good (or bad) one for court scandal. A few months earlier, a friend told Pepys that Lady Castlemaine, the king's chief mistress, had staged a mock marriage with another reputed mistress, culminating in the king's taking Castlemaine's place in the bridal bed. The same source supplied another story to illustrate the scandalous lives of courtiers. It is an account of a miscarriage: while the maids of honour were dancing at a ball, one of them miscarried a child 'but nobody knew who, it being taken up by somebody in their handkercher'. Pepys later heard more horrific details: Charles had taken the 'child' to 'dissect it', 'making great sport of it' and complaining he 'had lost a subject by the business'.[12]

Pepys recorded such stories because they shocked and fascinated him, but also because they had, however indirectly, a bearing on his new job. In the summer of 1660 Mountagu, now ennobled as the Earl of Sandwich, had got Pepys a post as Clerk of the Acts to the Navy Board. This job brought with it a new home by the Navy Office in Seething Lane, near to the Tower of London. It also brought new wealth, and a new set of colleagues to impress and to feud with. Pepys threw himself into the role, mastering the administrative business of the fleet and capitalizing on the opportunities for advancement that the position offered. He acquired additional lucrative appointments, such as working on the committee that oversaw England's new colony in Tangier. During all this, court gossip provided clues as to who was in favour and influencing policy, and who was on the decline. When Sandwich began to neglect his work to pursue an extramarital affair with a young woman, Betty Becke, Pepys feared this was damaging Sandwich's interest for 'the world doth take notice of it'.[13] He eventually took the risky step of writing to his patron to warn him – it led to a cooling of their relationship. Meanwhile, the king's growing reputation for neglecting state affairs ultimately threatened the navy's efficiency and its funding. 'Chance without merit brought me in' wrote Pepys of his naval role, and 'diligence only keeps me so'. That diligence included gathering all sorts of information that might improve his prospects.[14]

Disasters

Pepys's commitment to his job extended to remaining at the Navy Office during the plague, after other members of the Navy Board had evacuated the capital. This was the time of the Second Anglo-Dutch War (1665–7), making Pepys vital in maintaining communications. His bravery earned him the respect of the king and the duke of York, who was Lord Admiral. It also meant Pepys was on hand to capture how, as the plague spread, the extraordinary came to seem ordinary. In September 1665 the city was desolate and the landscape strange: 'But Lord, what a sad time it is, to see no boats upon the River – and grass grow all up and down Whitehall-court.' By October, he realized that he barely registered a corpse being carried by him: 'but Lord, to see what custom is, that I am come almost to <think> nothing of it', he wrote.[15] Readers have always enjoyed Pepys's capacity to not lose sight of personal matters amid his discussion of terror and upheavals. His most famous entry on the plague, 3 September 1665, begins with him dressing for church:

> *Lords day*. Up, and put on my coulour silk suit, very fine, and my new periwigg, bought a good while since, but darst not wear it because the plague was in Westminster when I bought it. And it is a wonder what will be the fashion after the plague is done as to periwigs, for nobody will dare to buy any haire for fear of the infection – that it had been cut off of the heads of people dead of the plague.[16]

Along with the pleasures of fine clothes and wigs, this proved to be a profitable and delightful year for Pepys, especially once he had moved to the safety of Greenwich and joined fellow evacuees in dancing and partying. New friendships were made here, including with the actress and singer Elizabeth Knepp. Summing up the year, he wrote 'I have never lived so merrily (besides that I never got so much) as I have done this plague-time.'[17]

If Pepys's account of the plague in 1665 is celebrated, it is his description of the Great Fire of London in 1666 that has truly secured his fame. Beginning with being woken in the small hours on 2 September by his maids who had spotted 'a great fire', he captures the chaos, the horror, and the entrancing spectacle of the fire as, over five days, it spread across the city. Pepys reports that it was he who warned Charles that the only means to slow the fire would be the drastic step of making firebreaks by pulling down houses. Samuel, Elizabeth, and their friends then spent the first evening watching the blaze from across the river:

> as it grow darker, [it] appeared more and more, and in Corners and upon steeples and between churches and houses, as far as we could see up the hill of the City, in a most horrid malicious bloody flame, not like the fine flame of an ordinary fire. [. . .] We stayed till, it being darkish, we saw the fire as only one entire arch of fire from this to the other side the bridge, and in a bow up the hill, for an arch of above a mile long. It made me weep to see it.[18]

The time for being a spectator soon ended. Pepys desperately moved his own gold and goods, before resorting to burying his naval papers, wine, and parmesan cheese in the garden. This famously eccentric decision was, in fact, eminently sensible. Pepys and his colleagues were at a loose end, waiting to see if the fire would destroy their homes: burying their remaining expensive goods to protect them from the flames and from looters was at least doing *something*. The Navy Office and Seething Lane remained standing. The cheese was recovered a few days later.[19]

Pepys's unrelenting curiosity and his gift for evocative detail are never so apparent as in his entries on the fire. The sights, others' reactions, and his own responses struck him as fascinating and disconcerting: 'But strange it was to see Cloathworkers-hall on fire these three days and nights in one body of Flame'; 'Strange to hear what is bid for houses all up and down here'; 'But it is a strange thing to see how long this time did look since Sunday, having been alway full of variety of actions [...]. And I had forgot almost the day of the week.'[20] On the fourth day of the fire, he walked out across the city to survey the damage. There, he was forced to pay 'twopence for a plain penny loaf'; saw his cousin's house 'in fire'; collected from a chapel, as a souvenir, some melted glass that had turned 'like parchment'; and witnessed 'a poor Catt taken out of a hole in the chimney joyning to the wall of the Exchange, with the hair all burned off the body and yet alive'.[21] In less than four sentences, he touched on the impact of the fire on the economy, his family, London landmarks, and on animals. Characteristically, Pepys's focus in recording here is also not quite what we might anticipate: the curiously transformed glass and 'poor' cat's fate merited more words than the destruction that had hit his cousin's family. At this point in the disaster, his account implies, seeing yet another home burnt did not have much of an impact; seeing the injured cat rescued did and, centuries later, that is a moment that readers too remember. It is a good instance of how anecdotes from the diary can take on a life of their own. This cat now features in historians' descriptions of the fire, narrates an online video aimed at primary schools, and has inspired at least two children's books.[22]

Londoners in the 1660s had the misfortune of living in interesting times, and Pepys had the good fortune to document them. In June 1667 the war came perilously close to home when the Dutch fleet sailed up the Medway and burnt the great ships anchored at Chatham. Pepys feared the Navy Office would be attacked by the Dutch, the French, or by mobs of incensed citizens. He hurriedly sent his gold and his journal ('which I value much') to safety.[23] After this national humiliation, peace was made. Turning catastrophe to his advantage, Pepys carved out a new role for himself defending the beleaguered navy at the parliamentary enquiries into the war's failures.

Sex

Public tumult, national disasters, and political machinations make for gripping reading and intriguing history, but so too do Pepys's accounts of private tumults, personal calamities, and domestic scheming. Elizabeth Pepys, like her husband, was busy adapting to their changing status: she studied genteel skills and managed their expanding household of servants. Elizabeth is never named within the diary but appears only as 'my wife' – a sign of Samuel's attachment but also his possessiveness. Sometimes, in affection (and especially when he felt he had wronged her), he described her as 'my wife, poor wretch'.[24] This became one of his most recognizable phrases. They fought frequently over Elizabeth's desire for 'money and liberty', for she wanted to spend their new wealth and to have more freedom to travel about town than her jealous husband allowed her.[25]

Samuel could be jealous. Elizabeth, with much greater cause, was too. She rightly suspected that his relationship with their friend, the actress Elizabeth Knepp, was not innocent. However, she was unaware of the extent of his sexual activity inside and outside their home. During the 1660s, Pepys had sexual contact with, among others, Nell Payne, Jane Birch, and Susan (servants in his household); Mrs Daniel (a sailor's wife); Elizabeth Bagwell (wife of a ship's carpenter); Betty Mitchell (a family friend); the sisters Frances and Sarah Udall (who were servants in a tavern); and the sisters Betty and Doll Lane, who were shopkeepers. Many of these relationships were transactional (such as sexual favours for a husband's promotion), some were for mutual pleasure (which did not rule out a transactional element), and some were coercive and violent (of which more later). Matters took a dramatic turn on 25 October 1668 when Elizabeth walked in on Pepys and her paid companion, seventeen-year-old Deborah Willet. Pepys described this using the mixture of languages that he sometimes employed to protect sexual passages, so I have added some translations in square brackets:

> My wife, coming up suddenly, did find me imbracing the girl con my hand sub su coats [with my hand under her skirts]; and endeed, I was with my main [hand] in her cunny. I was at a wonderful loss upon it, and the girl also.[26]

The effects of Elizabeth's grief, rage, and retaliation upended Pepys's control over his life and his diary. During the Great Fire, he had worried about losing track of the days; when struggling with the fallout from his behaviour in November 1668, he actually did.[27] Deb was, discreetly, fired but Pepys continued to hunt for her around London.

For much of the nineteenth century, readers were not permitted to read about Pepys's sex life. The full details only became available in 1976, when Robert Latham, William Matthews, and their editorial team finally succeeded in getting all of Pepys's entries into print. Nonetheless, Pepys's private life was a source of avid interest from the first. This was not just because it seemed that scintillating information was being withheld (it was), but because these suppressions raised questions about what information was historically valuable and which groups of readers, if any, should be allowed access to it. Despite editors' best efforts, sex and censorship have been major themes in the reception of Pepys's diary, and they are major themes of this book. I am concerned, too, with evasions and suppressions in responses to the diary that cannot be solely traced to editorial censorship – that is, with aspects of the diary that readers have, historically, not recognized or preferred not to discuss. Chief among these are the records of Pepys's enjoyment of sexual violence, and his references to his growing interest and involvement in the slave trade. As with questions of editorial censorship, investigating this content and responses to it reveals changing perceptions of history and of whose experiences count as valuable. Pepys's inclusion of this material means that – if the principle of including sexual content in a history is no longer so controversial – his record nonetheless remains a provocative and controversial source.

Endings

Pepys reluctantly ended his journal on 31 May 1669, believing that keeping it was damaging his sight. He also feared that blindness would mean he had little left to write about. To be forced to end his diary was, he grieved in his final entry, 'almost as much as to see myself go into my grave'.[28] This sense of loss is widely echoed in writing about Pepys. The rest of his life has attracted far less interest than the 1660s, though it was amply documented and scarcely less eventful. Thousands of his personal and professional papers survive, including other journals he kept – though none as detailed or as intimate as his 1660s diary.[29]

Pepys did not go blind, but he soon had more to mourn than the end of his journal. Elizabeth died of a fever in November 1669. From hints in his surviving papers, it is apparent that he continued contact with the now married Deb Willet and, in 1670, began a relationship with Mary Skinner, a merchant's daughter. She would remain – in his words – a source of 'Steddy friendship and Assistances' until his death.[30] Meanwhile, his impressive rise to power continued. In 1673 he was appointed Secretary to the Office of Lord High Admiral; later, he became Secretary for the Affairs of the Admiralty, a role which saw him reporting directly to Charles II, on a level with a Secretary of State.[31] In these decades, Pepys's achievements included establishing measures to clamp down on corruption (with strictly limited success); overseeing a huge programme of naval reconstruction; and instituting an exam for lieutenants (a means of ensuring those in charge of ships actually knew something about sailing rather than, say, having been appointed due to high birth or high bribes). He saw his naval work as fundamental to his legacy, and his achievements in this respect were admired well before his diary was public.[32]

Pepys's political and social success was punctuated by dramatic reversals. His fortunes were closely tied to those of his chief patron, James, duke of York. As Charles had no legitimate children, James was the heir to the throne. He was also, from the early 1670s, known to be a Catholic. These two facts were not seen as compatible by many Protestants. In 1679, during the febrile atmosphere of the Popish Plot when alleged Catholic conspirators were being hunted down and executed, Pepys (though a Protestant) was arrested on a capital charge of treason. The main allegation was that he had sold naval secrets to the French, but behind this was the implication that he was part of a wider conspiracy to put James on the throne and forcibly convert the nation to Catholicism. He endured anxious months before the unfounded case collapsed. It was several years before Charles could reappoint him to the admiralty. In 1685, James became king.

Serving as Secretary for the Admiralty under Charles and James in the 1680s was the high point of Pepys's career. His networks and influence stretched around the world. Another sudden reversal ended this. In 1688, James's efforts to promote Catholicism by circumventing parliament prompted an uprising and an invasion by his son-in-law William of Orange. James fled the country. This 'Glorious Revolution', as it was remembered by the victors, was the last of the revolutions in Pepys's lifetime. He was forced out of the admiralty. As he was not prepared to swear allegiance to the new monarchs, William and Mary, he moved from being at the heart of power to being barred from holding civil office. Two further arrests on suspicion of treason and Jacobite plotting followed in 1689 and 1690.

Rather than scheming to overthrow the new regime, Pepys was instead planning his legacy. He had long hoped to write a history of the navy, but instead he settled for collecting and curating the library that would carry his name after his death. In 1703, dying from the bladder condition that had first tried to kill him over four decades before, he made his will. His library, he instructed, should ultimately go in its entirety to one of two Cambridge colleges, Magdalene or Trinity.[33] Magdalene was Pepys's first choice: it was the college that had given him his start and which he had continued to sponsor during his life. Among almost 3,000 books that he decided to preserve were the six volumes of his diary.

History and Literature

Three hundred years later, Pepys's diary is casually referred to as 'one of the greatest texts in our history and in our literature', and 'one of the great literary manuscripts of the world'.[34] This is impressive, especially given that on first publication its historical and literary credentials were both considered suspect. The acclaim for the diary today is the result of changing perceptions of history and literature. The diary's first editor Richard Griffin, third Baron Braybrooke, worked on it in the 1820s and 1840s. He was far from persuaded of its literary merits. Braybrooke warned his readers that the diary was sorely lacking in 'accuracy of style' and that they would form no glowing opinion of 'Mr Pepys's literary reputation'. The diary's 'indelicate' passages were also obstacles to any literary esteem. Braybrooke did not attempt to defend Pepys on that score, instead silently cutting most of them.[35] As a valuable historical text the diary's claims were stronger, but still contested. It appeared at a time when the topics and the people that constituted 'history' were expanding – and its publication drew attention to that transformation. In 1848, the *Gentleman's Magazine* pondered Braybrooke's comments on the passages he had added to his latest selection. Braybrooke seemed to imply that only episodes relating to 'kings or other public characters' had 'historical value'. In contrast, the reviewer believed, 'everything which exhibits the manners and condition of a people [...] is history; aye, and far more important and instructive history than the minutest narrative of the actions of royal or noble persons in which historical writers ever indulged'.[36] As we'll see, the early editions of Pepys's journal fuelled the development of what would now be termed 'social history' – before they were, in turn, used to attack social and literary history in the early twentieth century. In the 1970s, the publication of the complete edition of the diary coincided with trends in historiography (or the writing of history) which the diary's fame both benefited from and encouraged. Mark Salber Phillips has pointed to 'the preoccupation with affective experience and everyday life' in historical thought after 1968. 'Cultural history' and 'microhistory' came to the fore.[37] As part of these developments, the late twentieth century saw a renewed interest in diaries among both historians and literary scholars.[38] In recent decades the complete edition of Pepys's journal has enabled new scholarship on everyday life and ideas of the self.[39]

Although the diary has always struck readers as a strange text, it is a marker of its cultural success that much of what it offers seems deeply familiar. Pepys's diary does what we now expect diaries to do. 'A good diary', it has been argued, is written regularly and close to the events it describes; good diarists are spontaneous and frank; they write about themselves and they write for themselves, not for 'an outside reader'. If Pepys's journal 'fulfills all the conditions of what a diary should be', it is partly because influential scholars pronouncing on what a diary "should be" greatly admired Pepys's writing and employed it as their standard.[40] The wide appeal of diaries as historical sources, Jerome de Groot observes, comes from the fact they appear to offer 'a direct relationship with the subject'. They seem to lack the mediation and repression of official histories.[41] Pepys's diary has frequently been praised on this score: his expansive yet minute record, together with his frank accounts of private matters, mean that his diary has struck readers as a peculiarly complete and intimate account of a life. Phillips has discussed how a sense of 'affective proximity' can reduce our perception of historical distance.[42] This has been a common experience for readers of Pepys's diary. In 1848, Peter Cunningham was delighted by how 'the reader is taken into [Pepys's] inmost soul' and praised his skill in 'bringing vividly before a reader whatever is attempted to be described'. In 1914, Wilbur Cortez Abbott argued, 'It seldom happens among myriads of human relationships that anyone knows any of his fellows, however near and dear, as well as all of us know Pepys.' Pepys's diary, Abbott believed, brought the 1660s 'nearer to us than any other decade of English history'. Nearly a hundred years later, a commenter on the website pepysdiary.com, addressed similar sentiments to Pepys directly, speaking on behalf of the online community that had formed to read the diary: 'We all feel we know you personally, despite the 350 year gap, and regret we can never share a "merry" dinner with you.'[43]

These are powerful, pleasurable experiences of connection with one personality and with the past, and they have many counterparts across two hundred years of responses. They are, however, experiences prompted by dramatically different texts, most of which have omissions and all of which transform what Pepys wrote at a fundamental level by rendering shorthand into fluent English longhand. Setting aside the question of editorial mediation between reader and diarist, any sense of closeness to Pepys or celebration of his diary as uniquely comprehensive should be nuanced by considering what that seemingly comprehensive, seemingly frank record masks or omits – especially where this concerns the agency or the humanity of others in Restoration society. When we read a version of Pepys's diary today, we can choose to relish the unusually immediate sense of the past it gives. As I'll be arguing, we also need to recognize it as a candid but nonetheless calculated creation, and one whose changing forms have helped shape what 'history' means in Britain and beyond.

Chapters in This Book

A history of the diary has to start with Pepys himself. My first two chapters explore the puzzle of his intentions when writing (a subject of much debate) and what we can learn from his shorthand. In the reception of Pepys's diary, certain topics are routinely ignored because they are difficult, their ramifications inconvenient, or because readers have not had the resources to deal with them. For all three reasons, informed discussion of Pepys's shorthand is very rare. It takes effort and considerable resources for scholars to learn shorthand and to access the diary manuscript (or images of it). Shorthand is also the kind of topic that readers of the diary might not want to think too much about, not least because it disrupts the pleasing idea that in reading an edition of the diary we are getting direct, intimate access to Pepys's thoughts. When I point to such blind spots in the journal's reception, it is often because I have shared them. For example, I worked on Pepys's papers for years but only learned his shorthand when I came to edit a selection of his diary.[44] It proved well worth the trouble: reckoning with Pepys's shorthand adds a new layer of meaning to his diary and new insight into his intentions when writing it. To understand what the diary was for and why it survived also means examining Pepys's intentions at the end of his life, when he bequeathed his library 'for the benefitt of Posterity'.[45] Chapter 3 therefore investigates his ideas of history, and his plans for how his archive, and his diary, would be read.

Chapters 4 and 5 deal with how Pepys's plans came to fruition – or not – when the diary was published and popularized in the nineteenth century. The first edition of 1825 was a very limited selection chosen by Lord Braybrooke. Bowing to popular demand, he then published an expanded selection which came out in 1848 and 1849. More text was offered in Mynors Bright's edition in the late 1870s, and more still by Henry B. Wheatley in the 1890s. Over this period, Pepys became representative of Restoration history. His name became a 'household word' through newspapers, paintings, and children's magazines.[46] Driving this interest was speculation about what readers were not allowed to see, conflict between commercial and scholarly imperatives, and competing ideas of historical worth. It also began to worry some commentators that readers were having altogether too much fun with Pepys and his diary, to the apparent detriment of Pepys himself and a patriotic appreciation of English history.

By the 1930s, the diary was widely available in cheap editions, and Pepys was to be found in advertising, in biographies, and in historical fiction. Chapter 6 explores these manifestations, together with how the experience of two world wars gave the diary a new social importance and personal relevance. Although Pepys's diary was firmly installed as a classic of English history and literature by this time, readers still did not have access to the full text. Chapter 7 reveals the legal and editorial scheming that lay behind the publication of the complete text (1970–83), edited by Robert Latham and William Matthews. This version of the diary – a major feat and still the only full edition – was shaped by a desire to dodge both ridicule in the press and prosecution in the courts. That dodging was successful: it is the most respected edition of the diary today. The most widely read versions, however, remain the Victorian editions, which have had a new lease of life as electronic texts. Chapter 7 ends by bringing the story of the diary into the twenty-first century, looking at what happened when readers of one such website, pepysdiary.com, found themselves living through history during the COVID-19 pandemic.

My final chapter uses the knowledge of the diary's text and the reading traditions discussed over the course of this book to examine what is possible when reading Pepys's journal today. The focus is on reading the diary against the grain to draw out information that Pepys himself missed or obfuscated. This involves giving attention to Elizabeth Pepys, to certain of the women and girls with whom Pepys had sexual contact, and to several of the Black people who lived in or near Pepys's household. This apparently disparate selection of people do share certain things in common, including being barely mentioned or appearing not at all in official records. Their presence in Pepys's journal therefore adds greatly to its value as a record of Restoration society, although his references to them have historically proved difficult for readers to register and interpret. This diary, as readers are constantly discovering, is puzzling, amusing, unsettling, and intriguing. To fully appreciate what it can offer today, we need to get to grips with its past, and with the weird and wonderful things that readers have done with it.

CHAPTER I

Writing the Diary

Samuel Pepys neatly packed a good deal of information on to the first page of his diary. He began with gratitude: 'Blessed be God, at the end of the last year I was in very good health, without any sense of my old pain but upon taking of cold.' The source of that pain, the bladder stones that had nearly killed him two years before, went unmentioned – neither he, nor God needed the clarification. He then immediately turned to other topics: a summary of the members of his small household ('my wife', 'servant Jane'); the arrival of his wife's period which had ended hopes she was pregnant; the volatile political scene in London; and how he was hiding his own financial troubles from the world ('esteemed rich, but endeed very poor'). Running out of room, he just managed to fit in mention of his 'uncertain' professional situation (a result of the uncertain political one) and the name of his boss. It made for a pleasingly full page, with the lines satisfyingly spaced.[1]

In both its orderly presentation and its rapid changes of topic, this entry was a fair illustration of how Pepys would continue his diary in succeeding years. He had nothing to say here about his reasons for writing and he offered very little on the subject elsewhere. Quite why he kept his diary, and whether he ever intended anyone other than himself to read it, have been enjoyable sources of speculation for critics down the years and, indeed, are questions likely to strike anyone reading it. From the first, readers have been trying to explain why Pepys recorded his life in such detail, and especially in such damaging detail: why take the trouble to record 'the most trifling particulars'? Why record evidence of 'petty weaknesses', vanity, greed, corruption, spite, and adultery? 'Self-love' has been a popular explanation from the start: if diary writing requires an element of this, Pepys has been seen as possessing a 'perfect childish egotism' and a nostalgia for his own past that give his diary its distinctive qualities.[2] Relieving his mind of 'burthensome secret[s]', or engaging in puritanical self-scrutiny to prevent moral lapses have also been suggested as motives.[3]

With the development of psychological theory and the concept of the unconscious, Pepys's habit of noting his sexual activities was interpreted as an alternative to repressing them, by distancing himself from responsibility in the act of writing. Others have seen him as instead using the diary to delight in sensuality.[4]

The issue of whether Pepys ever intended his diary to be read or published has similarly divided opinion. The more thoughtful considerations recognize this as raising two separate questions: what Pepys intended when writing, and what he subsequently decided. There is an overwhelming consensus that, at the time of writing, he wrote only for himself.[5] Few commentators have questioned this – the editor William Matthews was one, although his comments on this score were judged so doubtful they did not make it into the introduction to the complete diary.[6] On the matter of what Pepys ultimately intended for his journal, some critics see him as deliberately ensuring it would find readers; others (especially early commentators, amazed at its contents) argued that the diary's inclusion in his library was an oversight.[7]

Pepys's motivations for writing emerge more plainly if his diary is approached not as a unique and striking survival, but as one curious record among many. It is impossible to get a full picture of what Pepys was up to in his private diary without recognizing its relationship to his wider, obsessive record-keeping. His diary grew from, and was part of, his network of texts: bills, financial notes, letters, a book of anecdotes, and office papers among them.[8] While he was unusually fanatical in his record-keeping, Pepys was not unusual among his contemporaries in seeing the value of a journal. What he was seeking to achieve with it becomes clearer when we compare his diary with life-writing by others, including his friends and allies. These examples can show how he adapted existing methods, as well as illuminating the features that have made his diary so evocative for readers. From its first page Pepys's diary served multiple ends, and those ends would change with its writer.

Occasions

Pepys referred to his record as a 'diary' or, more often, as a 'journal'.[9] The kind of life-writing that shared characteristics with 'a diary' could be found under a variety of names in the seventeenth century, including 'diurnal', 'entring book', and 'memoirs'.[10] Diary keeping was growing among men and women across the social spectrum. By the time Pepys started, there was at least one manual on diary writing available. Most diary keepers probably picked up their methods and their ideas from family and acquaintances, for there was no presumption that a diary would necessarily be private.[11] Diaries were often intended to be shared. Peter Mundy (c.1596–c.1667), a Cornish merchant, wrote that he had recorded his travels 'Journall Wise', partly 'to pleasure such Freinds (who mightt come to the reading thereof) Thatt are Desirous to understand somwhatt of Forraigne Countries'. The occasion that prompted Mundy's journal was his trip to Constantinople in the 1620s. He continued recording his voyages, ending with his time in London in the late 1650s and 1660s, when he found the city as strange – if not more so – than what he had seen on his travels.[12] At the same time as Pepys and Mundy were describing the curious sights of Restoration London, Pepys's patron, Edward Mountagu, Earl of Sandwich, was also keeping a personal journal. Sandwich's journal upends modern preconceptions about personal diaries, for he sometimes had other people keep it for him. Pepys's friends John Creed and William Howe were among the clerks who entered material.[13] Spanning the early 1650s to shortly before his death in 1672, Sandwich's ten folio volumes began with naval notes soon after he became a member of Cromwell's Council of State, marking a new phase in his career.[14] The volumes went on to encompass remarks on his travels, court gossip, outgoing letters, navigation calculations, and cold cures. He had no regular routine of diary keeping; instead information was entered as Sandwich saw the need. Like Pepys's diary, this was therefore a highly miscellaneous record, but in its sporadic, shared maintenance it had very little in common with the one kept by 'Mr Pepys of the Navy Office' (who is mentioned by Sandwich a handful of times).[15]

The occasion that prompted Pepys's own diary keeping is, in one sense, obvious. The first of January 1660 was the first day of a new year in a new decade, and it looked very much like the month might see the start of yet another new regime.[16] The turmoil of the mid century was a significant prompt for many journal writers, who were trying to fathom the truth out of conflicting accounts or who wanted to chronicle events for posterity. In 1659, for example, Thomas Rugg, a barber living in Covent Garden, began a 'diurnall' titled 'Mercurius Politicus Redivivus' ('Political News Revived') that was 'for Future Satisfaction & Information'. It combined his own eyewitness accounts with reports from newsletters and printed newsbooks.[17] At this time Pepys was himself providing a news service. He wrote regularly to Edward Mountagu to keep him up to date on family news and public opinion. As Claire Tomalin has argued, these letters allowed Pepys to hone his reporting skills, picking out examples of speech or sights that conveyed the mood of the capital.[18] Pepys's diary was his personal record of such events, relating his own 'uncertain' state to that of the nation's. If the national turmoil was an encouragement to start recording, Pepys's discovery that he was at the very heart of events – an eyewitness to Charles's voyage home – must have been an incentive to continue his chronicling of high and popular politics. He had already contributed to the public reporting of the Restoration through one of his official letters, which found its way into the newsbooks in May 1660.[19] He also found himself with access to valuable information on political affairs of the kind that would go unmentioned in printed news or in his contemporaries' history writing. This, too, he chose to preserve.

'Blessed be God'

While Pepys had interests in common with writers, such as Rugg the barber, who focused on news and politics, his diary's opening paragraph also implies that devotional practices influenced his record. 'Implies' is the word here, for if 'Blessed be God' made for a religious beginning, what followed over the course of nine years was, to say the least, not notably devout. Good health and healthy profits prompted him to thank God.[20] God's forgiveness was asked when Pepys recorded behaviour that he knew to be sinful, though this generally comes across less as imploring God's mercy than as acknowledging the behaviour was not something he was proud of. For example, in 1662, when his colleague Sir William Penn pledged to assist him: 'I did (God forgive mee) promise him all my service and love, though the rogue knows he deserves none from me, nor I entend to show him any; but as he dissembles with me, so I must with him.'[21] Far from signalling penitence for a sin, this was an explanation of why his falsehood was justified and necessary.

Religious practices influenced Pepys's writing, but he shared the methods of pious diarists, rather than their motivations. Pious diarists sought to recognize 'all Gods gracious dealings' in their own life through regular self-scrutiny, thereby learning to better avoid sin and please God.[22] In 1686, Sarah Henry, the 22-year-old daughter of a clergyman, began her diary by setting out its purpose:

> It is in my thoughts to do something in the nature of a Diary, being encouraged by the advantage others have gained thereby, and the hope that I might be furthered by it in a godly life, and be more watchful over the frame of my heart, when it must be kept on record.[23]

This form of religious self-scrutiny often drew on other practices of evaluation. As historians have noted, writers of pious diaries frequently employed the language of accounting when, for example, enumerating God's blessings and mercies.[24] Among them was the London craftsman, Nehemiah Wallington (1598–1658), who kept many notebooks about his life that were intended as aids to godliness for himself and his family. His methods included writing 'Artickles [. . .] for the reformation of my life', each with a fine that was due to the poor if he broke it. Any breach was then registered with a dot against the relevant article in his notebook. From this, we can tell that he was rather better at keeping his pledge to 'rise beefore six of the clocke on the Lords Sabbath day' (with six failures costing him a quarter pence each), than he was at keeping his vow to 'be not angrey with my wife but upon some just occasion' (seventeen failures). Wallington was keen to deter himself from arguing with his wife, since he set a higher fine of halfpence a time for it.[25]

Pepys too was engaged in self-scrutiny for improvement, turning the practices of piety to more worldly ends. Like Wallington, he made vows to God to improve himself and paid fines to the poor box for breaches. Again like Wallington, these covered matters such as late rising and quarrels with his wife (being wealthier, Pepys's fine for quarrelling was two shillings and six pence).[26] He recorded these vows in a notebook and monitored his progress in the diary. Pepys's vows, however, were primarily intended to spur him to a more successful life. His nature, he rued, was to 'esteem pleasure above all things' and this tendency, unrestrained, threatened his finances, his peace of mind, and his reputation. 'Prudence', meaning emotional and economic restraint, was necessary in managing his own behaviour, as well as that of his wife and household.[27] He therefore took vows to curtail activities such as wine-drinking and play-going, finding this practice 'keeps me most happily and contentfully to my business – which God continue'. Hewing diligently to his duty might please God, but that was not how he expressed his motivation. When, for instance, he took a vow to 'laisser aller les femmes for a month' (to leave off women), the purpose was not to avoid sin but to 'fallow my business', because without such restraint it 'and my honour thereby, lies a-bleeding'.[28] Business and honour, rather than guilt and a godly life, were the terms in which he evaluated his behaviour in his diary.

Self-Accounting and Composition

Concern for managing his business – his occupation, duties, and finances – was foundational to Pepys's diary keeping. He was far from unusual in this. Adam Smyth has argued that financial records were 'one of the most common forms of personal documentation or self-accounting' in this period, and a profound influence on life-writing.[29] In Pepys's case, his diary helped him to track his expenses, rein in his spending and, as he grew wealthier, strategize about how to use his money for maximum effect. In 1663, he and Elizabeth determined that the expense of his being 'modish' would repay the investment. A spending spree ensued on a wig and velvet cloak. Pepys explained (twice) in this day's entry that the expense was justified, for it was done 'not prodigally, but only in Cloaths, which I every day see that I do suffer for want of'.[30] The diary also helped him justify his income. Much of Pepys's new wealth was acquired legitimately, through wages and presents that came with his administrative posts, but the line between a fitting gift and an outrageous bribe was a fine one. Wary of criticism, he recorded why a transaction could be argued to fall on the right side of that line – and how he might evade trouble when it manifestly did not. One day, Captain Grove, whom Pepys had recently helped to a new posting, handed him a letter. Realizing there was money inside, Pepys waited till he was alone to open it 'not looking into it till all the money was out, that I might say I saw no money in the paper if ever I should be Questioned about it'.[31] It was literally a paper-thin defence, but one worth memorializing lest he have cause to deploy it.

Pepys's journal helped him rationalize (in both senses) his finances, and it developed directly from his financial record-keeping. While working on the complete edition of the diary, William Matthews examined Pepys's method of composition and came up with some surprising conclusions. Since the diary's publication in 1825, it had been commonplace to state that Pepys's writing was unpremeditated and haphazard.[32] Matthews showed that it was no such thing. During each day, Pepys kept shorthand notes on his expenditure, with brief comments on whom he met and what he saw. Some of these survive since he bound them into the diary volumes instead of writing them up in full. On a visit to Oxford in 1668, he logged the pounds, shillings, and pence spent touring the colleges:

So to see Christ Church with my wife I seeing several others very fine alone with *WH* [Will Hewer] before dinner and did give the boy that went with me <before dinner>	0 –1–0
~~After dinner with my wife and landlord to the schools~~	
Strawberries	0–1–2
Dinner <and servants>	1–0–6[33]

Notes like these ones were the scaffold on which Pepys built his diary entries, drawing too on other records, such as his personal and official letter books. As the neatness of the diary manuscript indicates, he drafted his text before he entered the final version – Matthews argues that the process sometimes involved five stages.[34] He did not always 'set down' events each day, but normally managed it at least every few days and he became uneasy if this remained undone for more than a week.[35] The volumes into which Pepys wrote his final copy seem to have begun life as notebooks purchased at different times from a stationer. They are not uniform in size and there is no standard length, either in pages or time. His first three volumes finished halfway through a year, at the end of June, but this method ended with the fourth volume which contained 1665 and 1666 (not the most orderly of years in London). When Pepys judged a volume complete, he had it bound up in calf covers with gold tooling. In accordance with his will, after his death gold stamps were added to the books in his library, marking them as the property of Samuel Pepys, Secretary for the Admiralty under Charles and James (Figure 1.1).[36] By the early eighteenth century then, the diary looked much like the other books in Pepys's finely presented library – and very little like the ephemeral notes and notebooks that he had worked with on a day-to-day basis.

Nonetheless, Pepys's practice of taking shorthand notes on his spending and activities shaped his final diary entries. It encouraged his habit of tracing events from morning to evening, sometimes with additional news and observations at the end. Stuart Sherman points out that this was highly unusual. Pepys's journal is the first surviving English diary to track days from start to finish systematically and also the first to move day by day across its entire run.[37] In the early months of the diary, the structure of the financial notes on which Pepys built his entries shows through clearly: sums paid in alehouses, eating-houses, or during other financial dealings are often noted. Over the years, it remained the case that certain activities were more likely to feature in the diary than others because they had involved expenditure, even though the sums themselves were not given. The purchase of a book, for example, was more likely to be registered than its subsequent reading.[38] However, as Pepys continued, his journalistic skills developed and the financial underpinnings of this record became less evident. He increasingly elaborated on his notes, dwelling on what was 'most observable' in the day, or relaying the content of conversations.[39]

Pepys's accounts of conversations form part of another type of accounting which dominates the journal. Mark Dawson has persuasively argued that Pepys used the diary to evaluate his social progress and to advance it, for it allowed him to better understand how others saw him. The diary is therefore a record of 'social accounting', 'constantly noting social debts,

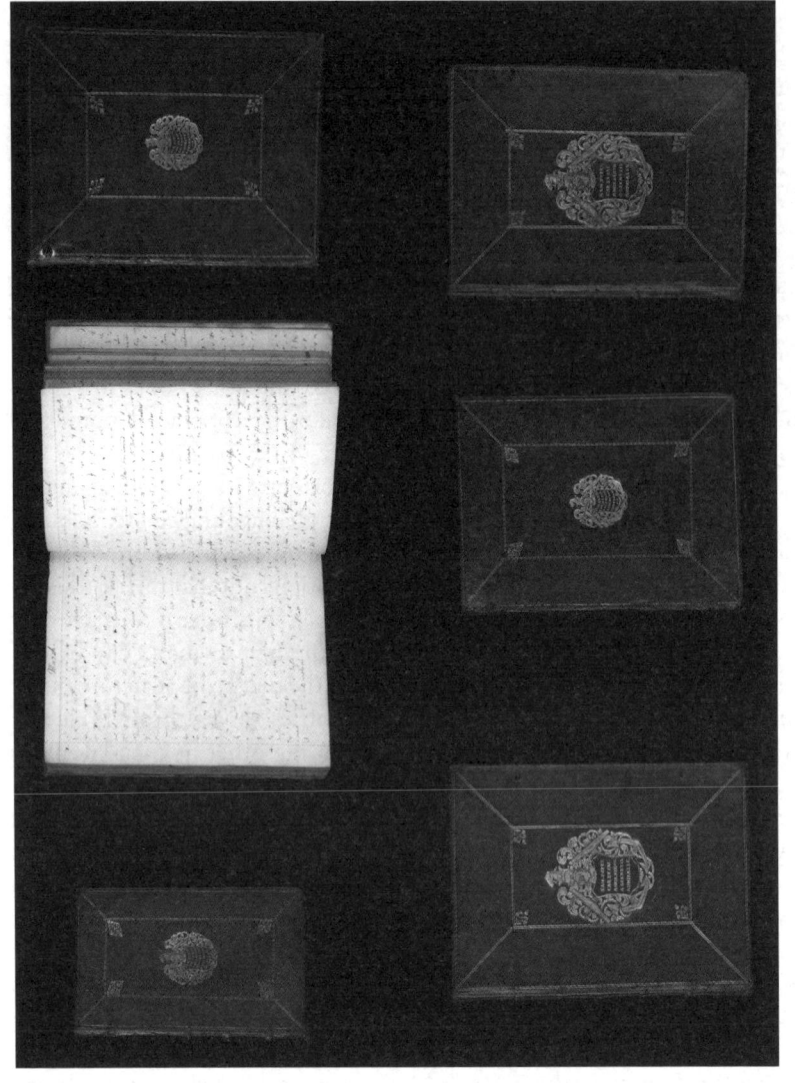

Figure 1.1 Samuel Pepys's diary volumes. PL 1836–41.

credits, and assessing Pepys's status'.⁴⁰ Pepys's decisions to dwell on certain episodes or supply seemingly superfluous facts often make more sense when seen in this light. One Sunday in late 1663, for instance, he and Elizabeth were visited by relatives, two of whom then stayed on to eat. This could have been summarily dealt with by a phrase such as 'Judith Scott and her husband stayed for supper.' Instead, he wrote in some detail about entertaining 'my two Cosens Scotts, he and she', noting that they were visiting his house at Seething Lane for the first time:

> we were as merry as I could be with people that I do wish well to but know not what discourse either to give them or find from them. We showed them our house from top to bottom, and had a good turkey roasted for our supper, and store of wine. And after supper sent them home on foot; and so we to prayers and to bed.⁴¹

Evidently entertaining these relatives was rather awkward: Pepys had little in common with them professionally (Benjamin Scott was a pewterer) and he usually met them only in the company of wider kin. Revisiting the events of the evening was about quelling his uneasiness over whether he had behaved suitably as a host: he had failed to 'give' his guests suitable conversation, but he had given them 'good' food and ample wine. Their mode of transport home was worth a mention because this too was part of hospitality, and implicitly revealing as to status. What Pepys does not explain is that the Scotts lived in St Sepulchre's parish, far from his home in Seething Lane.⁴² On a cold December night, the couple had risked walking through the city rather than – as someone of higher status might have done – hiring a hackney carriage. Pepys's phrasing, 'we [. . .] sent them home on foot', suggests he had arranged for, and possibly funded, a link-boy with a torch to light the way. In writing up the day's events, he was assessing how he had performed in his roles as cousin and host, and reassuring himself that he had done well enough, though not dazzlingly.

Control

Pepys's efforts at self-improvement via the diary were not confined to financial or social accounting. He recorded his recent past to shape his future. From its inception the diary was a tool for effecting change and providing reassurance in multiple areas. Its miscellaneity stemmed from its being a general store of information for Pepys's own benefit, especially a store for the kinds of information that had no obvious alternative place in his record-keeping system. It was part of a network of related texts and one of its defining features was that it did what other records could not. The diary became a catch-all for material that Pepys could not safely or easily log in his financial accounts, in letters, in notebooks, or in official records.

Pepys's concern about his health, apparent in the first line of the journal, is a case in point: he was deeply anxious about a recurrence of his bladder stones and, physically and psychologically, needed ways to deal with that threat. Taking a moment to be grateful for the absence of his 'old pain' at the start of his diary was one form of relief. To the disquiet of his early editors, another was to attend closely to his 'cods' (testicles) and to log patterns of farting, pissing, and shitting. His most terrifying experience with ill health was a 'great fitt of the Colique' which became, in Robert Latham's words, 'one of the best-documented attacks of flatulence in history'. Over nine days in October 1663, Pepys recorded growing stomach pain, the temporary relief of 'six or seven small and great farts', alarm at more pain when he 'went to try to shit', and so on. Recording was part of an effort to work out which treatments were beneficial. Having finally gained relief, he wrote down 'Rules for my health', which included using enemas and not straining on the privy.[43] Faced with this fearful situation, the diary had allowed Pepys to track his symptoms, assess remedies, and come up with solutions to ward off a recurrence. Whether or not these were successful, the act of recording had evidently provided some solace: it acknowledged his pain and cast him as an active participant in seeking relief, rather than a helpless sufferer.

The diary appears to have served comparable functions in his professional life, acting as means to exert control over his circumstances or – failing that – to offer the peace of mind that came with establishing there was nothing more to be done. During the 1660s, the Navy Board had inadequate funds, inefficient bureaucracy, and incompetent officials. As Clerk of the Acts, Pepys could do nothing about international wars and court factionalism, and his options in dealing with exasperating colleagues were limited. As with his comment (mentioned earlier) about the need to dissemble with Penn, he used the diary to note and rationalize his tactics. Sometimes the only relief that diary keeping could provide was a space to vent his spleen in safety. When provoked, Pepys had a fine line in sarcasm. In March 1668, rumours were flying about the parliament's investigations into the mismanagement of the Dutch war and the disgrace that no doubt awaited the Navy Board members. Recording these, Pepys first mimicked the tone of the gossips, then scoffed at the senility of his colleague Sir John Mennes, swiped at his other colleagues' corruption, and ended by implying that even their best efforts at corruption were not up to standard:

> W Hewers tells me, he hears this morning that all the town is full of the discourse that the Officers of the Navy shall be all turned out but honest Sir Jo. Minnes – who, God knows, is fitter to have been turned out himself then any of us, doing the King more hurt by his dotage and fally [i.e. folly] than all the rest can do by their knavery if they had a mind to it.[44]

Clearly this kind of comment had no place in the official records Pepys maintained, although those records were tracking the enduring problem that was Mennes. Later in 1668, Pepys began to journal his efforts to oust Mennes by adding 'memoranda' on this subject to his office letter book – minus the sarcasm of his personal diary. One such official memorandum ended by noting that, while he had fallen 'short of what I had laboured for' in attempting to get his superiors on side, he had done his 'utmost'.[45]

For Pepys, the act of recording and reflecting held out the promise of control in situations where he was otherwise helpless. As the letter book memorandum implies, this included the reassurance that came from preparing for the worst, if all other measures had failed. When, on 19 October 1666, the Board warned the duke of York that there were no funds left to supply the war effort, Pepys felt the need for a personal record of this warning. He detailed the conversation in his diary and remarked: 'This I set down for my future justification, if need be', emphasizing he had noted 'the very words' spoken.[46] This was prescient of him, for he was indeed called on to account for his actions. In January 1670 he supplied a 'particular' (personal) defence of himself to the committee that was investigating miscarriages during the war. In it he wrote: 'I challenge any man to assign one day from my first admission to this service in July 1660 to the determination [i.e. end] of the war August 1667 [. . .] of which I am not at this day able upon oath to give an account of the particular manner of my employing the same.'[47] He could, of course, make this claim in his particular defence because, in addition to his work papers, he had kept a particular diary.

Pepys's diary retained its importance to him because, unlike his other records, it was eminently adaptable to circumstances. When he needed a place to vindicate himself against political enemies, log useful gossip about a colleague, work up an amusing anecdote, or reflect on how to manage his wife's behaviour, his diary could serve him, and in as much detail as he saw fit. While many of the uses he developed concerned his self-betterment, the journal's importance as a store of moments of joy grew over time. His delights ranged from watching 'with great pleasure' as a plasterer worked on his new music room to leisure trips on the Thames with Elizabeth ('by water all the afternoon up as high as Moreclacke, with great pleasure, and a fine day – reading over the second part of *The Siege of Rhodes* with great delight').[48] Even during the Great Fire there were pleasing curiosities worth treasuring up – such as the transformed glass he first collected, then recorded. A treasure of a different kind stored in the diary was a macabre story told to him in August 1665. A maidservant, sick of plague, had escaped quarantine and roamed the countryside. Her frightened master believed her dead until he 'met the wench walking over the Common, which frighted him worse then before'. Further dark comedy followed when a gentleman took her for a lady heading to an illicit rendezvous and got a near fatal shock when he accosted her.[49] This kind of anecdote was worth remembering, not least because it might serve as conversation to 'give' others. Pepys's extramarital sexual encounters were also worth preserving, though if the diary is to be credited, these were few and far between for its first few years. That changed. When he ended his diary on 31 May 1669 he described it as the obverse of his official work records: its irreplaceable purpose was now documenting pleasure and, specifically, illicit pleasure. Due to his failing eyesight, he explained, any future record would need to be kept by his servants and contain 'no more then is fit for them and all the world to know'; anything requiring more secrecy 'cannot be much, now my amours to Deb are past, and my eyes hindering me in almost all other pleasures'.[50] The kind of diary he now imagined he would be compelled to keep was much more like that of his first patron, Sandwich, assisted by clerks: it would be personal but no longer private.

History and Pleasure

By its close, Pepys's diary had become an impressively malleable resource, weaving together his competing interests in business and delight. His eclectic mix of priorities combined to create vivid episodes which appear to close the historical distance between his past and readers' present. We can see how this works – and start to consider the issue of whether he ever wrote for anyone other than himself – by taking a close look at one of his most famous entries. On 23 April 1661, Pepys attended the coronation of Charles II. Also in Westminster Abbey was his future friend and fellow diary keeper, John Evelyn (1620–1706), who took a different approach to recording this spectacle. Indeed, comparisons with John Evelyn are an important part of how Pepys's fame as a diarist was established. Even before the diary was in print, its publisher was advertising the connection to Evelyn's much respected memoirs as means of burnishing Pepys's reputation.⁵¹ On the coronation Evelyn wrote:

> 23 Was the *Coronation* of his *Majesty Charles* the *Second* in the *Abby*-Church of *Westminster* at all which Ceremonie I was present [. . .] he went by Water to Westminster *Abby*: when his *Majestie* was entered, the *Deane* & *Prebends* brought all the *Regalia* [. . .]
>
> after *Sermon* the K: tooke his *Oath* before the Altar, to <maintaine> the *Religion, Mag: Charta* & Laws of the Land: Then the Hymn *Veni S[ancte] Sp[iritus]*, then the *Leitany* by 2 Bish[ops]. Then the L[ord] A[rch] B[ishop] of Cant[erbury] (present but <much> indisposd & weake) said, Lift-up your hearts: Then rose up the *King*, & put off his robes & upper garments; & was in a Wastcoate so opened in divers places as the A: Bishop might commodiously anoint him, first in the palmes of his hands, then was sung an *Anthem* & prayer, Then his breast, & twixt the shoulders, bending of both armes, & lastly on the crowne of the head: with apposite hymns & prayers at each anoynting: Then closd & buttned up the *Wastcoate*, which was don by the *Deane*.⁵²

Evelyn's solemn tone matches the solemnity of the occasion, as does his elevated register ('commodiously', 'apposite'). His credibility comes from detailed, factual reporting and his impersonal stance. All we learn of his own experience at the Abbey is that he was present 'at all'. This, as you might expect, is not the case with Pepys. His entry began at Lord Sandwich's lodging in Whitehall, where he had stayed over, sharing a bed, to get an early start:

> 23. I lay with Mr Sheply, and about 4 in the morning I rose.
> *Coronacion day*
> And got to the abby, where I fallowed Sir J. Denham the surveyour with some company that he was leading in. And with much ado, by the favour of Mr. Cooper his man, did get up into a great scaffold across the north end of the abby – where with a great deal of patience I sat from past 4 till 11 before the King came in. And a pleasure it was to see the Abbey raised in the middle, all covered with red and a throne (that is a chaire) and footstoole on the top of it. And all the officers of all kinds, so much as the very fidlers, in red vests.
>
> At last comes in the Deane and prebends of Westminster with the Bishops (many of them in cloth-of-gold Copes); and after them the nobility all in their parliament-robes, which was a most magnificent sight. [. . .]
>
> The King in his robes, bare-headed, which was very fine. And after all had placed themselfs – there was a sermon and the service. And then in the Quire [i.e. choir] at the high altar he passed all the ceremonies of the Coronacion – which, to my very great grief, I and most in the Abbey could not see. The crowne being put upon his head, a great shout begun. And he came forth to

the Throne and there passed more ceremonies: as, taking the oath and having things read to him by the Bishopp [...]

But so great a noise, that I could make but little of the Musique; and endeed, it was lost to everybody. But I had so great a list [i.e. desire] to pisse, that I went out a little while before the King had done all his ceremonies, and went round the abby to Westminster-hall, all the way within rayles, and 10000 people, with the ground coverd with blue cloth – and Scaffolds all the way. Into the hall I got – where it was very fine with hangings and scaffolds, one upon another, full of brave [i.e. fine] ladies. And my wife in one little one on the right hand.[53]

Pepys, unlike Evelyn, is concerned with the time and effort involved in becoming a witness: rising early, sneaking into the abbey, and the wait till 'at last' the bishops arrive. The mechanics of how he got into the Abbey contribute to a lively description, but they also serve Pepys's interest in social accounting. He did not have the status to secure a prime seat legitimately, so had to rely on Mr Cooper's favour. As he was now under obligation to Cooper, the man's name and position made it into this record.

When it came to the ceremony itself, Pepys does not supply Evelyn's level of visual detail, chiefly because to his 'great grief' he could not see it. Principal sights and pleasing sounds from the ceremony, he is clear, were inaccessible to most present. It is Pepys's attention to his own body (not the king's) that is most striking here. Even today nipping out for a 'pisse' is the kind of detail that might be left out of a personal diary describing a dignified state occasion. However, Pepys mentioned pissing to explain why he missed part of the ceremony and why he ended up navigating the abbey – for him, moving among the crowds proved a more exhilarating experience than witnessing the ceremony from afar. What we get at this point is equivalent to a long tracking shot recreating the varying focus of Pepys's attention: what he saw as he followed the railings; a wide pan to register the size of the crowd; a closer focus as he notices the fine ladies, and then a zoom-in as he spots his wife among them. In this entry, Pepys attended to what he could not see and hear, as well as to what he could: to the disappointments of the day, as well as its delights.

In Pepys's and Evelyn's accounts we get two different kinds of authenticity: Evelyn describes what happened at the coronation; Pepys describes what it was like to be at the coronation. If Evelyn's reporting sounds official, it is because much of it (including the description of the anointing) closely follows an account in one of the officially licensed newsbooks, the *Kingdomes Intelligencer*. A few details are added, such as Evelyn's observation on the Archbishop of Canterbury's poor health.[54] Lifting materials from printed texts was not unusual for diarists – Pepys seems to have done it at least one point in his wider coronation reporting – but it testifies here to Evelyn's eye for future readers and his sense of creating a historical record.[55] He copied out this passage into his surviving papers many years after the event, at a point when he was writing for future generations of his family.[56]

Pepys's method, in contrast, is grounded in his own experience and senses. It presents a credible and seemingly complete account through noting when those senses (and his ability to discern events) failed. After an evening of celebratory boozing he retired back to his lodging:

> no sooner a-bed with Mr. Sheply but my head begun to turne and I to vomitt, and if ever I was foxed it was now – which I cannot say yet, because I fell asleep and sleep till morning – only, when I waked I found myself wet with my spewing. Thus did the day end, with joy everywhere.[57]

Pepys wrote this entry up on the evening of the following day. However, trying to recall the effects of his drinking affected his tenses here, re-creating his disorientation (correctly, it should read 'if ever I was foxed it was *then* – which I *could* not say *then*'). In a characteristic shift at the end of this passage, he summed up the general joy, juxtaposed with his own less-than-joyful situation. This is the kind of abrupt change of tone and subject that earned Pepys a reputation as an unintentionally comic writer. He repeats this manoeuvre again at the very end of the entry. Apparently feeling a grand sign-off was called for he declared that 'the pleasure of the sight of these glorious things' could not be surpassed, followed by:

> 24. Waked in the morning with my head in a sad taking through the last night's drink, which I am very sorry for.[58]

Significantly, when Pepys assessed what the coronation meant it was the 'joy' and 'pleasure' it had offered him, not its political significance to Charles's realms. There are brief moments (including the climactic reference to 'joy everywhere') when Pepys's narrative reads like one of the accounts of celebrations published at the time in pamphlets and newsbooks. However, to serve such a purpose it would have had to be drastically redrafted to reduce its writer's presence and remove the lows of his experience. Those lows were important to him. The inclusion of his exit for a piss and his undignified spewing makes it manifest that he was writing here for himself – for himself as he wrote, recollecting this important day, and for himself as a prospective future reader, wanting to vividly recall this experience when memory had faded. He therefore sought to record those highs and lows, pleasures and pains, the one adding piquancy to the other.

Writing with Purpose

During the nine years that Pepys kept his diary, its value and its purposes changed. He turned the conventions and methods seen in religious diaries and financial recording to his own ends. His was a peculiarly flexible record, partly because one of its roles was to take on functions not fulfilled by his other forms of record-keeping. As such, its purposes developed to include assessing and improving his social status and his health; strategizing in relation to work and family problems; storing up potentially useful anecdotes and gossip; formulating pre-emptive defences; and relishing licit and (increasingly) illicit pleasures. This was a dynamic text, both in the sense that it evolved in response to Pepys's changing needs and in that it was intended to act upon him, stimulating favourable change in him and for him. The favourable changes he sought came not through focusing on goodness or godliness but on honour and prudence – conducting himself in the wisest manner financially, emotionally, religiously, and politically.

While many early modern diarists expected to be read by others, the reader that Pepys imagined for his diary was clearly himself, though himself in different futures. He shows evidence of expecting to consult his diary in the upcoming months and years (to recall anecdotes, delights, justifications and, if needed, to testify to his diligence). Simultaneously, his summary of his position in his first entry, along with his detailed, embodied descriptions, indicates he also wrote for himself in the distant future: for an older man who would need prompts to remember exactly where he had once stood – literally so at important moments such as the coronation. That older Pepys would need no reminder of what the 'old pain' meant, but he might well need his memory jogging about the exact political situation on 1 January 1660.

Reading with a mind to Pepys's priorities in this record helps make sense of the puzzling swerves and changing focus of individual entries as he set them down in their final form. His hawkish eye for matters of social status, or his desire to supply entertaining conversation, for example, can explain why certain episodes or details were worth revisiting via writing up and why they were worth memorializing for those hypothetical near-future and far-future selves. This kind of close reading can also uncover what may be opaque to us but was plain to Pepys: obligations incurred, tacit evaluations made, and even his omission of information that was too obvious or too inconvenient to explicitly acknowledge. To pursue the issue of his sense of readership and more fully explore the history he offers, however, we need an additional approach. I have so far, like almost all writers on Pepys, treated the diary as if it were a printed longhand record or a free-floating, unchanging 'text'. This misses the wealth of insight that comes from considering its original form. As I hinted when discussing the orderly presentation of Pepys's very first entry, the appearance of his diary clearly mattered to him. He valued the physical characteristics of books, just as he valued capturing the experiences of physical presence in his reporting. The next chapter follows his lead in giving careful attention to the six manuscript volumes that make up the journal.

CHAPTER 2

Shorthand and Secrecy

The secrecy of Pepys's diary has, ironically, helped win it millions of readers. Since the diary was first published, Pepys's use of shorthand has been taken as a powerful voucher for his accuracy and credibility. As Pepys's first editor put it, shorthand allowed him to record 'his most secret thoughts' with 'exactness' and without fear of discovery. (For an example of what this shorthand looks like, see Figure 2.3 on p. 43). Publishers portrayed Pepys's efforts at disguise as part of the diary's allure: early editions were advertised as 'deciphered' from the 'original short-hand MS.' or from Pepys's 'MS. cypher'.[1] Readers' interest naturally focuses on the secrets hidden, rather than the 'cypher' that hides them. Yet Pepys's shorthand itself conveyed meaning and it was integral to how he conceived of his diary. He signalled this in his final entry. Continuing the diary in its current form, he wrote, would be 'to undo my eyes', but the alternative could only be inferior. He imagined he would have it

> kept by my people [i.e. servants] in longhand, and must therefore be contented to set down no more then is fit for them and all the world to know; or if there be anything (which cannot be much, now my amours to Deb are past, and my eyes hindering me in almost all other pleasures), I must endeavour to keep a margin in my book open, to add here and there a note in short-hand with my own hand.[2]

Here he was clear that the chief virtue of shorthand was masking information not fit for 'all the world to know'. By 1669 he had come to see private information (especially his 'pleasures') as the chief reason for his diary's existence.

While Pepys regarded shorthand as vital to his purposes, it has generally been seen by commentators as interesting in principle, but not necessary to engage with in practice. Nineteenth-century editors had almost nothing to say about Pepys's 'cypher' – it was the enticing idea of a code cracked that mattered. Their silence stemmed chiefly from ignorance. In the first hundred and forty years of the diary's publication, only one of the men who oversaw a major edition could read shorthand: Mynors Bright, who produced the 1870s text. The others – Lord Braybrooke (in the 1820s to the 1850s) and Henry Wheatley (in the 1890s) – relied on transcripts that were the work of others. In the 1960s this changed: William Matthews was employed to work on the diary because of his shorthand expertise, while his fellow editor, Robert Latham, learned to read it on the job.[3] Matthews's description of Pepys's manuscript in the introduction to the complete edition is the sole authority for most contemporary discussion. Today only a handful of people in the world can read Pepys's shorthand. It remains extremely unusual for anyone writing on Pepys to have spent time with the six volumes of his manuscript, let alone read any of it. This has led to misconceptions about just what is possible using shorthand and how easy Pepys's text is to understand.[4] A detailed investigation of Pepys's use of shorthand in the diary, his secrecy, and what that secrecy reveals is long overdue.

Considering the diary as a shorthand text means upending some of the assumptions that underlie how it is usually understood. As readers, if we think about shorthand at all, it tends to be as a kind of cover that Pepys added to his text, one which has to be removed to expose the original meaning in English. Instead, the reverse is true. The shorthand *is* the original text, and the English we read in printed editions is constructed from it: it is the printed English longhand that has to be "seen through" if we want to better appreciate the information Pepys's diary conveys. Pepys's diary volumes have other properties that are lost or mediated in printed editions; for example, the layout, longhand, and his varying use of shorthand all carry meaning. Most notoriously, part way through his diary, Pepys began to use a mixture of English, French, Spanish and other languages to write up some of his sexual encounters. A reader of the manuscript therefore must contend not only with Pepys's shorthand, but with his idiosyncratic polyglot shorthand. It means we need to ask not just 'what does this passage mean?' but 'what might it mean that it takes this form?' Getting to grips with Pepys's methods can be tricky, but it rewards the effort – not least because it contains clues about his thoughts on whether his diary might, one day, find readers.

Shorthand in England

Many people in seventeenth-century England judged shorthand a skill worth learning. The ability to note down speech quickly using symbols had both personal and professional uses. Visiting London in 1641, Jan Amos

Komenský was struck by the 'large number of men and youths' who took shorthand notes of sermons, a phenomenon he regarded as peculiarly English.[5] Besides being a fashionable aspect of devotional practice, shorthand was a desirable skill in administrators, although it was far from essential: in 1668, Sir William Coventry, Pepys's ally who himself used shorthand, was seeking a new clerk with 'shorthand if it may be'. In the 1660s and 1670s, Pepys had men working under him in the Navy Office who used various shorthands, including Will Hewer, the man who became his surrogate son.[6] Men and women wanting to acquire this skill could do so via paying a tutor or purchasing a manual. Rival shorthand teachers vigorously advertised their systems on posts around London and published books describing their methods.[7] Pepys chose to learn one of the most popular systems, Thomas Shelton's 'Tachygraphy' ('swift-writing'). Like many shorthands, this had been devised with sermon note-takers in mind and contained special symbols for their convenience. Pepys could have picked up shorthand as a boy in London but, since Shelton and his publishers targeted university students, he probably learned it at Cambridge in the 1650s.[8] It must have looked like a sound investment of time and money: shorthand was good for recording university lectures and debates; it would be a useful skill in his likely line of work as a clerk; and – since it saved on paper and ink – it was a money-saving measure in the long term.

When Shelton advertised tachygraphy's benefits, the first he noted was its 'secrecie': it allowed a man to write down 'that which he would not have every one acquainted with [...] for his owne private use onely'. Its other advantages were 'brevitie, celeritie, and perpetuity' (meaning, he explained, preserving 'things of good use [...] which otherwise had bin lost').[9] All of these attributes made shorthand appealing to Pepys as a tool for diary keeping, but secrecy was particularly important. He was not alone in this. As researchers have shown, shorthand was used by other contemporary journal keepers to protect their thoughts. Starting her diary in 1686, Sarah Henry wished she had 'the advantage of writing characters' to help 'keep it private'; while the teenage Isaac Newton at Cambridge, and the alchemist George Starkey were among those who recorded their sins (including sexual sins) in shorthand.[10]

Recent writing on Pepys's diary has been sceptical about how much protection shorthand offered him. Keen to correct the view that shorthand was a mysterious code, writers are now more likely to argue that the contents were barely protected at all, even stating that learning Shelton was 'standard practice' in England.[11] The truth lies in the middle. Sold on bookstalls for over sixty years across the century, Shelton's tachygraphy was emphatically not a secret code and to call it a 'cipher' is misleading. If Pepys had wanted to use a code, he would have done so: he devised personal 'Characters' for his employers George Downing and Edward Mountagu to keep their correspondence secret.[12] Pepys also chose not to take full advantage of the concealing properties of shorthand for, like most shorthand users, he generally wrote place names and proper names in longhand. A page of his diary is very clearly a diary: it has the month in longhand, dates in the margins, and each page has an assortment of longhand words that provide clues to its content. On the other hand, the fact that shorthand offered privacy was, as his closing comments confirm, crucial. Keeping his diary locked in his study was the first line of defence but, if that measure failed, shorthand protected the diary from being easily understood by the people most likely to happen on it: his household servants and Elizabeth.[13] While it was possible that Elizabeth might go through his papers during his lifetime, the more serious risk was that, if he died unexpectedly, she would inherit the diary. His wariness about her as a potential reader helps explain a much-noted quirk of the diary: Pepys never names his wife. Elizabeth is never 'Elizabeth' or an initial, she is always 'my wife', and 'my wife' is in shorthand.[14] Pepys's habit of referring only to 'my wife' shows the value in which he held her and his sense that her identity was inseparable from his own, yet it also owes something to the principles of shorthand. 'My wife' was four strokes of the pen in Shelton's symbols – an economy that meant there was no real impetus to devise a special symbol for 'Elizabeth'. Since his habit with names was to default to longhand or longhand initials, getting into the practice of avoiding Elizabeth's name when writing ensured against a slip into longhand: she would therefore remain invisible to would-be readers – and to herself, should she discover the diary.

Reading Pepys's Shorthand

This brings us to what a reader sees on Pepys's page and how difficult his shorthand actually is to read. Shelton's system has a symbol for each letter, which is simple enough. However, it also has symbols for pairs of consonants that commonly appear together and for common prefixes and suffixes (such as 'pro-' or '-ing'). There are symbols, too, for common words and for words or phrases likely to appear in sermons. Many symbols do double duty, standing for a letter, a cluster of letters, or a word. For instance, the symbol for 'n' is –, which is also the symbol for 'and'. (Shelton beat 'Fish N Chips' advertisers to this abbreviation by several hundred years.) Shelton also encouraged users to choose symbols for their own common words, which Pepys duly did for words such as 'Mr' and 'home'.[15]

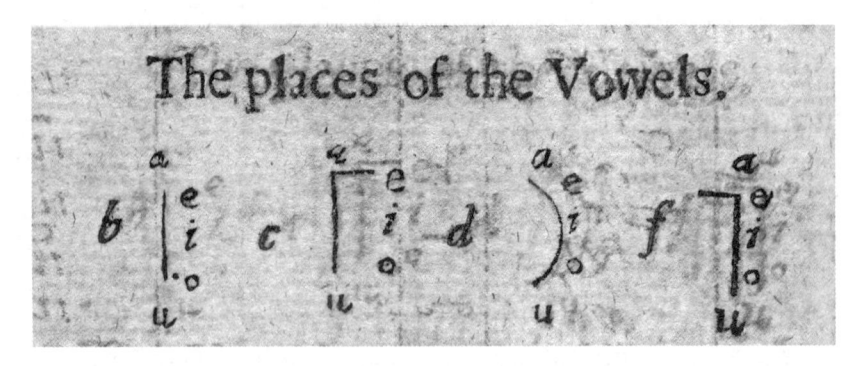

Figure 2.1 From Thomas Shelton's *Tachy-graphy* (1660), p. 4.

While Shelton allocated a symbol to each letter of the alphabet, he had a separate procedure for handling vowels in the middle of words. These are not normally written with a symbol, but are instead shown by the positioning of the symbol that follows the vowel. In Figure 2.1, Shelton illustrates vowel positions around the symbols for b, c, d, and f, by marking the place with the longhand vowel letter. When a writer takes their pen off the page mid-word and starts a new symbol (rather than joining symbols together), this signals a vowel, and where they position that new symbol tells you which vowel precedes it. For example, the symbol for 'c' with a 't' symbol directly above it (at 12 o'clock) means 'cat'; 't' at 2 o'clock is 'cet'; at 3 o'clock 'cit'; 5 o'clock 'cot'; and at 6 o'clock 'cut'. When a vowel comes at the end of a word it is shown by a dot in the relevant position. Words ending in 'y' are spelt with 'i' instead. Finally, to aid speed in writing, Shelton requires users to spell phonetically and remove letters that are 'superfluous'– meaning letters that are not sounded, not strongly sounded, or which can be easily deduced.[16] This applies to double vowels: for instance, 'about' becomes 'abot' and 'book' becomes 'bok'. Terminal 'e' is also a common casualty: 'slope' would be written 'slop'. In this system punctuation is almost entirely absent: Shelton suggests the writer only needs a sign for a full stop and can make use of question marks and brackets.[17]

This is, overall, a very flexible system: it can handle multisyllabic words, proper nouns, and (if not always smoothly) foreign words. However, Shelton's method does have certain ingrained difficulties, even when the reader is experienced and the writer, like Pepys, careful. First, a number of the symbols closely resemble other symbols. For instance, 'him' and 'then' are both variations of < . Meanwhile, the sign for 'b' (|) is also the sign for 'but' and happens to resemble the sign for 'them' (a slightly longer vertical line) ... and so on.[18] It is easy for a slight movement of the pen or a random blot to accidentally transform a word, and easy for writers to mix up symbols. Second, as the vowel positions rely on fine discriminations, it is not always easy to determine which vowel a writer intended. Finally, shorthand relies on cutting out letters and this incompleteness leads to ambiguities. How a writer chooses to abbreviate words can throw up a range of possibilities: the shorthand 'slop' could, for example, mean 'slop', or 'slope', or 'sloop'. If a writer has been precise and the reader is tuned into their idiosyncrasies, has a sound grasp of the context, and has understood the last few words, matters are straightforward, but lose the thread of meaning and it can be difficult to reconstruct what was intended.

To get a sense of how shorthand works in practice, we can take the start of Pepys's most famous entry, the first day of the Great Fire, 2 September 1666, shown in Figure 2.2. Literally, what Pepys wrote was this (with longhand shown in bold):

> 2 **Lords day** Sum of our mades siting up lat la nit 2 get things redi against our fe 2 dai **Jane** called us up abot 3 in the morning 2 tell us of a gr fir they se in the city. So I ros and slipt on mi nit gon and went 2 her windo and thought it to be on the bak sid of **Markelane** at the ['further' crossed out] furthest but being unused 2 such firs as fallod I thought it far nuf of and so went 2 bed again and 2 sleep.[19]

With very little experience of reading shorthand, it becomes easy to see '2' as (most often) 'to', and to recognize that 'dai' is 'day' and 'mi' is 'my'. Certain of the highly abbreviated words here, such as 'fe' for feast and 'gr' for 'great', are signs found in Shelton's manual (i.e. the symbol for 'gr' is also the symbol for 'great'). Pepys also employs some of his own formulations: 'la' for last, and 'se' for see/saw. With more exposure to Shelton's recommendations and how Pepys implements them, even seeming gobbledegook like 'mi nit gon' becomes legible: 'my night gown' is meant. The bizarre-looking 'fallod' is made up of the symbol for 'fall/full', and the symbol for 'd' in the position of an 'o'. What Pepys meant was 'fallo'd' for 'fallowed': in modern spelling this would be 'followed'. When skilled editors, such as Latham and Matthews, render the passage for their readers, it becomes:

> 2. *Lords day*. Some of our maids sitting up late last night to get things ready against our feast today, Jane called us up, about 3 in the morning, to tell us of a great fire they saw in the City. So I rose, and slipped on my nightgown and went to her window, and thought it to be on the back side of Markelane at the furthest; but being unused to such fires as fallowed, I thought it far enough off, and so went to bed again and to sleep.[20]

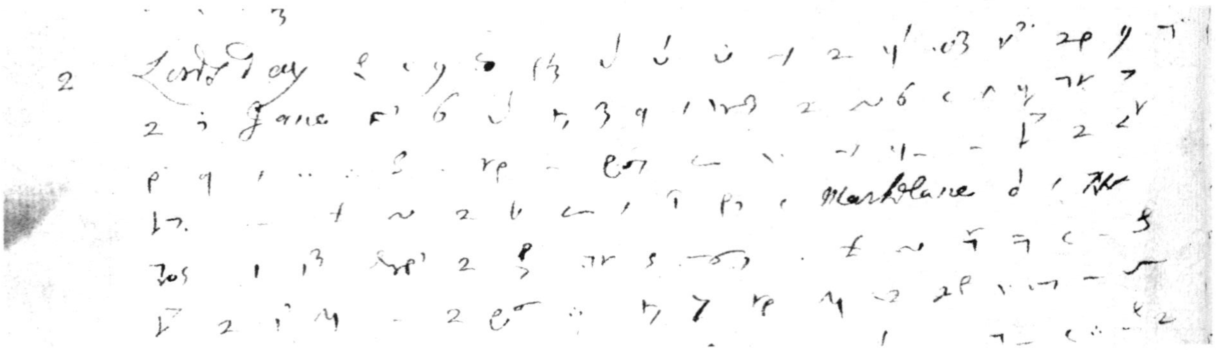

Figure 2.2 Diary of Samuel Pepys, 2 September 1666. PL 1839.

Comparing this amended transcription with the more literal one above conveys just how much work editorial teams have performed to make Pepys's shorthand legible for audiences. This work is far from visible in printed texts and has often been downplayed by editors, due to lack of knowledge (they didn't do the work themselves), modesty, or a desire to instil faith in their edition. In their public statements Latham and Matthews emphasized the reliability of their text (arguing Shelton's was a simple system, Pepys's hand legible, and even his polyglot straightforward) and often made light of the challenges. Their unpublished editorial papers are much clearer about the difficulties they faced, with lists of Pepys's personal symbols and the editors' lengthy discussions over how to render the text. Even whether to signal the longhand caused them much trouble – Latham ultimately decided not to do so. They chose to modernize the shorthand spellings, except where they felt the shorthand indicated a seventeenth-century variant spelling with a distinct pronunciation: so 'fallod', for them, became 'fallowed'.[21] Other editors and transcribers determined differently, without explanation. Mynors Bright in the 1870s generally favoured more antiquated spellings, seeking to create a seventeenth-century flavour: in his version of the Great Fire, Pepys was alerted by his 'mayds', slipped on his 'night-gowne', and thought the fire was 'on the back-side of Marke-lane at the farthest', not expecting what 'followed'.[22] These are small judgement calls but, across thousands of words, cumulatively powerful, contributing to readers' impressions of Pepys as a peculiarly modern and accessible diarist or as a charmingly quaint writer.

The fact that Pepys wrote in shorthand created great difficulties for editorial teams but it has resulted in versions of a seventeenth-century text that are more than usually easy for readers to understand. Shorthand meant Pepys's editors could not aim at immediate fidelity to the original and were instead compelled to implement their own decisions on spelling, punctuation, and grammar. Unlike, say, the editor of Evelyn's diary (quoted in Chapter 1) who sought to preserve a detailed impression of the manuscript by reproducing Evelyn's spellings and leaving abbreviations unexpanded, editors of Pepys have had to be more radical in their interventions. They create, rather than replicate, an English text and the results are editions extensively tailored to contemporary tastes. As Aaron Kunin observes, Pepys's diary can therefore seem 'magically transparent' in comparison to other early modern diarists' prose.[23] Transcribers and editors had free rein to determine the best combination of strikingly direct, fluently conversational, or "authentically" antiquated language to please their target audience.

While Pepys's use of shorthand required editors to reshape his text, it had already fundamentally shaped his prose. William Matthews thought the immediacy of shorthand note-taking propelled Pepys away from the ornamental, Ciceronian style that he deployed in official documents, towards a 'simple, quasi-conversational manner'.[24] This does not mean Pepys wrote as he spoke. The features of a shorthand system encourage certain language choices. Even for a proficient user, Shelton's method exerts a subtle pressure towards the words 'frequent in use' for which Shelton had created simple symbols and towards words which can be easily written.[25] It is no coincidence that Pepys's most characteristic phrases (ones that, down the centuries, imitators and parodists would echo) are extremely quick to write in shorthand. For example, his habitual way of beginning an entry is 'Up and to ... ': in shorthand this is three simple symbols amounting to three pen strokes. 'And so to bed', his famous phrase for ending his day, is five strokes, with the first three words each having their own single symbol: − S 2 |$^?$. His much repeated (and much mimicked) verbal tic, 'But Lord ... ' is two strokes. Another favourite 'But strange to see ... ' is similarly straightforward. His highs and lows of emotion are often introduced by 'with great' (with great delight/pleasure/sadness, etc.): 'with' and 'great' each have their own symbol, and each is one continuous stroke. Overall, Shelton's system encouraged Pepys towards easy and familiar symbols and less multisyllabic language, thereby shaping his idiosyncratic, accessible style.

Shorthand, intended to obscure sense, therefore ultimately contributed to the clarity of Pepys's diary for readers in two respects: it steered Pepys towards short, common words and it compelled editors to adapt his language and grammar to their own period, offering their readerships prose that (however archaic it might seem) was modernized. There is a third sense in which Pepys's language is clear: in his manuscript, he laid out his text with precision. His lines are carefully spaced and his characters usually well formed. Matthews observes that Pepys also preferred to end entries at the end of a page.[26] Pepys's care with shorthand characters and his manuscript's layout was a reflection of his own character. In 1663 he noted in himself a growing refusal to 'be pleased with anything unless it be very neat'.[27] As Latham remarks, the neatness of the diary seems to have had emotional importance for Pepys.[28] An aesthetically pleasing text presented an orderly life over which he could exert a firm hand, even – or especially – if events felt beyond his control. His orderly approach distinguishes him from the many writers who used shorthand in ways that indicated their purpose was "notes to self": where the legibility mattered less because familiarity with your own scrappy hand and your memory of the substance would be enough to make things clear.[29] Pepys's neatness signalled the value of the content and that the 'self' reading it might be many years in the future. It also, ultimately, held out the possibility of the diary's being legible to other readers.

Deeper Secrets

Shorthand was not the only protective measure that Pepys employed in his pages, nor was it the only indication of his sense of who might read them. The diary covers a wide range of sexual activity from solitary fantasies and masturbation to anatomically specific descriptions of who did what to whom. Midway through his journal, Pepys began to change the way he recorded some of these episodes. Early in the diary all such passages were in English shorthand, as when, in September 1663, he took Betty Lane on a pleasure trip to Lambeth: 'and there did what I would with her but only the main thing, which she would not consent to, for which God be praised; and yet I came so near, that I was provoked to spend' (i.e. ejaculate). In later entries, there was less concern with God's providential oversight of his sexual encounters, and more concern for the diary being overseen. In January 1664, he began to write some of these shorthand passages in French, starting with another encounter with Betty Lane at 'the cabaret at the Cloche in the street du roy [. . .] je l'ay foutée sous de la chaise deux times' (at 'the tavern at the Bell in King Street [. . .] I fucked her under the chair two times'). In June 1666, he began switching languages, producing a polyglot of French, Spanish, English, and Latin, with occasional words from other tongues. Meeting the now-married Betty Martin at her home, he 'did what je voudrais avec her, both devante and backward, which is also muy bon plazer' ('did what I would with her, both front and backward, which is also very good pleasure').[30] Next, around May 1667, he decreased his use of longhand overall. At the same time, he began to add extra letters into English shorthand about sex, and a few days later combined this technique of garbling words with his polyglot shorthand.[31] The effects can be seen in his account of how he had ceased to worry about Elizabeth Knepp resenting what he had done 'quand yo was con he**l**er in ponendo her mano upo**l**on mi**n**i cosa'. This is a mix of English, French, and Spanish. Into three English words he has added extra letter symbols ('l' twice and 'n' once, shown in bold). Because of the way Shelton's shorthand uses a symbol's position to indicate a preceding vowel, this in fact adds additional syllables (el, ol, in). With Pepys's extraneous letters removed what we get in Latham and Matthews's text is: 'quand yo was con her in ponendo her mano upon mi cosa'.[32] Finally, when translated it becomes, 'when I was with her in putting her hand upon my thing'.

Clearly Pepys went to great lengths to cover up this phrase, and others too. However, he was not at all consistent in his concealment. Some of the polyglot passages, although they allude to illicit relationships, do not contain sexually explicit material; in other sexual passages he used only shorthand. He also sometimes used longhand for names and words that should have been in shorthand if concealing the nature of the passages was the sole concern. This has led Matthews and others to argue that the polyglot was less about disguise and more about playfulness, or adding an air of continental, titillating sophistication to Pepys's sex life.[33] While this is a persuasive explanation for the foreign language use, it remains crucial not to underestimate Pepys's efforts at disguise. The manuscripts of early transcribers, who found the shorthand suddenly descending into gibberish, demonstrate that Pepys's tactics caused serious issues. Mynors Bright's transcript shows that, on encountering passages in French, he first assumed Pepys was using a 'different cipher' (another shorthand). After transcribing more entries, he deduced it was French, but was again stumped when Pepys shifted to a polyglot. As he explained to readers in a preface, the introduction of '*dummy* letters' then saw him 'nearly giving up in despair', and he was only able to solve it by systematically removing alternate letters (and not always then).[34] Pepys's shifting languages may have heightened his pleasure, but they also heightened his defences.

Other Readers?

With knowledge of Pepys's polyglot and shorthand tactics, we can look again at how his diary was meant to be used and whether he anticipated a readership. Most simply, the words Pepys chose to write in longhand can be telling. Here, again, is his account of Charles's coronation that we saw in Chapter 1, this time with the longhand in bold:

> But so great a **noise** that I could make but little of the **Musique**, and endeed it was lost to every body. But I had so great a list to **pisse** that I went out a little while before the king had done all his [messily written 'ceremonies' deleted] ceremonies and went round the **abby** to **Westminster hall** all the way within **rayles**, and 10000 people, with the ground **coverd** with **blue cloth** – and **Scaffolds** all the way. Into the **hall** I got – where it was very fine with hangings and **scaffolds** one upon another, full of brave ladies. And my wife in one little one on the right hand.[35]

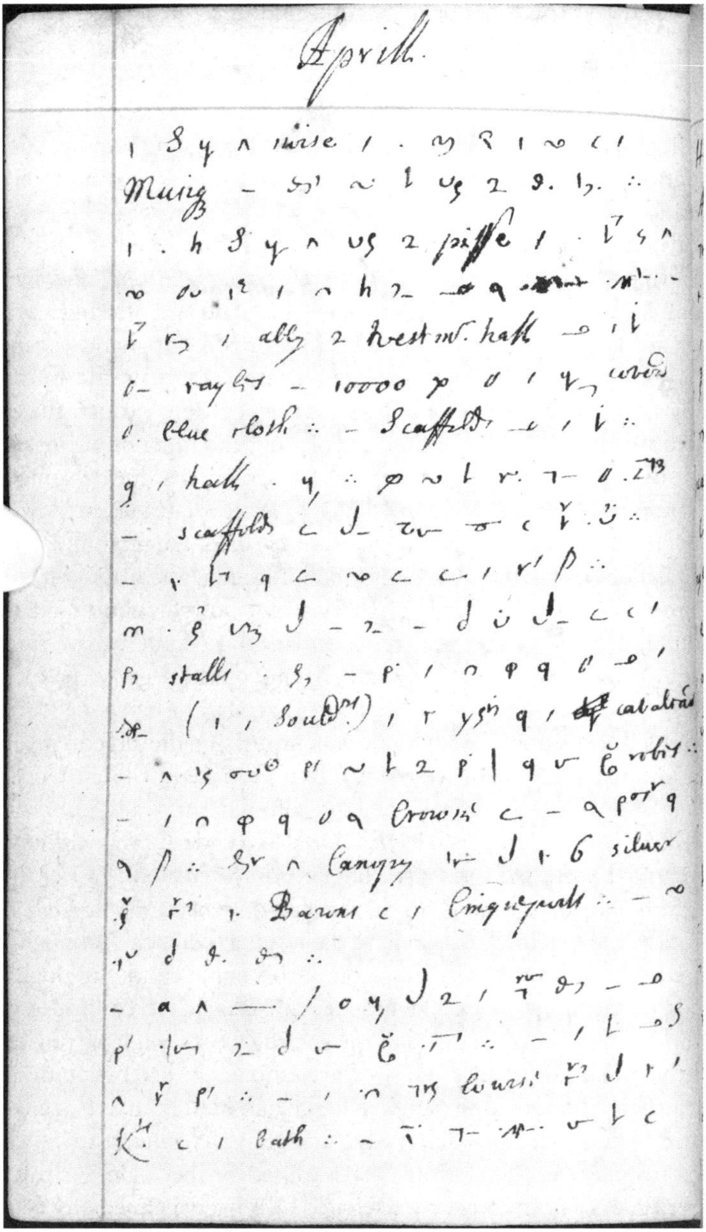

Figure 2.3 Diary of Samuel Pepys, 23 April 1661. PL 1836.

Figure 2.3 shows this diary page, beginning 'But so great . . . '. There is an unusual amount of longhand in this passage. Several words are placenames, which are normally written in longhand, but that explanation does not work for most examples here. Sometimes Pepys opted for longhand as it was easier than recalling the relevant symbols, but again that is no adequate explanation: words such as 'rayles' and 'blue cloth' are simple to do in shorthand, as indeed is 'pisse'. Since Pepys wrote 'pisse' in longhand, he evidently had no qualms about announcing that need – and indeed apparently wanted to stress it. Collectively, what the longhand seems to be doing in this excerpt is acting as a navigation aid and offering a precis of the text for a reader (Pepys himself). The words in longhand encapsulate Pepys's experience and his trajectory: the noise drowns the music; the pressing need to piss sets off a sight-seeing expedition through the Hall.

There are other examples in the diary of longhand functioning in this way. Indeed, its role as a finding aid seems to be active even during some of the diary's most private episodes. In late October 1668, Pepys sat down after several chaotic days to record how Elizabeth had caught him with Deb Willet. When he described the event, he put the fact he wanted to conceal most from his wife into a mix of garbled and polyglot shorthand. In the Introduction, I quoted this passage in Latham and Matthews's version with some additional translation, but what Pepys put on the page was far more of a challenge to readers (Figure 2.4). He wrote that, after he had gone to have his hair combed by Deb, Elizabeth found him 'imbrasing the girl con my haland sub su kimots and ended I was with mili min in heler kiloni'. Ungarbled, translated, and with the phonetic spelling adjusted, this reads 'imbracing the girl with my hand under her coats [i.e. skirts] and endeed I was with my hand in her cony' – 'cony' is a variant spelling of 'cunny' (vagina).[36] Over the next fortnight he insisted to Elizabeth that he had only been kissing Deb, before Deb told Elizabeth the full extent of their sexual contact. Although Pepys disguised that act in the diary, he wrote Deb's name clearly in longhand at the start of this episode (See Figure 2.4, mid-page). He continued to put 'Deb' and 'Willet' into longhand in the coming weeks, while he pursued her despite his wife's surveillance. This was even though he had previously grown more cautious about writing names in longhand. Had Elizabeth at any point laid her hands on the diary, the manifest references to 'Deb' on 25 October 1668 and after would have caused further pain. At this time, however, Pepys's need to clearly reference Deb overwhelmed any consideration of the risks. The repeated use of her name in longhand emphasized her central role in this episode and signals that he wanted to be able to locate these passages. It also shows that (despite his recognition that Deb had

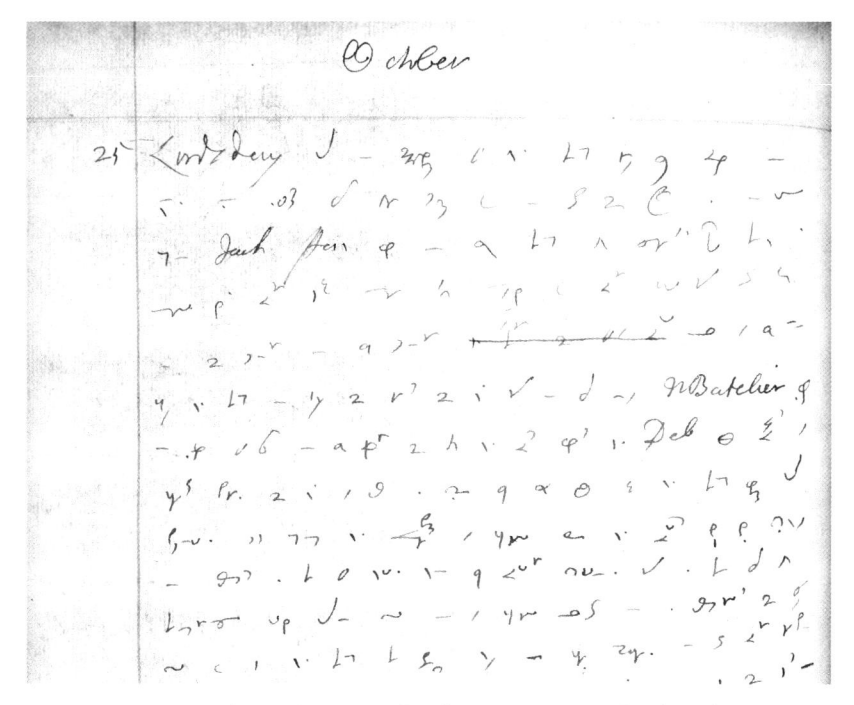

Figure 2.4 Diary of Samuel Pepys, 25 October 1668. PL 1841. The phrase beginning 'and endeed' is three lines from the bottom, at the start of the line.

suffered at his hands and been made 'my sacrifice'), his concern for her did not extend to masking her name within the text – he left her exposed.[37] His mention of Deb Willet on the final page of the diary, 'my amours to Deb are past', aptly captures the contradictions of his encoding approach and the appeal it had for him. 'Amours' is in longhand, but 'Deb' is now in garbled shorthand ('Deleb').[38] This was his last gesture at disguise before he ended his shorthand record, and the last thrill of writing a (barely) hidden name.[39]

Despite the inconsistencies in Pepys's secretive measures, his changing combinations of shorthand, longhand, polyglot shorthand, and mixed garbled and polyglot shorthand show that he strengthened his protective measures over the course of the diary. He did so, at least in part, because he was increasingly conscious that his diary might be read. After the death of his brother Tom in 1664, he had experienced what happened when private papers were passed to family members who were unfavourably discussed in them. Among Tom's papers, Samuel had found 'base letters' from their younger brother John. He was enraged at the 'very foul words' John had written about him and the 'plots' his brothers had been contriving together against him. As a result, he broke off contact with John for over two years.[40] During the Great Fire in 1666 and again in 1667 after the attack on Chatham, Pepys was impelled to send his diary volumes out of his custody, leaving them with others for safe keeping. By mid 1667 his growing influence, and the failures of the navy, had also made him a target for political enemies: he saw colleagues arrested and sent to the Tower, putting their papers at risk of confiscation.[41] The risks in keeping such a sensitive record had been repeatedly brought home to him.

The danger of hostile readers grew over the 1660s, but so too did the reasons for Pepys to consider that the contents of his diary should not remain entirely private. Through twists he could never have anticipated when he began writing, he had become an eyewitness to major historical events and court machinations. It would have become increasingly apparent to him that the diary contained material that could inform a published history – especially as he was coming to think of himself as a potential historian in relation to his naval work. As early as 1661, he set about writing a 'little treatise' on history and law concerning the king's claims to control of the seas around the British Isles, which he intended to circulate among navy officials. Friends and colleagues encouraged his ambitions as a historian. In 1664, when a new war with the Dutch was fast approaching, William Coventry suggested that Pepys write a history of the previous war during the 1650s. Pepys was delighted, feeling this project would suit 'mightily with my genius [i.e. character] – and if done well, may recommend me much'. Unlike his planned 1661 treatise, this history would have been destined for print. By 1668 he was considering writing a more ambitious 'history of the Navy', a project that would occupy him for the rest of his life.[42] Neither his treatise on the dominion of the seas, nor the history of the first Anglo-Dutch War, nor the grand history of the navy were ever completed – Pepys enjoyed researching and collecting material for histories far more than he loved actually writing them. However, in the 1660s and after, this kind of activity can only have sharpened his sense of how his personal diary might one day serve him as a source towards a naval history or, perhaps, serve someone else in a similar task. Close family, current enemies, and even distant generations were therefore all potential readers whom Pepys had cause to believe might have a strong interest in his diary. The possibility of these readers was clearly not enough to persuade him to adopt more consistent methods of protection, to avoid supplying damaging details, or to end the diary – its uses were too important to him for that. Yet, while its primary intended reader remained himself, his intimations of other readers developed as he wrote.

Shorthand Matters

Shorthand, though little understood, has been an enduring reason for the popularity of Pepys's diary. It has lent the diary an exciting air of mystery, while shaping a text which is highly readable. Shorthand influenced Pepys's direct, informal style and, by demanding unremitting editorial intervention, resulted in texts extensively adapted to their perceived audiences. When manuscripts are printed, some of the information conveyed by the material features of the original is inevitably lost, and this is more true of Pepys's diary than most other documents. His careful hand and regulated layout indicate, far more than any printed text can, that the diary was no spontaneous effusion and that its capacity to impose a neat order on his experiences was part of its purpose. As his eyesight deteriorated, his characters did too, and the diary had to end.

The use of shorthand and longhand in Pepys's entries often conveys how he expected to re-read them. This variation nuanced his statements and sometimes even undermines them. Coming amid his statements about his continued efforts to get Deb Willet's 'maidenhead', Pepys's concern for her during the events of October and November 1668 rings hollow enough in printed editions.[43] In his manuscript his repeated writing of her name in longhand at this time makes that resonance even louder. Blazoning his interest in her within the text and catering to his own future convenience in navigating this record took priority over any concerns about guarding her name. Pepys's efforts at ensuring the privacy of his diary's contents were erratic and the signs are that his sense of a potential readership beyond himself was similarly inconsistent. Yet his escalating protections, the manifest historical interest of his diary, and his own growing sense of himself as a historian who merited an audience, all strongly imply that his recognition of a potential readership increased as he wrote. Three decades later, he set about to turn that possibility into a certainty.

CHAPTER 3

Saving the Diary

Between ending his diary in May 1669 and his death almost thirty-four years later, Samuel Pepys gave much thought to how posterity would think about him. His deep concern for his reputation makes it all the more remarkable that he decided his scandalous, seditious diary should be preserved. That decision – which is, on the face of it, baffling – transformed Pepys's fame and it continues to transform how Restoration society is understood. He ran extraordinary risks in choosing to save his journal volumes (risks which only grew after the diary's end) and he took extraordinary steps to mitigate those risks. The puzzles of the diary's survival and what Pepys thought posterity should do with it are bound up with his understanding of archives and with the historical narratives that were available to him and his contemporaries. Today, the diary is seen as Pepys's most important achievement, but he saw it as a small part of a greater legacy that would preserve his memory and achievements for future generations. The diary was absorbed into his library, as six of the 2,971 volumes he left in his will 'for the benefitt of Posterity'. When writing his journal in the 1660s, Pepys gave little consideration to readers beyond himself. However, in 1703 when he laid out the 'Scheame' for the preservation of his books, he certainly had designs on future readers – which means he had designs on us.[1] To reckon with the explicit and implicit intentions of that scheme, which would ripple across three hundred years, we need to examine what prompted such an unusual and ambitious plan.

Dangers

A chief end of Pepys's diary keeping in the 1660s had been to help him refine his self-presentation, and thereby improve his prospects and his reputation. The diary's continued survival risked undoing all that he had worked for in this regard. In his diary, the diligent, honest, munificent gentleman and loyal servant of the king was revealed as a pleasure-loving, adulterous tailor's son, involved in some distinctly shady dealings and with plenty to say about the monarch's failings. Pepys's shorthand and his sporadic use of additional layers of linguistic protections defended this content only against casual observers: it would be no effective defence against determined readers, in his lifetime or after. From the 1670s, while Pepys's extraordinary professional rise continued, the stakes of keeping the diary intact rose too. As the Secretary for the Admiralty, he was now the target of frequent parliamentary and public scrutiny. His private life and the dubious profits he had accrued from naval work were recognized as weak points by his enemies. Most notably, these were used as part of a campaign to get Pepys charged with treason. In 1679, Pepys's Whig antagonists had him arrested as a conspirator in the Popish Plot (a non-existent scheme by Catholics to murder the king and take over the country). When it began to look like Pepys was winning in the law courts, his enemies sought to damage him further by publishing a pamphlet that trumpeted his corruption and invited speculation about the true nature of his relationships with sailors' wives and female friends.[2] As ammunition for such dangerous enemies, the diary would have been invaluable, not least because it contradicted Pepys's public affirmations concerning his devout Protestantism and his attendance at communion.[3]

After 1688, the risks of preserving the diary became acute, for the revolution that forced James II from the throne turned Pepys out of office and into a political dissident. He refused to swear loyalty to the new monarchs William and Mary, making him guilty – as he sarcastically put it – of the 'Sin of Jacobitisme'.[4] He was well aware that the new regime was keeping tabs on him, and that he and his papers were at risk of seizure. He was twice detained, in 1689 and 1690, on suspicion of treasonous plotting in James's cause and he feared other such 'surprizes' might follow.[5] Keeping damaging papers about him was potentially a threat to his freedom but it particularly risked their being used to discredit him and the monarchs he had served. William and Mary's reign endangered the part of Pepys's reputation which was founded on his reforms within the navy. William's supporters claimed that, rather than strengthening the fleet, James and his acolytes had undermined the nation's naval power, both deliberately (for nefarious Catholic purposes) and carelessly (through greed and corruption).[6] This was one element of a much wider campaign in which anti-Stuart narratives, once seen as seditious, were widely circulated and routinely printed. Long-established criticism of Stuart monarchs as tyrannical, extravagant, debauched and 'popish' was repurposed for anti-Jacobite ends. Charles II and James II had, it was stressed, been enslaved to the whims of lustful women and villainous Catholics (or lustful, villainous, Catholic women). Charles's alleged diversion of funds intended for the Anglo-Dutch Wars to his mistresses was a favourite example.[7] James's heir, born in June 1688, was claimed to be an imposter, a desperate gamble by conspirators to secure a Catholic dynasty. The most popular narrative on this topic – spread by word of mouth, manuscript, and print – was that the queen had faked her pregnancy and labour, with the supposed prince smuggled into her bed in a warming pan. In 1688, James had marshalled witnesses to disprove these allegations, but to little avail. Pamphlet wars on the topic continued for over a decade. Authors of 'secret histories' (novel-like accounts of behind-the-scenes politics) further embroidered this thrilling narrative by claiming to reveal new details of the fake prince's birth.[8] Throughout the 1690s, readers so inclined could read about the lascivious priests, cunning mistresses, murderous schemes, and bedroom antics that had preceded, and necessitated, the revolution.

Although Pepys had enjoyed reading earlier secret histories, he found this wave of anti-Jacobite propaganda repugnant and felt compelled to counter it.[9] The disputes around the navy prompted him to write his only published history. His *Memoires relating to the State of the Royal Navy* was privately printed for friends and potential allies in late 1690. The *Memoires* offered little by way of personal narrative but was instead a raft of documents concerning the shipbuilding programme that Pepys had run under James. It was designed to refute allegations of James's wilful neglect of the navy, and to cast the blame for deficiencies on his and Pepys's Whig opponents. Pepys's mastery of records was on display here, as was his craftiness, for he left out and misrepresented information to asperse his enemies. J. D. Davies has described this work, which was taken as objective fact by many naval historians, as a 'lesson in the manipulation of statistics and the historical record for political ends'. The book's select publication may, as Davies suggests, have been aimed at getting Pepys back into office or reviving his influence.[10] It was certainly aimed at making a pro-Jacobite account permanently available, as the work was on general sale the following spring.[11] Pepys, by this point, professed to have little faith in the public's ability to respect true worth (including his own achievements) – he thought only the opinions of a 'few good men' were worth valuing. During the Popish Plot, he had written to friends about 'this depraved Age', in which 'faithfulness & uninterested diligence in Office' had earned him nothing but abuse, along with envy of his 'Imaginary profits'.[12] The motto he chose in 1690 for the title page of the *Memoires* implies his attitude had not altered. It was a quotation from Cicero, beginning 'What vexations therefore they escape who have no dealings whatever with the people!'[13]

Although the contemporary public were not to be trusted, Pepys had not given up on 'posterity'. Much of his historical activity towards the end of his life consisted of collecting materials and producing records that were to be made available to a select few contemporaries and to later generations. One of his main aims was to collect material for a grand history of the navy – a project he had contemplated in the 1660s and which he trailed for readers of the *Memoires*.[14] This would no doubt have followed the *Memoires* in defending James's care for the navy. In the 1690s and early 1700s, Pepys was also privately assembling evidence to disprove allegations that James's son was a fraud and gathering testimonies from Jacobite allies. For example, in 1695 he took notes of his 'conference' with one of the Protestant women who had been present at the prince's birth and who had no truck with claims of imposter babies.[15]

Pepys's concern to defend his own reputation and James's, with his activity in countering anti-Jacobite histories, make the diary's survival even more of a puzzle. In the political climate of the 1690s and 1700s, his personal diary was newly incendiary – much of the material in it tended to support, rather than counter, the attacks on the Stuart kings. Aside from accounts that testified to corruption among navy officials, including Pepys himself, it was full of criticisms of the sexual appetites, extravagance, and negligence of the royal brothers. This was a secret history that had rather too much in common with the 'secret histories' that were being used to asperse James. The possibility that a diary might be published by political enemies was, as Pepys knew, no abstract threat. He owned a copy of the private diary of Archbishop Laud, which had been seized on Laud's arrest in 1644 and extracts published to discredit and humiliate him. One of Pepys's favourite books, Thomas Fuller's *Church-History of Britain* (1656) used Laud's diary as a source and discussed the controversy over its publication.[16] There were, in short, a whole host of reasons for Pepys to decide that it was too dangerous and, indeed, plain foolish to keep his diary near him and then make it available to other readers as part of his legacy. Fending off those dangers would require cunning and confidence in his own abilities; fortunately, he was not short of either.

Controlling Archives

Power lies in creating and controlling records. In Michel-Rolph Trouillot's words, archives 'convey authority and set the rules for credibility and interdependence; they help select the stories that matter'.[17] Pepys owed much of his professional success, and his posthumous fame, to his talents in this area. As Clerk of the Acts and, later, as Secretary for the Admiralty, he devised record-keeping procedures to track supplies and voyages, and to deter corruption. Astute use of records required knowing when not to record, and when to destroy.[18] The copious paper trail that he left of his own life seems prodigiously complete, but this is misleading. His desire for order and his recognition of the harm his records might do to himself and others meant he reviewed and purged his papers on multiple occasions. In early 1664, finding himself 'in an humour of making all things even and clear in the world, I tore some old papers'. These included his romance 'Love a Cheate' which he had written as a student. In December that year, he again decided to inspect 'all my papers and books, and to tear all that I found either boyish or not to be worth keeping, or fit to be seen if it should please God to take me away suddenly'. This practice continued in later life. In the summer of 1692, following two recent arrests and bouts of illness, he secluded himself for three months to 'garble [i.e. filter], sort or putt into order' his papers. The purpose, he explained to a friend, was to rid himself of 'anxietys' caused by the political situation: the implication was that he was disposing of material that could be used against him. He also wanted to ensure his papers were of 'use either to myselfe or any that come after mee'.[19] Pepys's 1660s diary survived that garbling, and all the rest. His personal and professional papers, which exist today in a range of library and museum collections, are the outcome of these purges and, for the most part, are what Pepys considered 'fit to be seen'.

Pepys filtered his own archive defensively, and – when he got the chance – did the same with others' records concerning him. For example, while some of the papers of his two younger brothers who predeceased him remain today among Pepys's papers, the materials which most caught his eye – letters containing 'very foul words' about him – are not among them.[20] In January 1663, he recorded destroying Elizabeth's personal papers precisely because they recounted events in a way that persuasively discredited him. This entry is worth dwelling on because, while it most obviously shows the dangers of diary keeping, it also provides clues to why his diary was ultimately allowed to survive its writer.[21] Elizabeth was campaigning for a paid companion to ease her loneliness and raise her status. In late 1662, she had put her arguments in writing, but her husband destroyed this letter without reading it.[22] On 9 January 1663, the argument erupted again. Elizabeth dispatched Jane to unlock her trunk and bring her 'a bundle of papers'. As Pepys recounts it, Elizabeth

> pulls out a paper, a copy of what a pretty while since she had writ in a discontent to me, which I would not read but burned. She now read it and was so **picquant** and wrote in **English** and most of it true, of the **retirednesse** of her life and how unpleasant it was that, being writ in **English** and so in danger of **being** met with and read by others, I was vext at it and desired her and then commanded her to **teare** it.

Enraged, he snatched her other papers, which included financial documents and his old love letters to her, and ripped them one by one before her face:

> she crying and desiring me not to do it. But such was my passion and trouble to see the letters of my love to her and my **Will**, wherein I had given her all I had in the world when I went to sea with my Lord **Sandwich**, to be **joyned** with a paper of so much disgrace to me and dishonour if it should hath been found by any body.[23]

The multiple causes of Pepys's anger show how he approached the recording and preservation of private information. Elizabeth's letter was troubling because he recognized its truth: it was a just indictment of his failure to meet her needs. He twice mentions the alarming fact that it was written in 'English' (a word he often wrote in shorthand, but was in longhand here for emphasis). This made Elizabeth's complaints more easily understood by 'any body'. The tacit distinction was with his shorthand diary, but he presumably felt Elizabeth should have written in her other language, French – her keeping the letter locked up was not enough. Finally, what really upset him was that she had 'joyned' their papers together (the offending verb is longhand), undercutting his private and public records of their relationship.[24] Imagining the conclusions that readers might draw about him fuelled his rage. The only items that he allowed to survive were a financial bond, their marriage license, and his first love letter to her. With the exception of the diary's account, protected by shorthand, an archival narrative of Pepys's sincere devotion to his wife was therefore created. It was one that eliminated Elizabeth's hand, relying solely on official documents and Pepys's own writing.

The diary recorded papers and views that Pepys elsewhere eradicated, thereby contributing to the risks in keeping it. However, this episode also demonstrates Pepys's acute perception that a document's meaning was not determined solely by the information it contained: its meaning was also shaped by the documents that accompanied it. That recognition in turn contributed to his diary's survival. While the diary now circulates independently in printed editions and online, he intended it to be read as part of his library. By leaving it in this context, he signalled its value as a historical record, and sought to ensure that this personal history would be interpreted in the light of the documents that surrounded it. The implications of this for understanding the diary are considerable, but we can start with one example of the historical records held within the library which indicates how Pepys expected his diary to be interpreted in their light. It is also an episode that amply demonstrates just how cunning Pepys could be when it came to ensuring that his version of events occupied the record – and how he felt that, in professional matters, such deviousness deserved celebration.

In the summer and autumn of 1668 Pepys was coolly staging a coup at work. At this time, the duke of York was under intense political pressure to reform the navy's administration. Pepys seized the opportunity to advance his position by offering James a solution. He describes in his diary how, on 24 July 1668, he met privately with the duke to detail at length 'the weakness of our office' and urged him to call the members of the Navy Board to account. As Pepys records it, James encouraged him to write up this analysis as a letter. That letter (written by Pepys in the duke's voice) was then copied out by James's secretary and delivered to the board. Pepys did not detail the letter's content in his diary, but copies survive dispersed across archives, including in his library. The letter criticized each official on the board for failing in their duties – except, mysteriously, the Clerk of the Acts. The board members were required to respond with individual defences. Pepys, to keep up the pretence, wrote one too. On 26 October, the day after Elizabeth caught him with Deb Willet, the plot thickened. Pepys took on the task of writing a rebuttal to all of the navy officials' answers – which again was sent as from the duke.[25] To recap: this was a response by Pepys in the name of the duke, to Pepys's own defence of his conduct in office, which had been produced in response to a letter that Pepys had himself written. His layered pretence (which seems to have deceived none of his colleagues) alienated the other board members but brought him to new influence. He succeeded in securing his position as an authority on the navy, well beyond that expected of a mere Clerk of the Acts. He had also, crucially, cemented his value to the duke as a confidante and as an asset in fending off his critics in parliament and on the Privy Council.

Looked at from one perspective (that of Pepys's colleagues) these manoeuvres were a feeble attempt at deception and a spectacular act of backstabbing. To Pepys, it was a stratagem of which he was proud, and which merited extensive memorializing beyond the privacy of the diary. In

May 1669, he had copies of papers from this episode bound up, stating in his diary that seeing it 'makes me glad, it being that which shall do me more right many years hence then perhaps all I ever did in my life – and therefore I do, both for my own and the King's sake, value it much'. The volume, now in the Pepys Library, makes plain his authorship of both sides of the correspondence.[26] Meanwhile copies of "the duke's" letters survive in other collections, including the Admiralty archive, where they appear as the duke's work – there is no record of Pepys's involvement.[27]

Pepys wanted his own reforming zeal, his ingenuity, and his influence on record, so that they would be credited to him 'many years hence': an idea conceived in 1669 but which he enacted through his later plans for his library. The diary and the volume of letters in Magdalene therefore offer two complementary accounts of Pepys's involvement, one private, one semi-public. The shorthand diary gives the detailed, personal history of how this initiative evolved. His own volume of the letters attributes them to him, offering knowledge not available from other copies. The fact that both records are surrounded by other evidence of Pepys's care for the navy on the library shelves encourages an interpretation of his actions which downplays self-interest as a motive. When reading the diary, Pepys's scheme concerning the duke's letters can escape notice: it unfolds slowly and is interwoven with his dramatic descriptions of being caught with Deb and other sensational incidents (such as courtiers running 'up and down all the night with their arses bare through the streets').[28] If these other events have drawn readers' interest more than his stratagems at work, the cumulative effect of the library is nonetheless to emphasize his naval work within the diary, while making his flaws seem less significant, and even finessing what might appear to be moral failings (duplicity, corruption, pride) into commendable qualities.

The Library

Pepys's diary survived because the library's purposes could accommodate the presence of the diary, and because he had designed measures to control how that library could be used. This was a carefully crafted collection, in its contents and its functions. During Pepys's enforced retirement, when political revolution threatened his achievements and reputation, curating his library became an alternative occupation and a means of securing his legacy. In 1691, he began drafting papers on the functions of 'a Private Library', concluding that the contents should cover the 'greatest diversity' of reading its owner was capable of, tailored to the importance of each subject and 'the particular Genius of their said Owner'.[29] 'Genius' here meant 'character' or 'inclinations': a library was to be understood as a projection of its owner's personality and interests. In this vein, Pepys's final choice of books included, for example, his collection of shorthand manuals, drama in several languages, an impressive collection of prints, and very many books on the 'Sea, & Navy'. He made a point of seeking out printed and manuscript texts on the navy, creating a research collection for the planned history he never managed to get down to writing.[30] His love of the past found expression in the library's large selections of 'History' (covering countries, religions, and institutions) and 'Lifes', offering accounts of rulers, philosophers, poets, and other 'hommes illustres' (illustrious men).[31]

A library was not merely a selection of books, it was the physical appearance and the organization of those books. Pepys's delight in his library's appearance led him to commission an artist to record it, showing the fine bookcases he had designed (Figure 3.1). For him, the 'Aptness' of the furniture design; the 'Uniformity' of book bindings; the 'Regularity or Orderliness' of the books; and the 'Clearness' of the finding aids, all contributed to the library's usefulness and to the impressions that users received of its owner.[32] Pepys organized his library by size, creating a visual neatness which also helped support the books. Since the volumes were not shelved by title, author, or subject, this meant that finding aids became particularly important. The catalogues that Pepys created to locate works also communicated how those works should be read. He and the library workers under his direction spent long hours preparing these documents.[33] Together his subject catalogue (the 'Appendix Classica') and notations on the books themselves offered guidance – subtle and not so subtle – on how readers should interpret volumes. The Appendix Classica, for example, explained that 'a principal Aim' of Pepys's collection of Civil War sermons was 'the Transmitting to Posterity a true Notion of the Preaching so much in Vogue with the Populace of England during the late Rebellion'. Pepys's collection of the small, cheap books that were often sold by pedlars prompted another gloss. The catalogue characterized these chapbooks as 'Vulgaria, Consisting of the most Noted Pieces of Chivalry, Wit, Pastime, Devotion, & Poetry, in Vogue with the English Populace'.[34] Evidently Pepys did not want 'Posterity' getting the impression that he sympathized with the content of certain of the Civil War sermons, nor that he collected chapbooks solely because he enjoyed them (although his diary confirms he certainly did).[35] These were to be recognized as historical documents. The first volume of his ballad collection similarly began with an observation

Figure 3.1 Pepys's Library at 14 Buckingham Street, York Buildings, by Sutton Nicholls (c.1693).

from John Selden, 'More Solid things do not shew the Complexion of the Times, so well as Ballads and Libells.'[36] Pepys's understanding of 'History' and 'Lifes' was not limited to the works on high politics and illustrious men that featured heavily under those headings in the Appendix Classica. He had an antiquarian approach to history – an interest in studying common customs and collecting items which, while it was normally focused on the distant past, could be applied to preserving the present.[37] His library project was designedly self-centred, but it was not selfish: it was intended to communicate his character *and* that of the society in which he had lived, and to do so for the benefit of himself, his contemporaries, and their successors.[38]

In a library which reflected the particular genius of its owner, a personal diary was not necessarily out of place but, like other less conventional items, that place did require some glossing. His 1660s diary was one of several of his journals saved in his library. The others detailed his actions in relation to specific projects or during legal proceedings against him. Most were not listed separately in his Appendix Classica and were bound up as part of his 'Miscellany of Matters Historical, Political and Naval' or his volumes of Popish Plot papers.[39] In contrast, each volume of his 1660s diary was individually listed in the subsection of the Appendix Classica that was given over to the manuscripts of 'Mr. Pepys'. The diary volumes were the first items under this heading, described as his 'Diary in Short-hand'.[40] The Appendix Classica was compiled under Pepys's direction in late 1700, making it clear that by that date – if not before – he had determined that this diary would be part of the collection that would carry his name and reputation into the future.[41] The survival of the diary as part of his final collection was therefore no last-minute decision, nor oversight, but planned at least three years before his death. By identifying that the diary was in 'Short-hand', if not the actual shorthand system, the Appendix Classica pointed readers in the direction of Pepys's 'Short-hand Collection' (also listed in the Appendix Classica). There three manuals on the relevant shorthand system by Shelton could be found, the most useful of which was *Tachygraphy* (1691).[42] The keys to reading the diary would remain with it down the centuries.

The catalogue also hinted at why this 1660s diary was worth reading. The remaining five items in the section 'Mr. Pepys' were all exclusively concerned with the navy, including the item immediately following the 1660s volumes, another 'Diary' described as 'relating to the Commission constituted by K. James 1686 for the Recovery of the Navy'.[43] His 1660s diary, therefore, was offered to posterity as a text primarily useful for understanding naval history and the author's role in it. Yet, if readers were expected to approach the diary with naval history in mind, it is worth factoring in the presence of the cues in the Appendix Classica and in the library volumes which encouraged users to consider how items demonstrated 'the Complexion of the Times' and matters 'in Vogue with the English Populace'. The diary contained Pepys's personal history, along with major political events and the lives of (other) great men; but it also recorded public opinion and the activities of the populace. In this, it was very much in keeping with the expansive sense of 'history' urged elsewhere in the library.

For the library to function as Pepys intended, the whole – books, organization, furniture – needed to survive intact across the ages. To this end, he devised a 'Scheame [. . .] relating to the Completion & Settlement of my Library'. It was formally added as a codicil to his will in May 1703, the month he died.[44] Key to the scheme's successful execution was Pepys's nephew and principal heir, John Jackson, whom he had been training in bibliophilia and who would be the library's second owner. Jackson was instructed to carry out Pepys's final wishes for the collection, aided by Pepys's executor, Will Hewer. Experience, Pepys explained in the 'Scheame', had taught him that libraries transmitted within families risked falling into 'the hands of an incompetent Heire and thereby of being sold dissipated or imbezelled'. For the library's 'unalterable preservation and perpetuall Security' he therefore counselled Jackson to pass it to an Oxford or Cambridge college, and to Magdalene College by preference – the college that both he and Jackson had attended. He wanted the library to be housed separately in its own room, ideally in Magdalene's 'New Building'. (The codicil did not mention that Pepys had helped fund that building's construction.[45]) The library room and books were to be known as the 'Bibliotheca Pepysiana'. His glazed bookcases were to remain with the library, meaning that the books would be displayed according to his practice. The catalogues – essential to navigating the library – were specified as part of the donation. No books were to be added to the collection, except by Jackson, who was given some specific instructions on this point; thereafter, the library was to remain unchanged down the centuries and be in the 'Sole power and Custody' of the college's master. No books were to be removed from the room, except by the master. The master, stipulated Pepys, might be allowed to take up to ten volumes to his lodge, but he was required to sign them out. Breaches of these terms would result in the collection defaulting to Pepys's second choice of venue, Trinity College, which was to inspect the library yearly for failures on Magdalene's part.

This was an exceptionally thorough set of rules to keep the library 'entire, in one body, undivided' and it has normally been understood in those terms.[46] It had, however, other unspoken purposes: it determined who could access the library and how they would do so, in order to fashion readers sympathetic to Pepys's world-view and the contents of his papers. Volumes from the collection were supposed to be read within the Bibliotheca Pepysiana, amid the gilded, neatly ordered books, which were arranged on bookcases which Pepys had himself designed. Readers would sit surrounded by evidence of his taste, accomplishments, and generosity – in a building he had paid for, with access under the control of an institution which had a strong interest in protecting its benefactor's reputation. Pepys's plans for his library were not focused on his 1660s diary but, with considerable skill, he had put in place measures to influence its reception and defuse its more incendiary contents. Understood within his 'Scheame' for his library, the presence of his diary begins to look rather like a test: only readers who shared Pepys's interests and diligence were likely to be able to access this most intimate level of record-keeping. To read his diary, a man would need to be admitted to the library by the college authorities (it would be a man, as the college was not open to women). That scholar would first need to recognize that the diary existed. He might come across it on the shelves or, curious about the library's creator, he might find it under Mr Pepys's manuscripts in the catalogue. A would-be reader would then need to identify and learn Pepys's chosen shorthand (the manuals were on the shelves and the catalogue pointed to them), before spending the time and effort to work through his voluminous journals. If this scholar were really dedicated, and shared Pepys's interest in languages, he would be able to decipher the polyglot. All this would need to take place in Pepys's impressive library room or in the master's lodge, under the surveillance of college officials. Pepys placed no explicit restrictions on entry to his library or on the publication of its materials because he did not need to: he was trusting in the judgement of the master of Magdalene to guard his legacy and his reputation. Whoever the master might be down the centuries, he was unlikely to grant permission to publish any of the library's contents, including the diary, if that publication would seriously damage the prestige of the college or one of its most generous alumni.

Pepys can hardly have been unaware that parts of his diary would eventually be circulated in some form. Even to a library visitor who lacked shorthand, the fact that the diary contained accounts of famous events would be plain: the entry on Charles's coronation had the heading 'Coronacion day' in longhand, while the Great Fire entries for 2–7 September 1666 featured London placenames and words such as 'Firedrops' in longhand.[47] The main use Pepys seems to have envisioned for the diary – the use that his library prods readers towards – was for it to be winnowed for material that would be published in a naval history, a history which would pay suitable homage to the library's creator. Pepys had prepared protections to deter his diary's being used to his detriment, and he may have been further emboldened by words from his contemporaries on how private diaries should be received when published. Reflecting on the seizure and publication of Archbishop Laud's diary, Pepys's friend Thomas Fuller dismissed criticisms of Laud's incaution and focused instead on readers' responsibilities. Some commentators had attacked Laud for

> keeping such a Diary about him in so dangerous days. Especially he ought to untongue it from talking to his prejudice, and should have *garbled* [i.e., removed] some light trivial and joculary passages out of the same. Whereas sure the omission hereof argued not his carelessnesse but confidence, that such his privacies should meet with that favour of course [i.e. customarily], which in equity is due to writings of that nature.[48]

Keepers of private diaries, Fuller maintained, deserved to have the best constructions put on writing that was not intended to be published. Pepys was not leaving this to chance. He had confidence in a favourable reception because he had planned measures to determine who could access his papers, along with steps to influence those readers to do him right.

Best Laid Plans

The careful devising of a scheme is one accomplishment, its successful execution is quite another. In leaving the final arrangements to John Jackson, Pepys had wisely allowed for his plan to adapt to circumstances. Jackson was a dutiful heir: he set about making the last adjustments to the library and put in place a preliminary agreement with Magdalene. However, he made one serious oversight – he died without making a will himself. Pepys's concerns about the viability of a succession of familial custodians were therefore vindicated, as his scheme for the library almost fell at the first hurdle. Fortunately for Pepys's reputation and grand plans, he had another, overlooked, adherent: Ann Jackson. Ann was the wife of his nephew John. She was also Will Hewer's first cousin once removed and the sister of Hewer's main heir. She had known Pepys as a child, attending his funeral.[49] After her husband's death in 1722, Ann arranged to be appointed the administerix of his estate: she was the one who ensured the library reached Magdalene, and she agreed the covenant that bound the college to Pepys's terms.[50] Although she had ample reason to respect Pepys's memory, it would have been easy to neglect his wishes, for there were other demands on her. She had seven small children to care for, whose fortunes might have been better served by 'dissipating' the library by auction – the prospect that had so alarmed Pepys. She would have been well within her rights to do so, as Hewer and John Jackson's initial agreement with the college had specified they could withdraw the planned donation.[51] Instead, Ann Jackson chose to fulfil the project that had been initiated by Pepys and continued by her cousin and her husband. Additional help came from the Earl of Anglesey, a former fellow of the college. He paid for the library's transport and – in furtherance of Pepys's long-sighted plan – set up a fund to pay a librarian to tend the books 'for ever'.[52]

Despite John Jackson's failure to secure Pepys's legacy, the library arrived safely in Magdalene in 1724. Yet here too there were early signs that Pepys's plans would meet obstacles. The library's presence began to draw bibliophile tourists, but in at least one case Pepys's efforts to favourably influence his library's users proved counterproductive. Christian Gabriel Fischer, visiting from Prussia in 1728, was impressed by the library's neat arrangement, glazed bookcases, and gold-tooled bindings but, on learning of the conditions Pepys had imposed, was scornful:

> This library has no additions, nor can it be moved from the spot, but is kept in honour of the family. I view it as a monument of vanity. After some time, the whole thing may become obsolete, that little bit of gold completely blacken, and the usefulness of the library disappear.[53]

Fischer understood that the Bibliotheca Pepysiana was intended to magnify Pepys and his family name: since its creator had no direct descendants, the library indeed bore his name into the future. However, Fischer objected to Pepys's mandating that the collection be treated as an archival record that memorialized its creator and the knowledge of his time, rather than as a working library, which would develop to reflect current knowledge and the needs of its users. This seemed to him perverse and self-centred, rather than far-sighted and selfless. Fischer was the first of many to comment that Pepys's rules for the preservation and integrity of his collection curtailed its uses. That was, indeed, part of the rules' purpose. Yet, in ensuring that Pepys's curated books and papers travelled down the generations together, those rules allowed for the survival of the 1660s diary in its unmediated entirety – and for uses that Pepys could never have imagined.

Risks and Rewards

The fundamental reason why Pepys allowed his diary volumes to survive was that, in the course of writing, they became precious to him: by 1667 they were 'my Journalls, which I value much'.[54] They contained experiences and knowledge which he prized, which remained potentially useful to him, and which he could see would be valuable to others. But, given their potential to destroy his hard-won reputation, that value alone would not have been enough. It was his skills as a creator, manager, and manipulator of records that allowed for his diary's survival – and his confidence in those skills to shape posterity's verdict. In 1663, he had feared the disgrace and dishonour that would come to him if his papers appeared in uncontrolled contexts before 'any body'. In the 1690s he had also to contend with a hostile political climate and his lack of faith in the public to reward merit. However, by this point, he had the abilities and means to shape a collection, set conditions, and motivate an institutional custodian in ways that would not just keep his papers safe, but safeguard his name.

The inclusion of Pepys's 1660s diary in his collection risked undermining the library's role in magnifying his fame as an accomplished administrator and generous benefactor. Yet, in other respects the diary's contents suited well with his collection's purposes. The diary added to the layers of public, semi-public, and private history that the library held. It recorded the growth of the library's creator, his interests, and his professional success, together with a detailed, insider account of the development of the navy. Like the ballads and chapbooks that Pepys bound and preserved, the diary also documented the kind of history that did not merit the categorization 'history', because it was too ephemeral or (in both senses of the word) too vulgar: it recorded trivial, unseemly matters and the interests of members of the populace who were neither royal nor illustrious. For Pepys, that too was valuable. Pepys's affection for his journal, along with its potential uses within the library and the new protections he set up as part of his 'Scheame', collectively made leaving the journal a risk worth taking. This was a tremendous gamble, but it was a calculated one. It would, ultimately, more than repay the investment in terms of its benefits to posterity and to Pepys.

CHAPTER 4

First Publication

Pepys's diary was first published in 1825, just over a century after its arrival at Magdalene College. This text was profoundly different from the versions widely read today, although it established the terms on which Pepys and his diary would continue to be discussed. The first edition was launched on a society shaped by the Revolution of 1688 and by the triumphs of Pepys's opponents. The heirs of that revolution generally saw themselves as greatly advanced in manners and morals from the notorious Restoration period. For this reason, and many others, offering the entirety of Pepys's diary to the public would have been wildly inappropriate, commercially impractical, and, indeed, illegal. The first edition therefore contained only about a quarter of the whole diary. Titled *Memoirs of Samuel Pepys*, and including some of his 'private correspondence', it was a selection intended to make Pepys appealing and admirable to nineteenth-century readers. For the first half of the century, this was 'Pepys's diary', the only version of the text available.

The first edition and the reactions to it are the foundations on which all subsequent responses to the diary, knowingly or not, have built. However, this publishing triumph was not all that it appeared to be for, as we'll see, the main players in the *Memoirs of Samuel Pepys* saw the benefits of not disclosing the entire truth about Pepys or about their own roles in the diary's success. This has led to certain beliefs that persist today. In 1825, readers enjoyed and puzzled over the *Memoirs*, finding a variety of ways to make sense of it. Pepys and his journal soon attracted influential admirers, whose analyses would be much reprinted over the decades. Among them were Walter Scott, Francis Jeffrey (a periodical editor), and the young historian Thomas Macaulay. For early readers, a recurring question was whether this odd text made any significant contribution to historical understanding, and, if so, what that contribution was. Indeed, as critics have argued, prompting this kind of reflection was a significant way that the diary contributed to historiography.[1] By exploring the early impact of

Pepys's diary, we can discover its contributions to history and, in the process, see how successfully – or not – Pepys's 'Scheame' for preserving his reputation played out.

Reading about the Restoration

In the early nineteenth century, before the *Memoirs of Samuel Pepys* was published, what were the general impressions of the Restoration period and what, if anything, might readers have heard about Pepys? While historians writing in the late eighteenth and early nineteenth centuries took various perspectives on the merits of the civil wars and Restoration, they usually took a dim view (to say the least) of the later Stuart kings. Charles II was known as a king whose easy manner and affability had won him loyalty, despite his 'debaucheries', his neglect of state affairs, and his absolutist tendencies. James II, if more serious-minded, was widely condemned as a bigoted man, bent on becoming an absolute monarch.[2] The revolution that unseated him had established parliament's right to determine the succession and had led to a limited monarchy by law: in the 1820s, the right to the throne of the current monarch, George IV, derived from these events. The prospect of James II's descendants retaking the crown had long receded, but accusations of 'Jacobitism' were still occasionally flung about in political rhetoric when, for example, an opponent was seen as having too indulgent a view of corrupt monarchs. In the wake of the French Revolution and amid demands for major parliamentary reform, the civil wars and revolutions of the seventeenth century seemed full of warnings for the present.

In the 1820s, readers seeking information on the later seventeenth century could derive it from recent historians or from Restoration authors whose popularity had kept them in print. A principal source on the period's politics was the Earl of Clarendon's *History of the Rebellion* (1702–4), an account of Charles's reign from the man who had been his chief advisor. Dramas and satires were also seen as revealing about the manners of the time. Samuel Butler's satirical attack on puritanism, *Hudibras* (1663), for example, remained much admired and imitated.[3] Increasingly, readers were also offered memoirs and diaries from the period. Pepys's diary was printed at the beginning of a trend for publishing eyewitness, biographical accounts of the seventeenth-century – a trend which Pepys's success helped fuel.[4] Anthony Hamilton's *Memoirs of the Life of the Count of Grammont* was already established as the chief source on Restoration scandal. When *Grammont* was first published in English in

1714, the title page had promised 'the amorous Intrigues of the Court of England'. Later editions dropped this scandal-mongering subtitle but kept the author's announcement that he had prioritized '*Amusement*' rather than '*Chronology*'.[5] Its historical accuracy was justly regarded as suspect. Far more dependable, in both credibility and respectability, was the newly published journal of Pepys's good friend Evelyn. *Memoirs Illustrative of the Life and Writings of John Evelyn* appeared in 1818, to much acclaim. The publisher was Henry Colburn, who would go on to publish the 'memoirs' of Pepys. When Pepys came onto the scene in the 1820s, he joined the scandalous Grammont and the more decorous Evelyn, and these became the two poles against which he was frequently measured.

Prior to his diary's publication in 1825, Pepys had been keeping different company. He was not forgotten, but what fame he did have was decidedly niche. In 1705, a short entry in a biographical dictionary on the lives of 'Great Men' described his life and set the tone for much of what would follow – chiefly because this was one of the few printed sources on him. Will Hewer, who helped to finance the *Dictionary*'s publication, almost certainly had a hand in drafting this account. It celebrated Pepys as the upright and incorruptible 'Father' of the navy (a phrase that would echo down the centuries), explaining that he had established the 'principal Rules' used in the navy and admiralty, and was responsible for 'Bringing-up' most of its officers. He had been a man of learning, and the owner of 'a Library of great Fame'.[6] The admiralty administration continued to remember Pepys. In 1810, John Barrow, who was then Second Secretary to the Admiralty, pointed in a book review to Pepys as the author of standing orders still used in the navy, and to his library as evidence of his achievements.[7]

Pepys's library, indeed, was the main source of his repute. A few items from it were published over the eighteenth century: his record of Charles II's escape after the battle of Worcester (1766); some of his ballads as part of Thomas Percy's *Reliques of English Poetry* (1765); and details of his collection of printed portraits.[8] James Granger's *Biographical History of England* (1769) drove the craze for 'grangerizing' books by adding portraits and extra images to them. Granger made extensive use of Pepys's print collection to document surviving portraits of notable people and – no doubt partly for this reason – included Pepys himself, repeating the praises of him from the 1705 *Dictionary*. Readers' best chance of encountering Pepys before his diary's publication was therefore likely to have been via Granger's much reprinted work, as one of the 'Commoners in Great Employments' under Charles II.[9]

The Library and the Diary

Pepys's library was preserving his memory and acting as a resource for scholars, just as he had intended. However, visitors gave the impression that this was despite Pepys's and Magdalene's best efforts, rather than because of them. In 1726, the shorthand aficionado Ralph Leycester accidentally happened on the diary while trying – and failing – to use Pepys's catalogue to find the collection of shorthand manuals. Although intrigued by the diary's shorthand, he did not want to 'be troublesome to the library keeper' so did not stay to decipher it.[10] In 1811, Thomas Frognall Dibdin, author of the determinedly eccentric *Bibliomania or Book-Madness*, ranked Pepys as 'a bibliomaniac of the first order and celebrity' for his ballad-collecting. Sadly, fellow bookfiends would find Pepys's library rules bothersome, for these limited access to his books. 'Oh, that there were *an act of parliament* to regulate bequests of this kind!', Dibdin lamented. While Dibdin had not been able to properly explore the library or find out much at all about Pepys's life, he had heard via his contacts that there existed in it 'a *Diary* of his life, written with his own hand'.[11]

The diary volumes, it transpires, had been located some years earlier by bibliomaniacal members of the extended Pepys family, who had been spreading the word and investigating publication. Martin Foys and Whitney Anne Trettien, whose research uncovered this project, have identified the writer and lawyer Sir William Weller Pepys as its driving force.[12] He was a descendant of one of Pepys's great-uncles. Also involved was William's brother, Sir Lucas Pepys, who circulated news of the diary around book collectors – this was how Dibdin had learned about it.[13] In William's surviving papers are several sentences from the diary's first volume, transcribed from the shorthand by one 'T. Cunningham', along with estimates from an unnamed publisher. Judging by these calculations, William was investigating printing the first volume of the diary in its entirety.[14] This got nowhere, probably because the challenges were not just technical, but reputational. In 1821, William remarked that Pepys had recorded 'his own vices' and that it seemed harsh 'to drag his Frailties' into the light.[15] The sentences Cunningham had transcribed were innocuous, but it seems that – years before the 1825 edition appeared – William Weller Pepys knew the diary contained content that would tend neither to Pepys's honour, nor to the 'honour of the family' (to borrow Fischer's phrase).[16] This project did, however, lead to the first sentence from the diary making it into print, apparently through Lucas Pepys acting as intermediary.[17] On 25 September 1660 Pepys noted: 'did send for a Cupp of Tee (a China drink) of which I never had drank before'. In June 1807 this was quoted by

Charles Taylor in an article about the 'History and View of the Tea Trade', with the observation that 'The love of novelty is a predominant feature in the British character.'[18] Once an exotic rarity, by the early nineteenth century Chinese tea was routinely drunk even in poorer households.[19] Taylor's comment was a token of things to come, since in later decades casting Pepys as representative of the national character would become commonplace. When the *Memoirs of Samuel Pepys* appeared in 1825, Pepys's first encounter with tea similarly caught the notice of several reviewers. They offered it as an instance of the diary's 'curious' content and of 'how far back we seem to be thrown' in reading it – an experience that, in bringing the reader closer to Pepys, brought home the distance between past and present.[20]

'The Decipherer'

Pepys's diary was finally published due to hard graft, the commercial success of Evelyn's diary, and judicious pragmatism by those involved when it came to revealing the whole truth. This pattern of tactical silences began with a glaring violation of Pepys's rule against removing books from the library – and covering that violation up. In 1818, the master of Magdalene, George Neville, gave the first volume of the diary to his uncle Thomas Grenville. Thomas, who was heading off on holiday, left the volume with another uncle, his brother William Wyndham Grenville (Lord Grenville), in Buckinghamshire. Lord Grenville was intrigued by the shorthand, which followed similar principles to the system he had learned as a law student. By deducing Pepys's letter symbols and some of the 'arbitrary signs', he was able to partially transcribe the first ten days of the diary. Excited, Lord Grenville wrote to his nephew to encourage publication. The journal, he thought, would 'form an excellent accompaniment to Evelyn's delightful Diary'. George should find 'some man who for the lucre of gain will sacrifice a few months to the labour of making a complete transcript'. His own involvement should be concealed from the transcriber, as 'it might not be right that he should know the MS to have been in my possession'.[21] Indeed, yes, as by the terms of Pepys's will the volume currently jaunting round Buckinghamshire and London was supposed to have got no further than the master's lodge, or else the whole library was forfeit.

George Neville followed his uncle's advice. In the spring of 1819, he hired John Smith, an undergraduate from St John's College, Cambridge, to work on the shorthand. Smith became the first person after Pepys to read the entirety of the diary. For much of the nineteenth century he would remain the only person to have done so. He ended up transcribing not for the 'few months' Lord Grenville had predicted but for nearly three years. For part of this time, he was also working as a journalist and as a minor university official. His work on the diary, he later stated, was 'usually for twelve and fourteen hours a day' and earned him only £200 total for his effort.[22]

From early on, Smith was cagey about how he accomplished the impressive feat of cracking the shorthand, and his later statements on this were downright disingenuous. Writing to a newspaper in 1858 to affirm his role as the manuscript's 'decipherer', he stated that he had first been assured by shorthand experts that transcription was impossible. With some 'imperfectly' transcribed passages from Lord Grenville, he had 'persevered, nevertheless', ultimately completing his 'arduous labours on the whole diary'. All of this was true.[23] From it and similar statements, Latham and Matthews concluded that Smith had deciphered Pepys's method himself. No one, they noted, had named Shelton's system until the 1870s. They therefore believed that Smith must have broken the diary shorthand using Pepys's account of Charles's escape from the battle of Worcester, which was in the library in both shorthand and longhand versions. In telling the diary's history it has become obligatory to note that poor Smith worked in ignorance of Shelton's manuals, which were close by in Pepys's collection.[24]

Not so, it turns out. Very early on in the transcription process, Smith had identified the system and got his hands on a Shelton manual. Before he learned to be discreet about his methods, he made a revealing note in his transcript. In the entry for 28 January 1660 Pepys had written 'I returned and went to Heaven where Luellin and I dined on a breast of mutton.' Smith, suitably puzzled, commented, 'The proper interpretation of the sign (∥) in the MS. is <u>heaven</u>, which I have inserted, but I have my doubts of it. It will probably turn up in the course of the narrative again.' This was the first time 'heaven' was used in the manuscript. It did, in fact, make sense, as 'Heaven' was the name of an eating house. Crucially, 'heaven' in Shelton's system is also an arbitrary symbol: it is not made up of letter symbols. The fact that Smith knew the symbol's meaning before he understood the context shows he had solid information on the arbitrary symbols by this point. As 'heaven' is not used in Pepys's Worcester transcript, that cannot have been Smith's source (ruling out Latham and Matthews's theory); nor was Grenville's brief transcript the source, for Grenville had not reached this entry. The place where you find lists of such word signs is in shorthand manuals. Another note shows Smith had the skills to navigate the library (or knew someone who did). The most likely way for him to have identified the correct system was to have looked up 'Short-hand' under 'S' in Pepys's alphabetical catalogue, which would have taken him, via the Appendix Classica, to the shorthand manuals that Pepys had bound together.[25] Using Grenville's 'alphabet', he could then have worked through the manuals, speedily ruling out those which did not fit the bill: the exact match was the 1691 edition of Shelton's *Tachygraphy*. In short, it looks as though, a hundred and sixteen years after Pepys's death, Smith did exactly what Pepys had laid the ground for a Cambridge man to one day do, and linked the diary to the manual on the shelf nearby.

It is unlikely that Smith entirely hid his identification of Shelton's shorthand from the Neville-Grenville family, but it served his interests to make sure the source of his expertise was not widely known. This was certainly the case in later years, when the family was keen to maximize the part played by Lord Grenville and when Smith needed to defend his own role. In 1858, in response to correspondence celebrating Braybrooke's and Grenville's contributions, Smith wrote to the press denying that the few passages Grenville had supplied amounted to anything like a 'key' to the shorthand. He stated that the diary had been made legible through his 'sole exertions', for which he had been poorly paid. (Smith was not asked, and so did not mention, that he had use of another key.)

Throughout his life, Smith was clear that he wanted credit as the 'decipherer', not the editor, of Pepys's *Memoirs*, and this was how his contribution was referred to on the title page.[26] Yet the nature of his work was, by any standard, editorial. In transcribing the shorthand, he made decisions about spelling, grammar, and punctuation. He supplied historical and linguistic notes for his readers.[27] Smith also made decisions about which passages were fit to be seen. He began by omitting sexual passages in French or polyglot from his transcript and replacing them with 'Obj' (meaning they were 'Objectionable'). This, he thought, was the best policy given the 'nature and meaning' of the passages and because, even when deciphered, they could be 'difficult to make out fully'.[28] Since this type of omission sometimes involved his cutting an entire episode, rather than just the offending phrase, there were episodes that no one else appears to have read until extensive work was done on the manuscript in the 1870s.[29] When Smith's transcribing reached May 1667, he gave up this censorship, perhaps because the cuts were becoming so frequent. He was quite capable of dealing with Pepys's garbled and polyglot shorthand – for example, he accurately transcribed Elizabeth's discovery of Deb and Pepys, with all that followed.[30] The neat transcript that Smith handed over to the master in fifty-four volumes was not absolutely complete, but it was more than enough to make the riches – and problems – of the diary plain.

'The Noble Editor'

Two men were largely responsible for what readers would see of the diary for most of the nineteenth century. Smith was one; the other was George Neville's choice of editor, his brother Richard, who was soon to become the third Baron Braybrooke. Braybrooke's chief qualifications for the job were that he was Neville's brother and a baron. This kept the editorial decisions in-house and lent the publication status. Braybrooke, or 'the Noble Editor' as reviewers called him, did not know shorthand and had no inclination to learn the principles: several decades later (by which point he had overseen two more editions of the diary) he declared that he had not 'the slightest knowledge of short-hand'.[31] Reading through the transcript, Braybrooke now found himself in the awkward position of trying to polish the reputation of a man, and a manuscript, about whose respectability he had serious reservations. On the one hand, the diary was a valuable, eyewitness account of major events, and he was genuinely thrilled by what he found there. 'This is very curious' he noted when, as one of the diary's very first readers, he discovered that Pepys had carried news of the Great Fire to Charles II.[32] 'Curious' has always been a favourite adjective to describe Pepys and his diary: it can mean 'inquisitive', 'odd', 'detailed', or (euphemistically) 'pornographic'. Here it meant 'exciting'. But, while Braybrooke was intrigued, the diary presented serious difficulties, for there was much about Pepys and his writing that did not fit contemporary ideals of authors, witnesses, or historical narratives. As Rebecca Steinitz has pointed out, the fact that Pepys's gentility was questionable made him a less than perfect authority for many nineteenth-century commentators. He was the son of a tailor, who showed demeaning obsessions with clothes and money.[33] Additionally, Pepys was repeatedly accused of Catholicism and had been a Jacobite – other potential lines of attack. There was also the problem of his literary failures, specifically what Braybrooke called his lack of 'accuracy of style or finished composition'.[34]

Faced with this situation, Braybrooke mounted a pre-emptive defence of a writer whose morality, politics, religion, frivolity, and grammar were all potential sources of embarrassment. He supplied a preface and a 'Life' which stressed Pepys's selfless toil in his country's service, his incorruptibility, and his unswerving Anglican faith. The diary, Braybrooke argued, confuted recent Jacobite historiography, since Pepys's account of writing the duke's letter of 1668, together with his published *Memoires* (1690), showed that the glory of reforming the navy was his, not James's. While Pepys's lack of literary polish and of discretion might seem demerits, Braybrooke urged readers to take them as signs of credibility. Pepys had 'hastily thrown together' an entry at the end of each day, showing an artlessness that evinced the 'unquestionable' veracity of his account.[35]

Where a diary entry posed a problem, however, the easiest solution was to leave that problem out. The standards of the day allowed editors to intervene freely and silently, and Braybrooke did so. Peter Looker observes that Braybrooke supported his account of Pepys's 'hasty' methods by actively removing much internal evidence that contradicted it: he cut Pepys's references to the work involved in diary writing and to writing up multiple days at once. This served to present the journal as unselfconscious, immediate reportage.[36] Alongside shoring up this argument for the diary's credibility, Braybrooke shaped the diary's contents to what he understood to be readers' priorities. Much that Braybrooke judged unbefitting to history or a gentleman did not make it into the *Memoirs*. In his preface, he explained that Pepys 'was in the habit of recording the most trifling occurrences of his life', so it had been 'absolutely necessary to curtail the MS. materially'. Braybrooke had nonetheless aimed to reproduce everything 'of public interest', while also including 'a great variety of other topics, less important perhaps, but tending in some degree to illustrate the manners and habits of the age'.[37] His selection duly foregrounded high politics and major events, with attention to fashion, the theatre, scientific discoveries, and the City of London's traditions. The *Memoirs* was not devoid of sex, because court scandal came under 'public interest'. References to Lady Castlemaine's nights with the king for example, made it in. To allow this kind of public interest material, silent changes were made to adjust Pepys's grammar and elevate his language: 'whore' became 'mistress', 'bawdy house' became 'brothel', and courtiers who ran around with their 'arses bare' were instead seen 'almost naked'.[38]

For any reader familiar with the complete diary, what is most striking about Braybrooke's selection is the absence of Pepys's day-to-day activities and private life. When it comes to Pepys's own sexual misconduct, there is silence: only hints of it remain in mentions of his wife's occasional jealousy. However, it is not just sexual or scatological references that are missing: Pepys's health, naval business, socializing, household management, and his discussions of family, servants, and colleagues are all dramatically cut. With these go much of the tension and the trouble in Pepys's life. In 1663, for example, Pepys never fights with Elizabeth and burns her papers in January; he has no terrifying 'fitt of the Colique' in October; Lord Sandwich never has an affair with Betty Becke so, in November, Pepys has no need to screw up his courage and warn him about the risks to his reputation. In 1668, Deb Willet is barely mentioned: their relationship and all the consequences that follow from it are cut. Men and women who did not meet the criteria of 'public interest' often had their existence entirely excised.[39] In this history, most of the female population of London were either scheming courtiers or actresses.

Braybrooke's prioritizing of 'public interest' hugely distorted the text, but the principles behind it are clear. More subtle, and less principled, was his tendency silently to remove Pepys's references to his own faults midsentence, while leaving the rest of a passage intact in ways that supported his presentation of Pepys as devout, honest, and industrious. For example, on hearing Lord Sandwich speak critically of Protestantism in 1660, Pepys described him as 'wholly scepticall as well as I'. Smith accurately transcribed this, but in the printed edition the phrase 'as well as I' – Pepys's statement of his own unorthodox tendencies – disappeared.[40] This is far from the only such instance and it was emblematic of Braybrooke's approach to defending his subject.

Pepys almost certainly would not have wanted his diary to be published this extensively. That said, the gist of Lord Braybrooke's editorial policy would likely have met with his approval, since it was geared to protecting his name and that of the college. Pepys's pride and his taste for fine books mean he also would have appreciated other publishing decisions. The *Memoirs* was issued as two royal quarto volumes (a large and prestigious format), with illustrations and a selection of Pepys's personal correspondence. This was modelled on the format for Evelyn's *Memoirs*. The publisher Colburn's advertising portrayed the two as companion pieces: Pepys was 'the intimate Friend of the celebrated John Evelyn' and his *Memoirs* were 'printed uniformly with Evelyn's Memoirs'.[41] At six pounds and six shillings, Pepys's *Memoirs* was also an extremely costly purchase. As one reviewer sarcastically noted, it had sufficient '*aristocratic* appearance and pretension' to 'warn away the *commonalty* of readers'.[42]

Reading Pepys's *Memoirs*

The commonalty of readers, however, did not need to lay hands on a copy of Braybrooke's edition to find out about Pepys. By the time the *Memoirs* went on sale in late June 1825, Colburn, who was notorious for his skills in 'puffery', had been busy drumming up publicity for months.[43] Many of Pepys's first readers would have known about him only through reviews in journals, which habitually reprinted long excerpts from works. On 2 July, the *Literary Gazette* presented its ongoing and extensive reviewing of the *Memoirs* as a public service for those unable to afford this expensive purchase or who were waiting for the volumes from their circulating library. The fact that Colburn was part owner of the *Literary Gazette* went discreetly unmentioned.[44] In reviews – Colburn-instigated and otherwise – the *Memoirs* was widely praised and Braybrooke with it. Smith's work as the 'decipherer' received far less notice, although he was commended by two papers. One of Smith's university colleagues suspected, with reason, that Smith had followed Colburn's lead and used his journalist contacts to plant a 'puff' of himself.[45]

Across a range of publications, reviewers emphasized the entertainment that the *Memoirs* offered, quoting Pepys's most 'curious' passages. Pepys's first cup of tea, as noted, was a favourite. Much commented on too, was Pepys's attention to clothing and wigs, especially his concern about infection-by-periwig during the plague. His failure to appreciate *Hudibras* and his disparagement of Shakespeare were remarkable. The alluring, outrageous actresses and mistresses of the king were fascinating (Lady Castlemaine and Nell Gwyn taking starring roles here).[46] Reviewers consistently stressed the financial and moral corruption of Charles's 'profligate court' – 'the licentiousness of which surpasses all credibility' warned (or perhaps promised) the *Literary Gazette*.[47] The *Memoirs* was, reviewers conveyed, a highly enjoyable miscellany. It was a view shared by the gentlewoman Harriet Yorke when she wrote in August to a kinswoman. Her husband had 'been very much amused with Pepys's Diary, & I think I have been still more' for it was 'an Omnium gatherum [a gathering of all things] much to my taste'. Of all its 'curious details', she found goings-on at the 'Profligate Court' particularly enjoyable.[48]

By September the *Memoirs* was a success. According to *The Examiner*, most readers agreed that the book was 'amusing, instructive, and in a very high degree historically valuable'.[49] Nonetheless, there was considerable disagreement as to how it was instructive and, especially, over its historical worth. Mark Salber Phillips, Peter Looker, and Rebecca Steinitz have all noted that the *Memoirs* fed early nineteenth-century debates about the nature of 'history' as a field of enquiry. Phillips argues that the classical understanding of history, which focused on great men and their political actions, had come to seem inadequate to explain the causes of change in a commercial society. The scope of historical narrative was therefore expanding to include discussion of commerce, arts, manners, and to feature groups, such as women, who were previously excluded. Memoirs and diaries were increasingly valued on this score.[50] Surveying the reviews of Braybrooke's first edition, Looker sees debates over how to regard the diary's 'trifling occurrences' as part of a wider struggle over history, 'class and elitism'. This was an important text 'over which competing historical arguments ranged, opinions were tested and, in turn, modified and influenced by the text itself'.[51] 'Texts like Pepys's diary', Steinitz similarly proposes, in fusing 'the mundane and the eventful, as well as the social and the political', were 'one impetus for the move toward social history most visible, of course, in Macaulay's *History of England* (1849–55). Macaulay's work, she notes, came out around the same time as Braybrooke's third edition of the diary.[52] In trying to make sense of the miscellaneity of Pepys's *Memoirs*, early commentators were drawn to discussing questions of censorship, character, and historical meaning that would become themes in readers' responses across generations.

Censorship of the diary attracted comment despite Braybrooke's discretion. In his preface he had made no mention that passages had been excluded because they were indelicate or obscene. Eagle-eyed readers might have noticed that he later referred in a footnote to Sedley's 'debauchery' on a tavern balcony as 'too gross to print'. Although Braybrooke was keen to avoid discussion of the unpublishable bits of Pepys, his publisher had other ideas. On 9 July, the Colburn-owned *Literary Gazette* offered excerpts from the diary illustrating 'the degeneracy of the period' and then remarked that there were 'a few memoranda' that 'the reverend editor' had 'with great propriety suppressed'. It was hinted these related to Pepys himself.[53] While asserting the *Memoirs'* politeness, this was also a way of inciting more speculation about the book. It worked. In October, the *Westminster Review* reported that Braybrooke had 'found it necessary, he tells us, to curtail the original manuscript in many places, and particularly where Mr. Pepys, it seems, had been unnecessarily explicit, and entered into details not exactly fit for the public eye'. Braybrooke's edition certainly had not said this, but wide-scale censorship on grounds of obscenity was now being presented, accurately, as fact.[54]

In March 1826, Walter Scott reported on the *Memoirs* for the *Quarterly Review*. Early on he digressed to discuss censorship, showing he too had heard rumours about the nature of Braybrooke's abridgement. Documents published for 'the antiquarian or historian', Scott argued, should be 'a literal transcript'. This was preferable 'even when decency or delicacy' might appear to demand omissions, otherwise doubts arose about the material's 'genuine character' and over the reader's ability to judge the author's character and those he depicted. Ultimately, Scott set aside such worries about the *Memoirs*. Since Braybrooke's edition presented Pepys's 'peculiar character' in a 'uniformly sustained' manner, Scott felt confident that Pepys 'had no crimes to conceal, and no very important vices to apologize for'.[55] It was a verdict that did not allow for consistent editorial excision of 'vices'.

These doubts resolved, Scott was free to treat the *Memoirs* as highly credible history and, simultaneously, as harmless literary entertainment. He recommended Pepys's diary as a rich 'mine' of information for a host of historically-minded readers. 'Antiquaries' interested in the theatre, in crime, in voyages, or in superstitions would find 'treasure' there, as would 'a lover of antique scandal' who wanted anecdotes with which 'to interleave a Granger, or illustrate a Grammont'.[56] Scott imagined that readers of the diary behaved as collectors, gleaning passages on their favourite topics without necessarily caring for any wider narrative. Meanwhile, the unfolding of Pepys's character was a narrative that Scott stressed was there for all to enjoy. The *Memoirs*, he implied, could be appreciated as a comedy of humours, with readers relishing and learning from the eccentricities of the lead character. Pepys's 'ludicrous vanity' over his clothing reminded him of 'the *humour* of one of Ben Jonson's characters', Fastidius Briske from *Everyman in his Humour* (1600), who valued his courtly finery more than his life. Pepys's 'humours', Scott continued, 'seem to us so diverting, that we cannot but carry on the same tracing out of petty vanity into another source of action' – which led to his detailing Pepys's excited purchase of a coach. Attention to the diarist's 'odd littlenesses', Scott indicated, would better enable readers to rise above such vanities in their own lives.[57]

In appreciating Pepys as a comic character, Scott was running against Braybrooke's presentation, though he was very much in step with other commentators. Columnists were not persuaded by Braybrooke's framing of Pepys as a serious, diligent man, nor as an exemplar of financial and moral virtue. Most agreed Pepys could claim only 'comparative purity', as against the very low standards of his time.[58] A good deal of the amusement the diary provided was at Pepys's expense. Joseph Snow in the *Gentleman's Magazine* reported that Pepys pondered his first purchase of a wig with 'laughable gravity' and that his desperate efforts to recover his gold (buried ineptly by his wife and father during the Chatham panic) were 'irresistibly ludicrous'. Francis Jeffrey in the *Edinburgh Review* similarly offered up a series of 'not very dignified' excerpts. It might seem unfair to expose Pepys's frailties, he remarked, but 'if a man will leave these things on record, people will read and laugh at them'.[59]

Finding comedy in the *Memoirs* was made easier because it contained no information that required readers to drastically revise their understanding of Restoration events or politics – at least this was the general perception. It was a view among Tories such as Scott, who felt that Pepys offered nothing 'of a very new or original character' to contradict 'historical facts'.[60] The sense that the diary supplied 'few particulars of any moment' on Charles's Restoration was shared by Jeffrey in the Whiggish *Edinburgh Review*, while William Stevenson in the Utilitarian *Westminster Review* concluded the diary did not offer 'much new light on the period'.[61] Harriet Yorke found that reading the *Memoirs* did cause her to revise her views of Restoration society somewhat, if only because accounts of the court that she had thought fictitious now seemed, unexpectedly, credible:

> One had always considered the witty & wicked Memoirs of the Comte de Grammont, as an exaggerated picture of its licentiousness, but really, the grave details of Evelyn & the Minute ones of Pepys, (who I think was somewhat of a Rake <u>at heart</u>,) prove that de Grammont only narrated in a more amusing way, & with the addition of a little more detailed scandal, all that was <u>really</u> passing.

Her husband Charles Philip Yorke, a former Lord Admiral, also found the profligacy of the Restoration striking. He 'had not an idea till he read this Work, to what an Extent of corruption & confusion all had arrive at' in the government, nor the 'total want of order' in the navy.[62] As Harriet Yorke's comments show, this was far from an unpleasant experience: reading about the depths to which society had sunk was shockingly enjoyable and, by implication, the modern government and navy were much improved, a cause for pride. The *Literary Gazette* advertised this appeal, sardonically. Pepys showed 'that age was unquestionably more wicked than the present', making it now 'some pleasure to reflect, that [...] there is at least a less open prostration of virtue in public persons and in private society'.[63]

The perceived lack of significant new 'historical facts' from Pepys on the period did prompt readers to consider where the historical worth of the diary lay and, in the process, to articulate alternative ideas of value that did not depend on high politics or great men. Snow in the *Gentleman's Magazine* declared of Braybrooke's volumes: 'Of their historical importance we think little', as the period was well known. Nonetheless, he continued, the *Memoirs* offered 'an interesting record of the fluctuations of public opinion respecting a return to monarchy'.[64] For Snow, a narrative which provided a broader social understanding of events had 'interest', if not 'importance'. Jeffrey was likewise 'rather disappointed' by the diary's 'political or historical parts' in the conventional sense. However, he argued, accounts like this one that revealed the 'manners and habits of former times' were 'indispensable'. The 'minute details', which 'History has so often rejected as below her dignity', illuminated the motivations of the 'central masses' of the people. Without this kind of knowledge, it was impossible to respond to any historical example with appropriate logic or emotion. Like Scott, he drew on ideas from drama and literary criticism to capture the appeal of the *Memoirs*. History might be written as 'grand Tragedy' or 'Epic fictions' – two elevated genres – but these were not a 'true' picture of the past: one needed 'some infusion of the Comedy of middle life', such as the *Memoirs* offered, to grasp 'the state and colour of the general existence'.[65] To Jeffrey, Pepys was not a great man by birth or on his own merits: this, however, made the diary peculiarly valuable, precisely because of its detailed depiction of 'middle' life.

Meanwhile, a small but vocal group of reviewers had a sharply different view about the historical worth of the *Memoirs*. As with other commentators, they did not see Pepys's account as overturning views of the vice-riddled Restoration; however, they maintained its political import had been missed. *The Examiner* argued that the *Memoirs* depicted the corruption of institutions under the Stuarts and the resulting 'seduction of a steady man of business' by bad example. This 'instructive' political history had been inconvenient for Tory reviewers as it confuted their 'principles of ancient Jacobitism' (meaning nostalgia for the Stuarts and, more generally, unfounded admiration for 'the higher orders'). 'Our Tory brethren' had therefore reprinted excerpts from the diary about the theatre and royal mistresses, calculatedly avoiding any selection 'which conveys a political notion of the times'. Read rightly, Pepys's account was an entertaining antidote to the Jacobitism found in the 'romances of Sir Walter Scott'. *The Examiner* believed attention to the diary's political narratives should therefore accompany appreciating the diary in other ways. Readers were asked to:

> procure it, not only as abounding with amusing anecdote and illustration of personal character; but as exhibiting the oppressive routine of a persecuting Church Militant; of a Nobility profligate and unprincipled beyond all example; of a Prince, a very hypocrite even in his no-religion.

This was a none too subtle invitation to map the politics and institutions of Charles II onto those of George IV.[66] In the *Westminster Review*, William Stevenson likewise argued that the diary was 'the secret history of Mr Pepys', alluding to the anti-Stuart 'secret history' genre current in Pepys's day. The *Memoirs*, he felt, could be read as an exposé of ministerial corruption and as an encouragement to parliamentary reform. Any complacent superiority about the present state of the nation when reading about Pepys's society was therefore misguided.[67] As he wryly remarked, that 'so valuable an exposition [...] of the practice of government, should have been ushered into the world, under the conduct of a peer, and the auspices of a college, was not to be expected'.[68] The historical value of the *Memoirs* therefore lay in its reformist politics although this, Stevenson joked, had wholly escaped its noble editor and Magdalene.

'A Book of the Highest Authority'

Pepys's *Memoirs* was prompting analysis of what qualified as historically significant and how the Restoration related to early nineteenth-century politics. As a source, it also soon began to influence the writing of history, in public and in private. Thomas Babington Macaulay's engagements with the *Memoirs* spanned decades, culminating in his *History of England* (1849–55), the work that made him one of the most influential British historians of the century. Looker and Steinitz have identified connections between the success of Braybrooke's editions and Macaulay's works, and these merit further exploration.[69] Macaulay's sense of his debt to Pepys is best conveyed by a terrifying nightmare he experienced in the late 1840s or 1850s. He dreamed that his young niece:

> came to me with a penitential face, and told me that she had a great sin to confess; that 'Pepys's Diary' was all a forgery, and that she had forged it. I was in the greatest dismay. 'What! I have been quoting in reviews, and in my History, a forgery of yours as a book of the highest authority. How shall I ever hold my head up again?' I woke with the fright, poor Alice's supplicating voice still in my ears.[70]

Macaulay's story points to the imaginative power, as well as the historical importance, that the *Memoirs* had for him. In 1831, he had written to his sister that Pepys's diary 'formed almost inexhaustible food for my fancy', leading him to invent long conversations between 'great people of the time [...] in the style, if not with the merits, of Sir Walter Scott's'.[71] Novels, such as Scott's, and memoirs, such as Pepys's, drove his historiographical thought and his writing of histories.

Writing for the *Edinburgh Review* in May 1828, Macaulay developed arguments about the counterproductive 'dignity' of history which his editor, Jeffrey, had expressed in relation to Pepys. 'Writers of history', urged Macaulay, needed to learn from the success of genres they viewed with 'aristocratical contempt' – such as memoirs, biographies, and even historical novels. Such books flew off the shelves because they engaged readers' emotions and imagination; they did not shrink from dealing with the lives of 'ordinary men', nor with 'vulgar expressions'. Meanwhile, in 'histories of great empires' and revolutions, 'the most characteristic and interesting circumstances are omitted or softened down, because, as we are told, they are too trivial for the majesty of history'. This was self-defeating, making historians' work both less enticing to readers and less effective in tracing a nation's progress in morality, wealth, and knowledge. 'The circumstances which have most influence on the happiness of mankind', he famously argued 'are, for the most part, noiseless revolutions. Their progress is rarely indicated by what historians are pleased to call important events.'[72] Looker describes this influential essay as a 'sustained articulation of some of the views expressed in the more progressive reviews' of Pepys's diary, and suspects that Macaulay had Pepys's writing in mind.[73] Macaulay's use of Pepys's diary in the next issue of the *Edinburgh Review* in fact makes that direct inspiration more than likely.

Macaulay followed his May manifesto with a review which practised what he preached. He set about demonstrating how history should be written via an analysis of the 'excesses' of Restoration England. When instancing scandals and the 'cold, hard ferocity' of the times, one of his main sources (though uncited) was Pepys's *Memoirs*. Braybrooke's censorship had, surprisingly, left intact Pepys's report of a woman's miscarriage at a court ball – perhaps because it seemed a particularly revealing instance of Charles's pernicious influence on his court.[74] Macaulay took this shocking episode and imaginatively embroidered upon it to increase its emotional impact on his readers:

> A dead child is found in the palace, the offspring of some maid of honour by some courtier, or perhaps by Charles himself. The whole flight of pandars and buffoons pounce upon it, and carry it in triumph to the royal laboratory, where his Majesty, after a brutal jest, dissects it for the amusement of the assembly, and probably of its father among the rest!

Here the details of Charles perhaps being the child's father, the triumphant parade of 'pandars and buffoons', and the father's presence at the dissection are all Macaulay's additions to bring home the appalling degradation of the court. Such anecdotes were ultimately valuable to him because they impressed his wider argument on his readers: it was essential to learn from the 'crimes and follies' of the past to avoid repeating the revolutionary crises which had dominated England under the Stuarts. The solution, he argued, was parliamentary reform to represent 'the middling class'.[75]

Macaulay's magnum opus, the *History of England*, was designed on the principles set out in his 1828 essays. In this, Pepys's *Memoirs* proved invaluable, particularly when it came to 'the history of the people' – a history that reached beyond the court and government. As it had twenty years before, the *Memoirs* supplied Macaulay with memorable examples of the vice of Charles's court.[76] Now, however, it also illustrated matters such as the development of provincial towns, the growth of the Royal Society, and the abysmal state of the roads. Macaulay had spent time exploring the Bibliotheca Pepysiana; he had much praise for its 'valuable collections' and for Pepys himself as 'the ablest man in the English admiralty'. The *Memoirs of Samuel Pepys*, along with Pepys's unpublished library manuscripts, his book *Memoires relating to the State of the Royal Navy* (1690), and his newly printed Tangier diary (transcribed by John Smith in 1841), were all cited as sources on the navy's development. Like Pepys, Macaulay saw ballads as vital evidence on the history of 'the common people'. Items from Pepys's ballad volumes were therefore instanced on matters as diverse as popular contempt for direct taxation, the 'vulgar' love of highwaymen, and Shrewsbury's reputation as a party town.[77]

In the course of his *History*, Macaulay heaped condemnation on James II and celebrated the revolution which had ended Pepys's career. Yet in many respects, this work fulfilled Pepys's hopes for his library. This was a hugely acclaimed history that praised Pepys's achievements as a naval administrator and as a historian. A Cambridge-educated scholar had immersed himself in the Bibliotheca Pepysiana, and the result was a book which interpreted Pepys's achievements based on Pepys's chosen sources. It quoted from the diary selectively, interpreting this private record in the light of the library's other holdings. Macaulay's use of the library to determine what was 'in Vogue with the English Populace' similarly respected Pepys's cues on how to understand his collections.[78] His expansive understanding of history was very much in keeping with Pepys's own. Ironically, therefore, Pepys's scheme for his library, which he had honed as a Jacobite dissident, was realized in a founding work of Whig history.

'Honest Pepys'

In 1825 the *Westminster Review* invited readers to imagine how Pepys would have responded to the publication of his diary, predicting he would have reacted with 'dismay'. The attention that reviewers gave to Pepys's 'weaknesses, and trifling adventures' would indeed have alarmed him.[79] Yet in other respects, his plans for promoting both learning and his name had worked out astonishingly well. Magdalene College had protected the library in accordance with Pepys's will; the edition of the diary sanctioned by the master had been shaped by that will. John Smith had conscientiously transcribed the diary, following clues that linked Pepys's shorthand to Shelton's. Braybrooke then made protecting Pepys's good name a guiding principle of his selection, presenting a version of Pepys tailored to contemporary ideas of credibility and taste. Colburn produced a high-status publication, and used his marketing acumen to impress Pepys's respectability and interest. The publication of the *Memoirs* had – it is true – entailed bending the rules, keeping strategically silent about inconvenient facts, and hyping Pepys under the guise of disinterested commentary, but since Pepys was no slouch at any of these himself, this was in keeping with his methods. Finally, the release of the *Memoirs* had begun to draw new scholars to Pepys's library, producing historical works to his benefit and posterity's.

There was a good deal of agreement among early readers on the merits of the *Memoirs*. Its miscellaneousness and 'minuteness' were assets: this was a text which could be mined for anecdotes or read as a continuing narrative of character or politics in ways that suited a range of interests. While treating Pepys as a highly reliable witness, reviewers were markedly more likely than Braybrooke to criticize and mock him. He was a curious, even contradictory, character. The *Memoirs* was seen as a narrative of Pepys's follies and self-interest, at least as much as his heroic industriousness. Readers discussed the diary's appeal in both literary and historical terms, drawing parallels with secret histories, historical novels, and comic drama. Its topical variety, the abundance of entertaining but 'trifling' incidents, and the fact it had been abridged, all fuelled discussion of its historical significance. For Macaulay and others, the *Memoirs* encouraged the writing of social history, along with the incorporation of techniques and topics associated with imaginative literature.

Away from the public eye, Pepys's diary also spurred another genre of history writing – although this was an impact that would not become apparent for some time. The *Memoirs* inspired readers in their own diary keeping. Walter Scott began his first regular diary in November 1825, a few months after reading Pepys's newly published *Memoirs*. His son-in-law later pointed to evidence that the one had inspired the other and recalled that Scott always had Pepys's 'queer turns and phrases on his lips'. Some of those phrases made it into Scott's journal: on 29 June 1826, he wrote 'J. Ballantyne and R. Cadell dined with me, and, as Pepys would say, all was very handsome.'[80] A couple of decades later Pepys's culinary minutiae were again prompting imitation. In November 1848, just as the *History of England* was in press, Macaulay returned to reading Pepys – probably the third and fourth volumes of Braybrooke's new edition, which were just out. Not coincidentally, he chose that month to restart his own diary, deciding in the first entry that 'I think that I will note dinners as honest Pepys did.'[81] 'Honest Pepys', as represented in the *Memoirs*, had become the Samuel Pepys that readers knew, and he was making his presence felt in a range of writing. This Pepys was intriguing, amusing, inspiring, and imitable – and they wanted more.

CHAPTER 5

Victorian Pepys

Samuel Pepys's diary began the Victorian period as a high-end publishing success and ended it as a popular 'classic' of British history. In 1875 Mynors Bright, releasing a new edition of the diary, confidently announced that 'Pepys' had become a 'household word'.[1] It was certainly true that swathes of the reading public now knew Pepys's name, but it was also true that no one quite knew how to say it. 'Peps' was how it was usually pronounced. Support was growing for 'Peeps', the pronunciation used at Magdalene College and by Pepys's closest relatives. Or perhaps it should be 'Peppis'? Or even 'Papes'?[2] Pepys's name, like his diary, was established as the subject of serious scholarly enquiry and of fun.

Demand for Pepys's diary, and more of it, saw three major expansions published during the Victorian period. Between 1848 and 1849, Pepys's *Diary and Correspondence* appeared. Edited by Lord Braybrooke, it was the first expanded text since the 1825 first edition. This put about 40 per cent of the diary into print. In the later 1870s, Bright's edition of the *Diary and Correspondence* made 80 per cent of the diary available. Finally, between 1893 and 1899, Henry B. Wheatley's *The Diary of Samuel Pepys* published all but 'a few passages which cannot possibly be printed' (about ninety passages were still judged unprintable).[3] Along with these costly editions, changes in copyright, in technology, and in literacy helped bring the diary to new audiences. For editors and publishers, this expanding readership was a mixed blessing: healthy sales were, of course, welcome, but answering readers' demands while balancing commercial and scholarly imperatives was far from easy. Meanwhile, much transmission of knowledge about the diary was going on elsewhere, in newspapers, exhibitions, magazines, and through word of mouth: each major edition saw a wave of creative and often mischievous activity.

Just as there were different ways to say 'Pepys', there were multiple versions of Pepys current in Victorian culture. These stemmed from the new diary texts and how Pepys's editors managed the fraught issue of censorship – which itself became a principal component of Pepys's fame. The effects of editors' 'suppressions' were wide ranging, for readers found various ways to deal with the puzzling and provocative absences in the available editions. New diary texts and the speculation about what was missing provided inspiration to painters, fiction writers, and parodists. The diary's growing status also manifested through its use in formal education and its role in informal education, notably in children's magazines and illicit reading. As had been the case in the 1820s, at the end of the century the diary was again being deployed in debates about correct and incorrect ways of doing history. For a vocal group of Pepys's admirers, his fame among the Victorians would come to seem rather too close to infamy for comfort.

Rival Editions

In the second half of the nineteenth century publishers competed to offer the best, or best value, editions of Pepys's diary. Until 1875 Braybrooke had, as one of his many critics put it, 'a monopoly of Pepys'.[4] Up to this point the only selections of the diary available were overseen by Braybrooke, and thus he mediated between Pepys and all other readers. Thereafter Braybrooke's family continued to control access to the diary: John Smith's transcript was in their possession, as was the mastership of Magdalene College and with it guardianship of Pepys's library. Braybrooke's brother was succeeded as master by Braybrooke's son, Latimer Neville, who remained in that role until 1904. The expanded editions of the diary by Braybrooke, Bright, and Wheatley that Magdalene sanctioned in the later nineteenth century were all multi-volume editions for readers of considerable means: each edition promised an improved text, and each volume cost over ten shillings. From 1870, however, a second market for much cheaper diary editions developed. In that year, *Notes and Queries* pointed to the publication of an edition at three shillings and sixpence and commented 'that most amusing if not most moral of gossips, Samuel Pepys, is about to gather round him a new class of listeners'. Further cheap selections followed. In 1875, Pepys's diary was available for one shilling in the 'People's Classics' series, advertised as 'a cheap and desirable addition to the library of the tasteful'. It was, nonetheless, 'not emasculated' (even thrifty, tasteful readers wanted sight of Pepys's private parts).[5] These cheap editions were possible because Braybrooke's 1825 *Memoirs* of Pepys and his 'second edition' of 1828 (a near identical text) were now out of copyright and could be used by any interested publisher.

In the late nineteenth century, wealthy readers purchased Pepys's *Diary* in editions by Braybrooke, Bright, or Wheatley; less well-off readers continued to read his *Memoirs*.

Braybrooke's New Editions (1848–1849 and 1854)

At the high end of the market, publishers drew in readers by promising more diary entries and more comprehensive annotations. Each edition claimed to be, or strongly implied that it was, the only 'complete' text. After no new Pepys for over twenty years, between 1848 and 1854 Braybrooke produced two new editions in rapid succession to answer demand. It was the first of these, the third edition of 1848–9, that expanded the diary text; Henry Colburn's advertising promised it contained 'the restored passages so much desired'.[6] When this sold out, Braybrooke and a small group of scholars expanded the notes for the 1854 fourth edition. In his 1848 preface, Braybrooke explained that he had faced widespread criticism for using 'the pruning-knife with too much freedom' in his 1820s editions. He therefore now presented all the diary, with the exception – and it was a big one – of entries 'devoid of the slightest interest, and many others of so indelicate a character, that no one with a well-regulated mind will regret their loss'.[7] (Braybrooke's implication that anyone who objected to his editorial choices was a mentally unbalanced deviant, suffice to say, proved unpersuasive.) He did not explain his criteria for passages 'devoid of the slightest interest', but this meant many episodes of naval business, including much about Pepys's involvement in a notorious scandal over the appropriation of prize goods in 1665. In this edition, Pepys was allowed to engage in rather more disreputable behaviour than before, but not disreputable language. In the 1825 edition, for example, he had reported getting to his lodgings 'pretty well' after drinking at Charles II's coronation. In 1848 he relayed for the first time his need to 'vomitt' after going to bed, but the follow-up account of waking 'wet with my spewing' was still too indelicate to feature. Nor, of course, was there any nipping out for a 'pisse' mid-coronation.[8] More of Pepys's domestic life was included, but his relations with women never went beyond flirtation.

Bright's Edition (1875–1879)

The first time that Pepys had an extramarital relationship was in the 1870s and even then it was a single lapse, with Deb Willet. Not coincidentally, this was also the first time that Braybrooke's prestige editions had a rival.

The new editor, Reverend Mynors Bright, was trustworthy from Latimer Neville's perspective (as master of Magdalene and custodian of the diary). Not only was Bright a reverend, he was a former president of the college, so could be relied on not to bring the institution into disrepute. Bright became the first person since John Smith to have read the diary through, for he had learned Shelton's shorthand. His edition was the first to publicly identify Pepys's system as Shelton's. In preparing his text, Bright had no access to Smith's transcript, which was still with Braybrooke's family.[9] Instead, he set to work using a copy of Braybrooke's 1854 edition, reading this against the diary manuscript and interleaving pages on which he wrote out the missing passages. When he got to passages that he regarded as obscene he practised his own method of censorship: he transcribed them only in shorthand, but removed any 'dummy' letters added for disguise by Pepys.[10] While Bright's published edition did offer more text than Braybrooke, he followed Braybrooke in principle and in practice when cutting. He too omitted 'material tedious to the reader' which, he explained, chiefly concerned Pepys's 'daily work at the office'.[11] When it came to Pepys's discreditable language and behaviour – with some notable exceptions which I will discuss later – Bright frequently defaulted to Braybrooke's choices on censorship.

Bright had a fraught time working largely solo on his edition and matters got worse on publication. In the 1870s, the copyright to Braybrooke's most recent editions was held by the publishing partnership of George Bell and Frederick Daldry. On learning of Bright's forthcoming work, they were furious at the idea of their valuable property being superseded by this more complete text, which was coming out with their rivals, Bickers and Son. Bell proceeded to throw all the spanners he could in Bright's works. He declared publicly that only his company could legally publish the diary, arguing that copyright in Braybrooke's edition was the same as copyright in the diary itself. Among other dubious assertions, this meant claiming that transcription from shorthand was literal copying. 'Messrs Bell and Daldry's impudence is considerable', wrote Latimer Neville to Bright.[12] The battle of Bickers (for Bright) versus Bell (for Braybrooke) went on in the press. Bickers touted Bright's 'complete' edition as correcting 'glaring mistakes' in Braybrooke, while Bell claimed Braybrooke's was the only 'genuine and complete Edition'.[13] Bright, already bruised, felt further insulted by a review in *The Athenaeum* concerning his first volume's notes (which he had scraped together at the last minute, after George Bell refused him the right to use Braybrooke's 1854 notes). Bright threatened to abandon work entirely. The eventual resolution of this disaster involved Bickers having to placate both Bright and the firm of Bell and Daldry. He paid for the right to use Braybrooke's 1854 notes in Bright's later volumes. He also reluctantly agreed (at Bright's insistence) that this edition would be confined to one print run. To help the exhausted Bright get the rest of the volumes to press the antiquarian Henry B. Wheatley was brought in.[14]

It proved a significant appointment – Wheatley had found his calling. Alongside his work with Bright, he threw himself into promoting Pepys. Struck by the 'want of annotation' in Bright's edition, he produced the first book-length work on the diary, *Samuel Pepys and the World He Lived In* (1880). This offered short chapters on topics such as 'The Navy' and 'Public Characters' – context that readers might seek, but which an edition's pages could not accommodate.[15] In the early 1880s, Wheatley fundraised for a memorial to Pepys. Elizabeth had a monument in St Olave Hart Street, put up by her husband. Samuel Pepys had none, and this now looked like a significant omission. With the monument erected, Wheatley was soon involved in further Pepys activity. Demand from readers made a new edition of the diary desirable, as did the copyright situation. Bright had died in 1883, leaving the copyright in his transcription to Magdalene. This meant that Pepys's manuscript and the most recent editorial work on it were now under the college's control, while George Bell and Sons held the rights to Braybrooke's 1848 and 1854 texts. The copyright in the 1848 expansion was soon to lapse, which must have focused minds. Combining forces, Magdalene and Bell agreed a new text should be published, with Wheatley as its editor.[16] It was this edition that would become the *Diary* for the next eighty years.

Wheatley's Edition (1893–1899)

As an editor, Wheatley had a significant, but not unprecedented, impairment: he could not read Pepys's shorthand. He did, however, have access to Bright's transcript and to a shorthand expert, Hugh Callendar, to help with passages that had proved too outrageous for Bright to transliterate.[17] Wheatley printed the vast majority of the diary and for the first time signalled omissions using ' ... ' – albeit not consistently. Still censored were Pepys's more anatomical descriptions of sex and his crude language. 'Wind' and 'stool' were fine; 'piss', 'farts', and 'shitting' were not.[18] Quite a bit of sexual content was printed because Pepys's ambiguous phrasing and/or his polyglot made it suitably inexplicit. Wheatley therefore included Pepys's many references to doing 'what I would' with Mrs Martin and how 'Deb. did comb my head, and I did toker her with my main para very great pleasure.'[19] Since Wheatley would have had a good idea from the censored entries what 'doing what I would' with Betty Martin often entailed, or where Pepys's hand likely was when touching Deb Willet, this was pushing the limits. Latimer Neville was far from happy, protesting repeatedly to the publishers about 'the gross indecency of certain passages, which have excited comments public as well as private of a wholly unfavourable nature'. The publisher Edward Bell counted such protests by arguing that Wheatley had faced considerable pressure from private letters and 'respectable journals' to print the whole. The college now had in place a formal agreement which gave it a proportion of the royalties. It was, Edward Bell tactfully implied, reaping the rewards of Wheatley's risqué decisions via the resulting quick sales and continuous demand.[20]

Wheatley was trying to accommodate scholarly conventions, commercial requirements, and popular enthusiasm for Pepys. One consequence was that he differed from his predecessors in how he represented the work of editing. Instead of one man and his small band of advisors trying to produce a definitive text, elucidating the diary was presented as an ongoing, communal effort. 'Lovers of Pepys are numerous', he wrote. He had therefore been able to appeal successfully to historians for help, and now asked 'the kind assistance of any reader' who could explain puzzles that remained unannotated.[21] This approach reflected a growth in journals that provided forums for exchanging knowledge, such as *Notes and Queries* (founded in 1849). Wheatley was confident about an enduring scholarly interest in, and a general affection for, Pepys.

Wheatley also reflected the contemporary reception of Pepys by encouraging appreciation of the diary as comic entertainment. In his prefatory material he quoted a speech about the diary's fame given by the poet and critic James Russell Lowell at the unveiling of Pepys's memorial in 1884. Lowell felt Pepys's naval work, while highly commendable, was really of little interest. 'It was not', he judged, 'Pepys the official who had brought that large gathering together that day in honour of his memory: it was Pepys the Diarist.' Culturally, Pepys had been a 'Philistine' and a '*Bourgeois*', yet this had led to 'one of the most delightful books' written in English or any other language. The writer's 'garrulous frankness' and '*naiveté*' meant there was 'more involuntary humour in Pepys's Diary than there was in any other book extant'. This diary, being full of unconscious irony and self-satire, had no rivals 'in its peculiar quality of amusement'.[22] In reproducing Lowell's views at length, Wheatley allowed for, and indeed encouraged, seeing Pepys as the unwitting butt of his own highly comic narrative. It was a striking contrast with Braybrooke's first edition, but this perception of Pepys was now deeply popular, and no later nineteenth-century edition could afford entirely to ignore it.

'Suppressed Passages'

Also unignorable was readers' continuing fascination with what had not been published. Editors were under continual pressure to produce the goods – or rather the bads, for interest focused on what 'was too naughty to be printed'. *The Athenaeum* claimed in 1876 that 'every one curious in social history has looked into every new edition with a hope of meeting with at least some traits of that naughtiness'.[23] Knowledge (or purported knowledge) of the missing passages was valuable social and intellectual currency. Over the years, details of what had been 'suppressed' leaked out. Tracking the culprits and who received this privileged information is tricky, but there are clues. Journalists agitating for more diary to be published drew their readers' attention to the fact that passages were in circulation via manuscript and word of mouth. In 1841, Leigh Hunt had told readers of the *Edinburgh Review* that after Braybrooke's first edition:

> The suppressed passages were naturally talked about in bookselling and editorial quarters, and now and then a story transpired. The following conclusion of one of them has been much admired, as indicating the serious reflections which Pepys mixed up with his levities, and the strong sense he entertained of the merits of an absent wife. We cannot say what was the precise occasion; but it was evidently one in which he had carried his merry-makings to an unusual extent – probably to the disarrangement of all the lady's household economy; for he concludes an account of some pastime in which he had partaken, by a devout expression of penitence, in which he begs the pardon of 'God and Mrs Pepys'.[24]

Pepys never refers to 'God and Mrs Pepys' in those words in his diary. The leaked passage could have been a fake, but it was more likely a genuine, if garbled, report of the entry for 19 November 1668. On this day, Elizabeth discovered that her husband had recently seen Deb and forced him to swear he would never do so again. He was more than usually penitent, ending: 'I do by the grace of God promise never to offend her more, and did this night begin to pray to God upon my knees alone in my chamber; which God knows I cannot yet do heartily, but I hope God will give me the grace more and more every day to fear Him, and to be true to my poor wife.'[25] Hunt offered his readers the entry's conclusion as a comic morsel, apparently without knowledge of what had prompted it.

After Braybrooke's expanded editions, the private circulation of omissions continued. In 1858, the *Illustrated London News* used the occasion of Braybrooke's death to renew complaints:

> Still we have not the *whole* of Pepys; – and why not? Lord Braybrooke was squeamish. There are suppressed passages current in learned societies that merit publication as Pepys had set them – not separately.[26]

The extracts circulating in the unspecified 'learned societies' (meaning institutions like the Society of Antiquaries or the Roxburghe Club), almost certainly derived from Smith's transcript, which had remained in Braybrooke's hands. Braybrooke was president of one such learned historical society, the Camden Society. Indeed, it seems that Braybrooke himself had been telling these stories as part of defending his editorial decisions. In 1871, a friend recalled having heard from him 'particulars of so immoral a character that they were obliged to be omitted in printing Pepys's Diary'. Pepys, the friend concluded, was 'a thorough scamp'.[27]

Many of Pepys's sexual and scatological references were fleeting and had little impact on his other activities. For editors, these were easily cut, leaving few 'traits of that naughtiness' for sharp-eyed readers to spot. However, suppressing one particular strand of narrative proved a crux. Pepys's relationship with Deb Willet and its discovery had consequences that reverberated through the last seven months of the diary. Cutting it led to practical issues of narrative coherence and to ethical issues concerning editorial responsibilities. Nineteenth-century editors had a duty to accurately represent the historical record, but this could conflict with a desire to treat historical individuals respectfully and the obligation not to expose readers to highly immoral content. How editors treated Deb Willet offers a good illustration of the changing content of the diary and the handling of competing ethical obligations. In 1825 Braybrooke had niftily avoided all difficulties via his general policy of removing the majority of Pepys's personal life. Deb Willet was barely mentioned. What both he and Bright attempted in later editions – removing the immoral conduct but leaving other domestic interactions intact – was more difficult and, arguably, more ethically dubious. More women and girls featured, but the nature of Pepys's relationship to many of them, and the reasons for their actions, was often absent. Braybrooke's 1848 text featured the first mentions of Mrs Martin and Mrs Bagwell (all innocuous), and offered fragments of the narrative about Deb, including Pepys's praise of her as 'mighty pretty' on her arrival. On 25 October 1668, Pepys had 'my hair combed by Deb'. There the entry, and Deb's narrative, ended.[28] No more was heard of her. Three months later, on 12 January 1669, Elizabeth had a sudden fit of jealousy and appeared at her husband's bedside with 'tongs red hot at the ends, [and] made as if she did design to pinch me with them'. Here Braybrooke added a footnote, which was retained by Bright:

> Mrs. Pepys seemed inclined to have acted on the legend of St. Dunstan, who –
> —"as the story goes,
> Once pull'd the devil by the nose
> With *red-hot tongs*, which made him roar,
> That he was heard three miles or more."[29]

If this implied that Pepys had done *something* to incite suspicion, removing the source of Elizabeth's disquiet made her appear wholly irrational. The footnote presented this as an amusing scene, turning rage and alarm into an occasion for editorial wit.

As already noted, it was not until Bright's 1877 volume that Pepys had an affair with anyone – and then it was just the one disastrous encounter with Deb. For Bright, this was too significant a relationship to cut, but he obviously had serious qualms about what was proper to include, leaving a broken and mysterious narrative. Readers discovered Pepys's infidelity only when Elizabeth did: on 25 October, 'my wife, coming up suddenly, did find me embracing the girl. I was at a wonderful loss upon it, and I endeavoured to put it off'. Silently omitted here is the explicit detail on how Pepys had been 'embracing' Deb, along with Pepys's comment that 'the girl also' was lost for words. Bright suppressed Pepys's further denials to Elizabeth, his guilt, his secret pursuit of Deb inside and outside the home, and his desire to have 'the maidenhead of this girl' – thereby concealing the extent of Pepys's duplicity.[30] Elizabeth, however, again abruptly appeared brandishing tongs. In Chapter 2, I noted that Pepys kept Deb's name in longhand in a number of these passages, advertising her presence rather than masking it with shorthand. In contrast, Bright removed many references to Deb Willet – such as 'the girl also' – in ways that cannot be fully accounted for by a desire to protect Pepys's reputation or readers' sensibilities.[31] In his cuts, he seems to have been attempting to protect Deb Willet's honour, as much as Pepys's.

The kind of suppressions that Braybrooke and Bright practised tended to remove the cause but preserve the effect. Careful readers noticed and wondered – especially those who were seeking 'naughtiness', sexual or otherwise. In 1881, Robert Louis Stevenson, writing on 'Samuel Pepys' for the *Cornhill Magazine*, puzzled over why Pepys had given his wife a black eye in 1664. It was 'one of the oddest particulars in that odd diary of his' that Pepys mentioned the injury 'in passing', but not how or why he had done it.

The oddness was Bright's, not Pepys's: Pepys had earlier described hitting Elizabeth during a quarrel over household management; Bright had cut that episode without removing the later parenthetical reference to it.[32] Stevenson attributed the lacunae to Pepys's famous idiosyncrasy, but he and other reviewers were increasingly impatient with these partial suppressions. He argued that the diary, as a 'historical document' and 'an established classic', should be published in full. Rather than seeing Bright's editorial caution as scholarly or gentlemanly decorum, Stevenson thought it 'more or less commercial': it was an effort to secure a larger readership by rendering the diary inoffensive. In doing so, he felt, Bright and Bickers failed to respect both the diary's historical status and the edition's readers. After stumping up twelve shillings for each of Bright's 'six huge and distressingly expensive volumes', he argued 'we are entitled to be treated rather more like scholars and rather less like children'.[33] The unspoken contrast here was with readers of the cheaper, heavily abridged reprints who had not established their scholarly interest or their social status through such a costly investment.

In the 1890s, Wheatley tried to avoid such criticism by giving – with the exception of a few phrases – almost the entirety of Pepys's relationship with Deb Willet and its aftermath, along with evidence of Pepys's other sexual relationships. In Wheatley's version 'my wife, coming up suddenly, did find me embracing the girl . . . . I was at a wonderful loss upon it, and the girle also.'[34] Readers were divided on the ethics of this approach. The reviewer for *Notes and Queries* tracked Pepys's 'corrupt and unscrupulous' conduct towards Deb Willet, approving of Wheatley's decision to leave a 'blank' (an ellipsis) at the culmination. Pepys, they argued, was a 'shameless and persistent libertine'; he, not editorial 'squeamishness', should be blamed for such 'blanks'. This reviewer was unusual in their harsh condemnation of Pepys, for having a fuller text does not usually seem to have prompted a re-evaluation of his character.[35] More typical was the *Saturday Review*, which, like Stevenson, was annoyed by editorial tampering with 'a classic': 'Let us have no more, in a *soi-disant* complete edition, of these childish and irritating points and aposiopeses'.[36] At the time of the diary's first publication, Walter Scott had been concerned that censoring such historical documents impaired readers' ability to judge character and therefore their historical understanding. In the late nineteenth century, the expanded, segmented publishing market meant that censorship of prestige editions, while still seen as harming historical knowledge, was increasingly attacked as a mercenary move. It insultingly infantilized elite purchasers, whose cash earned them access and vouched for their interpretative credentials. Price was a proxy for scholarly interest, age, and social status.

Imagining Pepys: Pictures, Fiction, Parody

Each time a major edition of the diary arrived, it sparked not just reviews but wider press coverage that popularized ways of interpreting the text. Imaginative responses to what was missing from the diary became an important part of this. For copy-hungry editors of newspapers and magazines, Pepys's diary was a gift that kept on giving. Most obviously, it was a text full of short, easily excerpted episodes that spoke to a variety of contemporary interests and perennial concerns, and which could be quickly deployed to make up column inches. One Thursday in 1849, for example, the editor of the *Morning Post* used an item headlined 'The Maiden's Defence' to fill a gap between stock prices and an advert for an 'Organic Vibrator' to cure deafness. Without commentary, he reprinted Pepys's account of how a 'pretty, modest maid' responded to Pepys's attempts to take her hand in church by pointedly taking 'pins out of her pocket to prick me if I should touch her again'. Pepys decided to 'forebear'.[37] This was a new inclusion in Braybrooke's third edition, as was an episode titled 'Pepys's wife' printed in the *Cheltenham Chronicle* the same year. Appearing in between church news and theories about cholera, it was the scene in which a jealous Elizabeth menaced Pepys with hot tongs.[38] This dramatic (and intriguingly mysterious) episode was in the process of joining moments from the fire and plague as one of Pepys's most recognizable entries.

The diary's appeal was visual as well as textual. Woodblock and lithographic illustrations were essential to many Victorian periodicals' efforts to boost circulation, and images of Pepys and his times proved highly marketable. One key moment came when a new portrait of Pepys was discovered. In 1666 Pepys had described how John Hayls had painted his portrait ('[I] do almost break my neck looking over my shoulder to make the posture', he noted).[39] In 1848, just as Braybrooke's expanded edition was published, Peter Cunningham identified and purchased this missing portrait (Figure 5.1). It was reproduced in the *Gentleman's Magazine* in 1851, and later in Bright's and Wheatley's editions.[40] This painting would become the dominant image of the diarist, overtaking Godfrey Kneller's portrait of a much older Pepys that had been painted in 1689.

Moreover, the excitement surrounding the 1848 edition prompted artists to offer diary episodes as subjects at prestigious exhibitions, pictures which were then given wider circulation in periodicals. The diary offered moments of dramatic sentiment that repeatedly drew artists, such as Pepys's report of Charles's poverty-stricken exile or the rescue of a child from a plague house.[41]

Figure 5.1 Samuel Pepys, by John Hayls (1666).

When painters imagined Pepys himself, they preferred domestic scenes, especially ones in which he cavorted with actresses such as Nell Gwyn and Mrs Knepp under his wife's nose. In 1851, Augustus Leopold Egg's 'Pepys' Introduction to Nell Gwynne' was given a prime position at the annual Royal Academy exhibition (Figure 5.2). Egg depicted the moment in 1667 when Pepys's party were taken backstage by Knepp to visit Gwyn ('I kissed her, and so did my wife'). The *Illustrated London News* lubriciously described

Figure 5.2 Pepys and Nell Gwynne, by Augustus Leopold Egg (1851).

the scene: 'Mr. Pepys is in the act of saluting Nell with a loud and enjoyable kiss [...] Mrs Knipp [is] so tempting that we should like to turn her round and have a look at her.'[42] Off to the left, Elizabeth looks anxious (not something mentioned by Pepys). Hot on the heels of Egg's success, Alfred Elmore offered the Royal Academy another scene of intrigue in 1852. The setting was an artist's studio. In 1666 Samuel, Elizabeth, Knepp, and Mary Mercer had visited John Hayls's rooms for Elizabeth to have her portrait painted ('while he painted, Knipp, and Mercer, and I sang'). In Pepys's account, this was a highly pleasurable experience for everyone. The resulting portrait, showing Elizabeth as St Katherine, had been engraved for the diary's first edition and reproduced in the 1848 text, so Elizabeth's image was familiar to readers (Figure 5.3). In Elmore's reconstruction of the diary entry, Pepys leans enthusiastically close to Mrs Knepp while singing (Figure 5.4). As often in the diary, Elizabeth is prominent, but her thoughts are hidden. *The Examiner* described the scene as one of sexy women, high comedy, and high discomfort for Elizabeth: 'Buxom Mrs Pepys [...] dares not un-St Katherine herself to look round at her husband as he throws himself into

Figure 5.3 Elizabeth, Wife of Samuel Pepys, Esq, by James Thomson (1825), after John Hayls (1666). Published in Braybrooke's *Memoirs of Samuel Pepys,* I.

the delights of music with his lady friends.' The *Illustrated London News*, however, saw it differently: Elizabeth showed 'a tone of sadness' at 'the neglect to which she is habitually subject'. In 1866 Elmore's picture was engraved for the *Art-Journal*, allowing its readers to put their own constructions on the painter's imaginings.[43]

Pepys's dealings with women had clearly caught the public imagination. Building on the diary's descriptions, these historical paintings drew attention to places where full description was wanting or where others' views, unmentioned by Pepys, could be conjectured. Historical fiction was another way to develop this way of reading. Just as the last volume of Braybrooke's 1848 edition was published, in autumn 1849, one of the earliest – perhaps *the* earliest – short stories about Pepys was printed. It appeared in the *New Monthly Magazine*. In the previous issue, the editor, William Harrison Ainsworth, had opined that 'a very large class of readers' would be 'sorely grieved to find that that most amusing work of its class,

Figure 5.4 The Wife's Portrait – Pepy's [sic] Diary, by Samuel S. Smith (1866), after Alfred Elmore (1852).

Pepys' Diary' had ended – especially as the concluding volume had proved more 'racy' than earlier ones (his term).[44] Entitled 'An Evening with Knipp' (*sic*), the story by Dudley Costello supplied that loss by offering more racy amusement. Set on 1 May 1667, it followed Pepys's attempts to arrange a pleasure trip with Mrs Knipp, dodging the suspicions of his wife and Knipp's violent, drunken 'bully' of a husband. In the diary, Knepp had complained to Pepys 'how like a devil her husband treats her', and Pepys heard she had once been found crying by a messenger. Costello expanded on these hints of a violent relationship. His story gave Pepys's viewpoint, along with those of Mrs Pepys, Pepys's footboy Jacke, and Captain Knipp, all of whom have grudges against Pepys and who, with exception of the Captain, receive some authorial sympathy for their mistreatment at Pepys's hands. The story culminates with Mrs Pepys and the Captain interrupting their spouses' partying: Mrs Pepys with 'the warlike spirit of an Amazon' strides in to order Pepys home. That night Pepys finds his wife at his bedside with 'a weapon as formidable as if it had been prepared by the Devil himself – nothing less than a pair of tongs, *red hot at the tips!*' In a scene 'worthy of Hogarth', he wrestles them from her and begs forgiveness, swearing never to see Knipp again. Meanwhile Knipp has locked her drunken husband out of their house, which leads to his being arrested 'and as a sequel to the adventure, it is recorded that he never attempted to beat his wife again'.[45] This story, inspired by several passages from the later 1660s, drew directly on Braybrooke's 1848 selection and footnotes.[46] Most notably it offered an imagined context for what one newspaper called 'the tongs adventure' of 12 January 1669 – an episode now notorious, but which (thanks to Braybrooke's cuts) had no obvious trigger in the published text.[47] Costello's story completed narrative threads that had been broken in Braybrooke's selection or were missing from the diary itself: he imagined a cause for Elizabeth Pepys's outrage and (in the subplot about Knepp's ill-treatment by her husband) supplied a poetic justice absent from the historical record.

Fiction inspired by Pepys was a rarity at this point. It was more common to get creative through parody. When, in 1875, Bright claimed that Pepys had become a 'household word', it was '*Mr Pips his Diary*', a famous parody from many years before that he instanced as proof.[48] This serial had first appeared in the satirical magazine *Punch* in 1849. Each week, a modern-day Pepys, driven by curiosity, fun, and occasionally by his wife, visited one of the crowded sights of London or enjoyed a typical middle-class pastime: a Royal Academy exhibition, a Sunday in Hyde Park, and a cricket match were among the entertainments covered. The column, by Percival Leigh, was accompanied by illustrations of the 'Manners and Cvstoms of the Englyshe in 1849' by Richard Doyle.[49] These showed the English public going enthusiastically and chaotically about their business. *Punch*, as Jane Goodall has remarked, portrayed Englishness as a 'bizarre and endlessly amusing phenomenon', and Mr Pips's reportage was very much in this vein.[50]

To imagine Victorian England through the eyes of Pepys meant enjoying English eccentricities and appreciating continuities with the past: many of Mr Pips's activities – trips to Hyde Park, to boisterous fairs, and to the clothes shops of the West End – were those pursued by Mr Pepys two hundred years before. Leigh's double-edged mockery swiped gently at Pepys and at *Punch*'s readers as a body. Certain eccentricities, such as obsessing over a bargain or the royal family, were enduring 'Englyshe' behaviours. On 5 September 1849, for example, Pips visited 'MADAME TUSSAUD her Wax Works', assiduously tracking the damage to his purse ('cost 2*s*, and a Catalogue 6*d*'). He gave as much attention to the behaviour of visitors as to the attraction itself, enjoying the sight of 'A Crowd of Dames and Matrons gazing at the Group of the Royal Family, calling the Children

"Dears" and "Ducks", and would, I verily believe, have kissed their Wax Chaps, if they had been suffered'. At the exhibition, visitors were offered history in the form of a sequence of famous figures, assembled with a tenuous grasp of chronology and decorum. Pips was tickled: 'CHARLES THE FIRST protesting against his Death-Warrant, and his Son backing him; and CARDINAL WOLSEY looking on. LORD BYRON in the Dress of a Greek Pirate, looking Daggers and Pistols, close to JOHN WESLEY preaching a Sermon, was likewise mighty droll.'[51] Madame Tussaud's Wax Works brought historical figures comically into proximity; Leigh's parody worked by more expertly closing the distance between nineteenth- and seventeenth-century England through Pepys's/Pips's viewpoint.

Parodying Pepys in this way was a winning formula. His distinctive style was easy to mimic: drop the first person pronoun, insert lots of periphrastic verbs ('did sing', 'do hate'), include some of his recognizable phrases ('mightily', 'with much delight', 'But Lord!', 'But strange ... ') – and end with 'to bed'. As crystallized in *Punch*'s parody, Pepys was ever mindful of fashion, spending, and women, absorbing everything around him with relish. He frankly welcomed others' misfortune if it benefited him, had an eye for the absurd, and was constantly trying to evade the surveillance of his wife. To add to the amusement, there was also the novelty (which soon became its own convention) of reversing the direction of the historical gaze. Instead of the present looking back at the past, this was – as Leigh explained – the past 'peeping' at the present.[52] This version of Pepys, and of Englishness, was a hit. Leigh's parody was repeatedly published into the twentieth century and won many imitators. From 1849 onwards, Pepys was to be found in many publications, commenting on contemporary student life, gossiping in Exeter, playgoing in Monmouthshire, and, in 1855, describing 'Ye Manners and Customs of ye Australians' in the *Sydney Morning Herald*.[53]

Education and Miseducation

Punch's depiction of Mr Pips touring the 'Distinguished Characters' at Madame Tussaud's rather implied that he might be one of them: Pepys writing his diary, near Wesley preaching his sermon.[54] Pepys's fame was not quite that high, but his role as a representative figure of the Restoration was growing. For young people, Pepys and his diary were becoming recognizable through his appearances in schooling and – as importantly – through knowledge picked up via informal education (which sometimes meant picking up a copy of the diary when no one was looking). Beginning in 1870, a series of Education Acts had expanded schooling provision; in

1880, education became compulsory in Britain for children up to the age of eleven. This ongoing expansion greatly increased the market for schoolbooks and children's reading.[55] Peter Yeandle has shown that children's exposure to history in school came chiefly through books designed to teach literacy that taught history in the process.[56] Schoolbooks, however, gave more attention to the events of the civil wars and to Cromwell (a 'very earnest' and 'strong' leader), than to coverage of the Restoration and Charles II. The plague and Great Fire were the focus, if the period was mentioned at all.[57] Pepys made an appearance in some of the advanced reading books aimed at those children who had stayed on beyond the compulsory leaving age. The diary was represented here as part of literary or social history: an 1872 School Board reader, for example, offered episodes from Pepys's account of the plague as part of a chronological arrangement of 'the best authors in prose and poetry'. Charlotte Yonge's *English History Reading Book* (1883), a social history for twelve-year-olds, informed them that Pepys 'had an office in the Admiralty' and that his diary 'tells of all the parties he went to, and of all the fine clothes he and his wife wore'.[58] The comparative neglect of Restoration history in late Victorian schoolbooks stemmed, in part, from the perception that Charles's reign had been a setback in the nation's political and moral progress. It had been a period of 'disaster and disgrace' for a society that prided itself, now more than ever, on its imperial might and which urged children of all classes to share that pride.[59] John Finnemore made this explicit in his *Famous Englishmen* (1902). 'During that reign England sank, in the eyes of the world, to the lowest point of shame and scorn she has ever reached.' The lowest point of this lowest point, he believed, was in 1667 when the Dutch destroyed the English fleet at Chatham – and he cited Pepys and Evelyn in support.[60]

If most children's opportunities to learn about Pepys through schooling were scant, they stood a rather better chance of reading about him through the informal education provided by the new crop of children's magazines. Pepys's diary was used to enliven history in staid and not-so-staid publications. In 1871, the *Juvenile Companion and Sunday-School Hive* featured a piece titled 'The Great Fire of London', which began by describing the 'very foul', plague-ridden streets of the metropolis. The Great Fire had destroyed these, along with St Paul's cathedral and 13,000 houses, but reassuringly:

> Such a fire would be impossible now, on account of the improved means of arresting and extinguishing fires. During the last century there has been marked advancement in arts, sciences, and general education. And we hope

the present youthful generation may far surpass its predecessors, in all that is true, and noble, and good.

This exhortation to further moral, technological, and urban planning advances appeared to be the climax of the article, but it was followed by 'some remarks of Samuel Pepys' describing the 'arch of fire' and 'the cracking of houses at their ruine'.[61] In contrast to the third person summary in the rest of the piece, these lines had been chosen for their evocativeness. It was a tacit invitation to look at the accompanying illustration of London burning and imagine the sight and sounds of the fire in a way that would impress the event, and perhaps the moral, on the memory.

While the *Juvenile Companion* prioritized the learning that could be gleaned from the fire, another publication, *Boys of England, A Journal of Sport, Travel, Fun & Instruction*, put instruction last on the list. This was a hugely successful weekly magazine that in the 1870s achieved a circulation of a quarter of a million readers, chiefly working-class boys.[62] In October 1876, the magazine's serial 'Comic Lives of the English Kings and Queens' reached Charles II. Right in the centre of the article was an eye-catching illustration captioned 'Mr. Pepys – Hys Diary. Published for Subscribers Only' (Figure 5.5). It showed a buck-toothed Pepys offering Charles II a large book entitled 'Pepys' Diary. Court Scandal, Charlie & Mrs Grundy' (Mrs Grundy was the archetype of priggish disapproval). The article's account of Charles's life highlighted exciting stories and egregious characters from his reign, via even more egregious puns. Charles was described as 'indolent' and greedy, with his court being worse in morals 'than any of the courts – or alleys either – in the worst parts of London'. Towards the end Pepys was casually introduced:

> Among other persons who lived in this reign was Mr. Samuel Pepys – or Peeps, as some folks call him. He is reported to have invented pepsine, and several other things; but we know he did invent a book which he showed to King Charles.
>
> But neither that monarch nor anyone else could read it for a number of years, so the king did not subscribe.[63]

Unlike much of the rest of the column, this jumble of wit was not a parody of historical commonplaces found in schoolbooks or histories for children, but depended on knowledge picked up from wider culture and adult sources. A lot was being assumed of readers here. The wordplay on Pepys/pepsine worked best if readers had heard the standard pronunciation, 'Peps', and recognized the word 'pepsine' (discovered in the 1830s, this enzyme was commonly used to treat stomach problems). The jokes

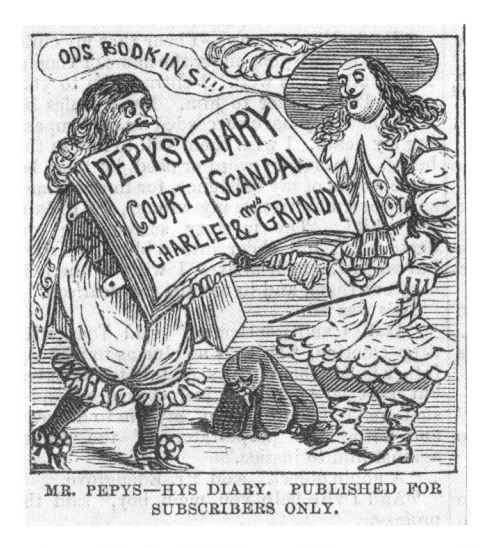

Figure 5.5 'Comic Lives of the English Kings and Queens, no. 33, Charles II', *Boys of England*, 20, 6 October 1876, p. 304.

about the diary relied on knowing it was in shorthand and that it had remained unread for decades – again, facts nowhere explained in the article itself. Finally, the caption 'Mr Pepys – Hys Diary' alluded to the *Punch* parody (which went under the title 'Mr Pips hys Diary').[64] As the main illustration, Pepys's diary here represented the Restoration and its infamous repute, but without any direct reference in the column to the scandals the diary contained. Apparently, a substantial slice of the readership of *Boys of England* – the boys themselves and older members of their family who shared the reading – was expected to be *au fait* with the publication circumstances of Pepys's diary, its scandalous reputation, and its prior history in parody. With cheap editions available and Bright's volumes currently appearing to a surge of publicity, these were fair assumptions.

Around the same time that the *Juvenile Companion* and the *Boys of England* were making very different uses of Pepys as engaging history, a ten-year-old girl, Elinor Glyn, got her hands on what she later described as 'an unexpurgated, early edition of Pepys' Diary'. Her response, or rather how she recalled that response in her 1936 autobiography, aptly captures the appeal, and the problem, of the diary's reputation in the late nineteenth and early twentieth centuries. Glyn found the diary while exploring her family's library on her own, driven there by frustration with the dull 'memorized question and answer' method of teaching favoured by her governesses and history textbooks. The diary she read was probably one of the mid-century Braybrooke editions, so hardly 'unexpurgated' but nonetheless fascinating. Pepys, she recalled 'awakened great interest in the Charles II period, and strengthened my Stuart proclivities'. To express her new allegiance she annotated her 'child's illustrated History of England', with 'Dear Good King' under Charles II's picture and 'Nasty old Beast!' under Oliver Cromwell's – not the positions generally taken by late Victorian histories.[65] By her 'Stuart proclivities' Glyn meant not just an esteem for Charles II, but her lifetime of rejecting convention – she grew up to be a successful and risqué writer of novels, screenplays, and this memoir, *Romantic Adventure*. In it, she cast Pepys's diary as an emblem of exciting, unorthodox history and a symbol of her own rebellion.

Reputations

As *Boys of England* and Glyn's recollections together indicate, by the end of the century, 'Pepys' had become a metonym for Restoration history, and especially for the 'naughty', scandalous (and therefore entertaining) perception of that history. This was, and would remain, a route to Pepys's further popularity. However, for some commentators, it was also a serious problem and symptomatic of wider, worrying trends in history. Pepys and his diary were certainly held in great affection, and his star had never been higher. The diary was recognized as a 'classic' of history and – although this was regarded as a less secure claim – as a classic of literature too. Pepys appeared in compilations of the 'best authors in prose and poetry', and writers such as Robert Louis Stevenson were prepared to defend his literary merit. A style, Stevenson argued, which was 'indefatigably lively', which dealt in 'the most fastidious particulars, and yet sweeps all away in the forth-right current of the narrative' *was* worthy of esteem, in spite of Pepys's 'childishly awkward' and 'ungrammatical' utterances. Yet, despite all this acclaim, early twentieth-century historians noted that even Pepys's professed admirers were prone to patronizing and insulting him (to Stevenson, for example, he was not just 'childishly awkward' but 'our little sensualist in a periwig').[66]

In 1914 Wilbur Abbott, an American historian, put forward the strongest formulation of this argument in an influential attack on the 'Victorian' understanding of Pepys. Abbott believed the diary's first publication had a transformative effect on perceptions of the Restoration period. From being 'a dull, tangled interlude between two revolutions', portrayed by the likes of Clarendon, the later seventeenth century had become 'the England of Pepys, amusing, intimate, incredibly alive'. 'The strange, surprising adventures' of Pepys rivalled those of Robinson Crusoe: his diary had the appeal of great fiction. However each expanded edition had revealed a Pepys more remote from Victorian sensibilities, and his reputation had accordingly sunk:

> Secure in its superior virtue and manners; relieved from the gay plumage of the seventeenth-century male; repressing the earlier liberties of English speech; and at least the open license of its morals; the Victorian age read, loved, despised, what seemed to it a garrulous, amusing man.

Abbott's attack on the Victorians for caricaturing Pepys has a basis in the sources, but it relied in turn on caricaturing the Victorians. He believed that they 'above all resented what [Pepys's] told of his dealings with women'.[67] Although readers may have disapproved of Pepys's behaviour, many were clearly intrigued and wanted more. Abbott's sense that the publication of the diary revolutionized perceptions of the 'dull' Restoration ignored the fact that early nineteenth-century impressions of the period – such as those of Harriet Yorke and Walter Scott – drew as much from the scandal chronicle of Grammont, recently reissued plays by Dryden, and satires such as *Hudibras*, as they did from the memoirs of politicians or grand histories.

Abbott's article was a call to arms. As he saw it, a battle was being fought over Pepys's reputation, with academic disciplines lined up on opposing sides. There were now, he explained, two competing versions of Pepys. The dominant version was a 'petty, childish, simple figure, evoked by literary critics from the Diary'. Abbott later designated this 'the social Pepys'. He argued that adherents of the social Pepys (such as Hunt, Stevenson, and Lowell) knew nothing of Pepys beyond what they found in his diary or editorial comments on it. Their priorities were therefore deeply mistaken. They had failed to 'realize the fundamental fact that Samuel Pepys was not a diarist who happened to be connected with the Navy Office, but was the greatest of all Secretaries of the Admiralty who happened, in his earlier years, to write a diary'.[68] The cultural fixation on the diary of Samuel Pepys, though it drew readers to the Restoration, had ironically become an impediment to a fuller understanding of Pepys and history – specifically, he implied, the popular understanding of Pepys drawn from his diary hindered recognition of the importance of the navy and empire in British history. In contrast, the 'correct' view of Pepys, employing sources such as state papers and naval records, had begun to emerge thanks to 'the development of naval history'. Understanding 'the serious Pepys' meant appreciating Pepys's role in 'England's greatest service', which had made the country a world power. Thus, while 'literature and the literary historians' had failed Pepys, he was being rescued by 'historical scholarship'.[69] This was an argument over academic territory as much as an effort to break from tendencies labelled 'Victorian'. Literature and history departments had recently been set up in universities, such as Abbott's Yale, and there was disciplinary ground to be staked out. In labelling the dominant interpretation of the diary 'the social Pepys' and associating it with (frivolous, intellectually lazy) 'literary historians', Abbott was implying that 'social' history could easily cease to be 'historical scholarship', and that 'literary historians' had scant claim to 'serious' history. The label 'the social Pepys' signalled the amiability of this way of reading Pepys and his history – it was widespread and popular, which made it pernicious if unchecked.

A Classic

At the end of the Victorian era, Pepys's diary was being sold as a classic of English history and, contrary to early condemnations of his style, of literature. Pepys had a low profile in formal schooling which may well have added to his appeal. He had achieved a name recognition that inspired a host of other works, including a book-length study, a short story, parodies, and articles aimed at children. Speculating about what went unmentioned in the diary texts (due to Pepys's own silences or to censorship) was one of the drivers of his fame. Admirers circulated rumours of suppressed passages, illustrated characters' unmentioned reactions, and invented fictions to fill in the gaps. It also proved tremendously entertaining to imagine what a Victorian Pepys might have to say. Parodies of the diary invited readers to enjoy some historical distance from the present, appreciating its oddities, while constructing reassuring continuities with the past. Mr Pips and his imitators were fun-loving, flawed observers who (unlike Pepys the diarist) did not deal in biting criticism of contemporaries. At the end of the century, Pepys was becoming emblematic of the Restoration, or rather a version of the Restoration that was reassuring and amusing: he was evoked as a witness to the plague, the fire, and the depravity that society had surpassed – and as a shorthand for the 'naughtiness', scandal, and gossip that still proved so attractive.

Amid all this activity, the diary – or rather the popular interest in Pepys as an intriguing, amusing character derived from his diary – could seem like an obstacle rather than an asset for the public's 'correct' understanding of history. Readers who favoured a 'social' interpretation of Pepys came under attack as salacious, irresponsible, and superficial – criticisms which are belied by the evidence of thoughtfulness, of layered wit, and of a critical eye for the present that is visible in many such reactions. It was, however, the case that a focus on Pepys as a humorous, naïve, and companionable writer easily bred contempt. This was taken not only as an injustice to Pepys, but as a failure to appreciate the importance of naval, imperial, and archival forms of history. (It also meant underestimating Pepys's craft in reportage and his skills in shaping historical records to his own ends, although no one was making those arguments.) Pepys was now in the unfortunate situation of needing to be defended from his own admirers.

In 1903, Henry Wheatley founded the Pepys Club, an exclusive dining group to celebrate Pepys's memory. The seventy members of this august fan club included aristocrats, cultural patrons, and Pepys scholars. In 1916, Wheatley spoke to the club on 'the Growth of the Fame of Samuel Pepys'. Having previously endorsed Lowell's attitude to reading the diary, he now endorsed Abbott. 'Our Club', he declared, 'may be considered as a sort of Missionary Society to educate the public that they are wrong in treating Pepys with affection, tempered with a lack of respect.' Uniting the 'two apparently inconsistent characters' of Pepys would be a challenge for the coming century.[70] In the twentieth century, the world in which Pepys was read would become volatile and dangerous in ways previously unimagined, giving his diary new, powerful resonances.

CHAPTER 6

War and the Diary

In the early twentieth century the fame of Pepys and his diary reached new heights. His diary was much reprinted, there was a rush of scholarly works around the tercentenary of his birth in 1933, and he appeared in theatrical hits and early radio broadcasts.[1] Perhaps the best marker of his fame, however, was that numerous brands decided that Pepys could be used to sell their products, ranging from cigarettes to sleeper-train tickets: his presence conveyed pleasure, amusement, and, inevitably, going to bed.[2] In 1922, for example, his ghost advertised Johnnie Walker's whisky. Pepys regretted that the drink had not been around in his day, for 'there would have been many another line to my famous diary – "Another JOHNNIE WALKER and so to bed"' (Figure 6.1). This campaign classed Pepys in the same category as other spectral converts to Johnnie Walker, such as Henry VIII, Elizabeth I, and (rather unexpectedly) Oliver Cromwell. If not a leader of his country like these others, Pepys nonetheless rivalled Charles II as a figurehead for his period.

Since its first publication, Pepys's diary had been accruing a host of associations. As his early twentieth-century biographers informed readers, the diary was a famously 'genuine' record of the past: it was a 'transcript of events' and an account of a character given with 'unparalleled' candour and sincerity.[3] It was also a subversive, naughty challenge to received ideas of authoritative, respectable history. His diary had historical prestige and it had merriment – not least because parodies had helped make its style widely recognized. Pepys was both a comical, self-involved fool and a serious-minded, selfless servant of his country. By the start of the twentieth century, these associations were joined by a strong emphasis on Pepys as a representative of 'the ordinary man' – meaning both the people of his time and his assumed readers. Peter Looker links this development to Pepys's being anachronistically seen as 'a member of the English middle class', a group which had grown in social and political power during the nineteenth century. Pepys, the seventeenth-century navy official serving his king, was

Figure 6.1 Johnnie Walker, Historical Spirit Series no. 14, *The Sphere*, vol. 91, 7 October 1922, p. i.

talked of as if he were a twentieth-century civil servant. Biographers and editors described him as 'the type of the average man'; 'average in character' and 'distinctly representative'; indeed, among writers, 'he alone is Everyman'.[4] In 1926, the publisher George Bell and Sons had great success with *Everybody's Pepys*, a selection of the diary featuring entertaining pictures by E. H. Shepard (who was, almost simultaneously, illustrating another amiable gourmand, Winnie-the-Pooh). 'Everybody's Pepys' meant the contents would appeal to – and be inoffensive to – a wide audience, but it was also a play on a now standard assertion about the diary: Pepys embodied universal human qualities, therefore everybody's Pepys.[5] In trying to make the diary attractive to an expanding readership, identifying Pepys as an approachably 'ordinary' everyman had an obvious commercial logic. However, the belief that Pepys represented his readers, especially his English readers, would prove ideologically useful to boot. Between 1900 and 1970, there were no newly expanded editions to fuel interest in Pepys's diary; instead, it was the experience of two world wars that transformed perceptions of his journal and its importance.

In the first half of the twentieth century Pepys's diary became a multi-media phenomenon, and – as people at the time commented – prone to appearing in unexpected places. The 1920s and 1930s, for example, saw a spate of diaries by Elizabeth Pepys, while in 1961 Pepys was the subject of a chart hit by Benny Hill, one of the most successful TV comedians of the century. (As the term 'pop culture' was coined in 1959, this would officially put Pepys at its inception.)[6] The fashion for Elizabeth Pepys's diaries early in the century was only possible because of his diary's popularity, yet it was also a sign that writers were not entirely persuaded by the versions of Pepys and of history being widely advocated. Around the same time, in the 1930s, a best-selling trilogy of Pepys biographies by Arthur Bryant was likewise presented as pushing back against popular views of the diarist. Bryant's account became celebrated and inspired many of Pepys's uses during and after the Second World War.

Pepys's ubiquity during wartime attracted contemporary notice. 'It is surprising', began a column in *The Scotsman* newspaper in 1942, 'how often Mr Samuel Pepys keeps cropping up in connection with the war.'[7] Surprising, but understandable. The experience of two world wars destroyed assumptions that had underpinned Victorian and Edwardian readings of the past. In the 1870s, a magazine writer could quote Pepys on the Great Fire and then confidently state 'such a fire would be impossible now, on account of the improved means of arresting and extinguishing fires'.[8] Readers of the diary during the Great War, suffering zeppelin attacks, had reason to fear this statement was not true; readers in 1941 knew it was not. The Second World War saw Britain's home territory attacked, along with mass evacuations, and huge destruction to the capital. Together these were ordeals that had not been seen on such a scale since the late seventeenth century. Pepys's diary, which described the Second Anglo-Dutch War, the plague, and the fire, alongside personal travails, took on powerful new meanings. After being recruited in various guises to aid the war effort, Pepys's reputation as author and as a famous Englishman was much improved – leading directly to his diary being adapted as a flagship BBC drama and to his chart success with Benny Hill. The diary in twentieth-century British popular culture would prove both a source of enduring comedy and a resource for coping with strange times.

The Great Romantic: Novels

In 1926, the editor of *Everybody's Pepys* joked that Elizabeth's diary, like her husband's, 'would have made good reading'.[9] At least one historical novelist had already reached that conclusion, and several more would take up the baton in the next few years. The 1920s and 30s saw a succession of "diaries of Mrs Pepys" appearing as novels and short stories. Their authors all imagined what would have happened if Elizabeth had found her husband's journal. Elizabeth Louisa Moresby (publishing under the pseudonym "E. Barrington") began the trend in 1921 with 'A Portion of the Diurnal of Mrs Elizth Pepys', and three novels followed in the next thirteen years.[10] This run would not be equalled until the 1990s, when a combination of a complete edition of the diary, feminist historiography, and a renewed literary interest in women's diary writing again led to multiple authors concluding a journal of Elizabeth Pepys was needed.[11] In the 1920s the triggers included the ready availability of diary editions and a tradition of speculating about Elizabeth's views. The interest in 'the tongs adventure' and Dudley Costello's short story had been early examples of this tradition, while Elizabeth and Samuel were now appearing as a bickering double act in pageants and plays.[12] Elizabeth had developed a reputation as a foil to her husband that was ripe for novelists' expansion.

With varying degrees of seriousness, novelists in the 1920s and 1930s used Elizabeth to critique the portrayals of Samuel Pepys present in biographies, essays, and other popular historiography. Pepys's status as an archetypally frank recorder was a target, as was the readiness of historians and literary critics to excuse his flaws (such as his 'extreme sensitiveness to female charms') by citing his 'candor' and other virtues.[13] The lack of attention to women in these histories was also, tacitly, criticized. When it came to historical commentary, genre aligned largely with gender: biographers and editors of Pepys tended to be male; authors of historical fiction about his wife, female.[14]

The belief that Pepys had written a comprehensive, credible record was sent up in Elizabeth Beatrice Brunner's novel *My Wife, Poor Wretch* (1928), which was subtitled 'Uncensored Episodes not in the Diary of Samuel Pepys'. These episodes were ones that Pepys had, supposedly, censored himself. In Brunner's story, the existence of Pepys's diary has never been a secret from his wife: 'Certainly she knew Samuel kept a journal. Live with a man day in and year out, share his room and bed, dress and undress with him, comb his wigs and wash his dirty socks and not know? And she half French and wholly a woman?' Elizabeth has learned shorthand and, from the diary, discovered the existence of her husband's 'hussies'. Yet she also deduces that much is his fantasy; when confronted, he confesses 'I have done more in its pages . . . than ever I did in life!' Elizabeth recognizes the value of the diary to posterity in recording Samuel's role as a 'hero in the plague and in the fire' but she is resolved not 'to go down into history as the poor wife, the poor wretch, the poor fool'.[15] The couple therefore come to an agreement: Samuel will add sections to his diary about Elizabeth's admirers and his jealousy, recording her beauty and her power over him. He also agrees to claim he is ending his diary because of his poor eyesight, concocting a tragic final paragraph. Brunner turned Pepys's frank, secret diary into a fabricated, collaborative effort designed for a future reading public. This was far from a serious suggestion, but it did imply that Pepys's much celebrated reputation for honesty and self-revelation deserved scrutiny.

A more serious – if no less inventive – critique of prevailing attitudes to Pepys's diary came from Moresby's fictions. Her short story, 'A Portion of the Diurnal of Mrs Eliz[th] Pepys', appears to have been the first ever fictional diary of Elizabeth.[16] This was expanded in 1933 (the year of Pepys's tercentenary) to become *The Great Romantic*, which was marketed, rather misleadingly, as a historical romance. Told in the third person, the novel covered multiple viewpoints, among them those of Samuel, Elizabeth, Lady Sandwich (wife of the Earl of Sandwich), and Mrs Becke (the Earl's mistress). Moresby retold episodes from the diary, reworking the details from perspectives other than Pepys's.[17] As in Brunner's story, Pepys's diary is portrayed as a highly unreliable record, both because of its writer's shortcomings and because it has been deliberately falsified. Pepys is shown consistently underestimating those around him, especially if they happen to be female. The mastermind of much of the political action is revealed to be a woman who hardly appears at all in his diary: the Earl of Sandwich's mistress, Betty Becke, here rechristened Rachel Becke.[18] Rachel successfully schemes to become mistress to the heir to the throne, enabling her to control both Pepys's career and the fate of the kingdom. Pepys gradually becomes aware of part of her plan but, we are told, decided to leave his knowledge of Rachel's power-grab out of his diary because it was 'too grave to be entrusted to the most secret cipher'.[19]

In offering an extravagant secret history behind the secret history of the diary, Moresby was having a good deal of fun while suggesting ways in which Pepys's impressively comprehensive record might be selective or silent, notably when it came to acknowledging the intelligence and the agency of others. Her sharpest critique, however, was directed at writers inclined to disregard or downplay the damage Pepys's actions could cause. In both the 'Diurnal of Mrs Eliz[th] Pepys' and *The Great Romantic* Elizabeth discovers and reads the diary. For her, it is no comedy but instead devastating. The disillusionment and distrust that she experiences weaken her health and, it is implied, contribute to her early death.[20] Moresby's novel was an implicit attack on commentators who were inclined to look indulgently on Pepys's infidelities or to stress his devotion to his wife after her death. Robert Louis Stevenson's famous essay on Pepys had, for example, imagined an elderly Pepys, with his 'period of gallantry' now behind him, revelling in 'the recollection of the love that bound him to his wife'. Moresby's novel instead ended with an elderly Pepys chuckling over the 'idle rogueries' in his diary, with no thought for Elizabeth: 'A girl, dead in her youth and beauty: a fretful child, jealous and over-passionate, what could she mean to an old man charged with all the interests and values of a long life? He did not even recall her now, as life's procession passed before him.'[21] This historical romance proposed an anti-romantic perspective on the diary, and encouraged a similarly sceptical view of contemporary works which lauded Pepys.

A Great Englishman: Biographies

The Great Romantic was published in the same year as Arthur Bryant's *Samuel Pepys: The Man in the Making* (1933), the first of his three biographies celebrating Pepys and his achievements. Bryant's approach exemplified certain of the interpretations that Moresby was contesting. He generally took a benign, ironic view of Pepys's corruption and cruelties, including those resulting from his 'roving love'. Pepys's least complimentary assessments of Elizabeth, Bryant offered as fact: she was 'somewhat of a fool'.[22] *The Man in the Making* was soon followed by *The Years of Peril* (1935) and *The Saviour of the Navy* (1938); the latter's title was a fair index of the claims Bryant made for Pepys. Pepys was depicted as on a trajectory of improvement, from being 'beset in youth by frailties all too common' to becoming a moral exemplar and 'our hero' (it was, perhaps, helpful that no detailed diaries of his private life survived from later decades). Through tracing Pepys's life up to his retirement, Bryant sought to 'challenge the legend of [the] amorous buffoon and gossip'. He was responding to Wheatley's call 'to unite the two apparently inconsistent characters [of Pepys] and see the greatness of the man'.[23] In this, Bryant achieved considerable success: his portrayal of Pepys was highly influential in succeeding decades, and the sales of his trilogy reportedly amounted to over two million copies.[24]

When writing new prefaces to his trilogy in the late 1940s, Bryant explained Pepys's achievements to his readers as threefold. First was the diary, where 'there is not a page in it that does not arrest the reader and quicken his perception of humanity'; then came Pepys's work on the 'civil administration of the Admiralty', which had shaped the navy's present form.[25] Bryant's attention to Pepys's naval career was the most valuable part of his writing, for this was an aspect lacking in the vast majority of biographies and, indeed, in the available diary editions. For example, during the Anglo-Dutch War, Pepys's patron the Earl of Sandwich had pre-emptively distributed cargo seized from Dutch ships to himself and his officers, with Pepys among those quick to try and turn a profit. This had led to a public outcry, to the near termination of Sandwich's career, and to many diary entries from Pepys on the affair. The notes to Wheatley's edition of the diary offered little help in understanding exactly what Sandwich and his allies had done wrong. Bryant, on the other hand, explained the breach of protocol and marshalled sources to show how this profiteering had taken place when the navy was desperately underfunded and sailors were starving. He noted Pepys's culpability, with readers invited to be amused at the diarist's avaricious excitement and impressed at his skill in evading blame.[26] In his account of Pepys's navy work, Bryant drew greatly on the unpublished research of J. R. Tanner, a Cambridge historian and Pepys expert. This was without full acknowledgement, as scholars at the time and since have argued.[27] Nonetheless, Bryant deserves credit for turning what was, on the face of it, an unenticing subject – naval administration – into suspenseful and popular history.

Pepys's third claim to greatness, Bryant argued, was as 'the father of the Civil Service'. He had laid down 'the moral standards, integrity and tradition of inflexible service' which had defended the country against corruption.[28] This was a new addition to Pepys's fame, reflecting both Bryant's estimate of the importance of the civil service to the British empire and his sense of 'English' values ('English' and 'British' being treated as synonymous). In *The Saviour of the Navy* (1938), Bryant stressed Pepys was 'above all things an Englishman – the very quintessence of that which we mean by English character'. Pepys's character was especially evident in his commitment to his duty, as seen in his decision to remain in London during the ravages of the plague in 1665, and seen again in 1688 when he continued in post as William invaded.[29] His English character was also apparent in his unfailing loyalty to the monarchy (unfailing apart from his youthful rejoicing in Charles I's execution). Bryant was moulding Pepys to his own Conservative politics. His celebration of Pepys encouraged British readers to reverence tradition and unity, and was intended to sway public opinion on contemporary issues. Participating in the 1930s debates over British rearmament, Bryant maintained the navy was essential as a deterrent. Pepys's life served to reinforce his point. As Reba Soffer puts it, Bryant cast Britain's history as 'the exceptional story of an oceanic Empire whose epic beginnings and continued progress depended upon British military and commercial mastery of the seas'.[30] Bryant's particular understanding of national tradition and unity meant he supported British rearmament while sympathizing with Nazism. While publicizing his third volume of Pepys, he was also publishing pro-Nazi and antisemitic work. He finally ended his support for Nazism in spring 1940, months after war was declared.[31] Bryant subsequently turned to bolstering the war effort, writing patriotic histories which traced precedents for British victory against the odds. His earlier Pepys biographies easily fitted into this new specialism.

Bryant's portrayal of Pepys as 'a great Englishman' came to the fore during the 1940s. When the second edition of his trilogy was published at the end of the decade, he argued that the war had altered the ways that Restoration history was understood, elevating Pepys's standing and giving him immediate relevance to readers' own histories. Hitler's forces had been destroyed 'with the aid of the instrument of force which Pepys spent his life in fashioning' (meaning the navy). The late seventeenth century now seemed much closer: Pepys's biography was a story of 'a European War, a Fire of London, an Economic Crisis and a Revolution. Since I wrote it we have experienced two of these and are passing through the others. It may help to set our ordeal in perspective to read with what courage Pepys faced these shadows.'[32] Evidently for Bryant the nation's ordeals had not ended with the war – he alluded to post-war deprivation and the landslide election of a Labour government. The lessons offered by Pepys's life continued, he argued, to have pressing relevance.[33]

Bryant's post-war prefaces aptly captured certain ways that Pepys's diary was deployed during the war, especially in his account of the parallels between the 1940s and the 1660s. However, his view of Pepys's heroic commitment to the nation through the navy and civil service was only part of Pepys's popularity in wartime, and – it seems – not the most significant part. Bryant's portrayal of Pepys's naval heroism was taken up in official propaganda, but the contemporary assessments of that propaganda's impact reveal its limitations. In 1941, the Ministry of Information produced a short film *Sam Pepys Joins the Navy* (1941), in which a young man of that name arrived to enlist. This prompted the following exchange:

> Officer [to the queue of enlisting men]: If this chap does as much for the navy as old Sam Pepys did, he'll be a pretty good man.
>
> Man in the queue: I didn't know Pepys had anything to do with the navy, sir, I thought he was the fellow who spent most of his time going to bed.
>
> Officer: Yes, according to his diary. But in 1673 Samuel Pepys was Secretary of the Admiralty and, what's more, he had the energy and the foresight and the guts to lay the foundation of the greatest navy the world has ever seen.[34]

The perception of Pepys as merely a diarist is here quickly addressed and corrected. While the explicit reference is to his catchphrase 'And so to bed', this exchange also alludes to, and counters, the idea that he was just an 'amorous buffoon'. After the queue (and the cinema audience) has been duly schooled, Sam Pepys is seen in a naval training montage. In an abrupt segue, the ghost of Samuel Pepys then steps down from his portrait in the Admiralty Office to express his approval of the new recruit and of the War Savings scheme. He is delighted to learn from an admiralty official that this allows ordinary citizens to finance the navy: 'Nice work John Citizen, keep it up!' It was an ingenious concoction, but not an entirely persuasive one. The Ministry of Information's report on the film noted that some of the audience thought their fellows knew little or nothing about Pepys and so would not have grasped the historical parallels – then, as now, Pepys was far from universally recognized. Other viewers liked the joking at the start of the film, but were less gripped by the ghostly touting of war bonds.[35] The responses were symptomatic of wider reactions to the diary in wartime: the evocation of Pepys as an exemplary figure in Britain's naval history generally proved less meaningful for audiences than other, less exalted messages that were taken from his life and writing.

War Diaries

The more compelling uses of Pepys and his diary during the two world wars were those which foregrounded Pepys's ordinariness, rather than his extraordinary life and achievements. By 1940, the concept of the 'ordinary' had gained a new rhetorical power. In this war 'ordinariness' was celebrated. To be ordinary was to be emotionally authentic, transparent, trustworthy, and neighbourly – and it was a term that usefully blurred class distinctions when unity needed emphasizing.[36] This prizing of ordinariness developed alongside a renewed interest in the merits of diary writing. Joe Moran argues that 'between the 1920s and the 1950s, diary keeping came to be imagined as one way of making sense of changing notions of the self, individual privacy and the value of ordinary life'. There was much debate on the radio and in newspapers about the art and aims of diary writing, and especially whether 'an ordinary, private life might (or might not) be worthwhile and interesting enough to record'. Diary keeping appears to have increased during the First World War and again during the Second.[37] Laura Carter sees these changing attitudes to the ordinary and to diaries as part of a new movement in social history promoted by educationalists, which she terms 'the history of everyday life'. Books, programmes, and exhibitions in this vein 'evoked subjective historical experiences for ordinary people in the present, [as] a way for them to understand their place in the changing, mid-century world around them'. She argues that the publication of historical diaries, such as Pepys's, in popular editions, was part of this phenomenon.[38] In the context of these trends, appreciating Pepys as ordinary and focusing on his documentation of everyday life took on greater affective power in wartime – and could be turned to serve the war effort. This was the case with Robert Massie Freeman's astonishingly long-running parody of the diary, which proved one of Pepys's most successful wartime deployments.

Freeman's witty engagement with Pepys ran from 1909 to 1946, with weekly columns in the journal *Truth* and, during the interwar period, in *Radio Times*. Writing in the persona of an upper-class, middle-aged descendant of 'our great Samuel', Freeman and his early collaborator Robert Augustus Bennett offered spoof diary entries on modern life. Initially, this was very much a *Punch*-style parody, with the focus on upper-class social occasions and Pepys's comical hypocrisy and parsimony. However, a running commentary on the news soon developed. It was during the First World War that the venture really took off. In September 1916, recent columns were published in book form as *A Diary of the Great Warr by Saml Pepys, Junr*. Demand was so fierce that the book was on its fifth reprinting by the end of the year, and two sequels followed in 1917 and

1919.[39] Freeman (now the sole writer) was still going strong in 1941 when another '"Warr" diary', *Pepys and Wife Go to It,* appeared – this was, in fact, book number seven.[40] Pepys junior, while still well off, had by this time become less conspicuously upper class. The editor of the volume asserted, with some reason, that over the last quarter of a century 'more people have read with enjoyment the modern Pepys than, over the same period of time, have habitually read his great prototype, the scholastic labours of Mr. Arthur Bryant notwithstanding'.[41] 'Habitually' was the keyword here – Pepys junior's weekly presence in magazines brought him regularly into British homes over four decades.

Pepys and Wife Go to It took its name from a slogan of encouragement, meaning 'to set about a job' (or, sometimes, the enemy). As ever, Pepys and his wife set about each other, but they also supported each other through the hazards, alarms, and excitements of wartime London. Pepys junior gave a good deal of attention to the incremental changes in daily life and the cityscape. On 17 October 1939, passing through Piccadilly Circus, he saw the famous statue of Eros was gone and learned that

> he hath been safely evacuated to a receptioun area. Which methought a signal tribute to his sculptor that his alone of all the Town's sculptured features sh^d have been thus honoured. But perchance, the more part of the others were too bulky. Moreover, certain of them rather asking to be bombed in the opinion of many. (p. 40)

As this suggests, Pepys junior often found cause to imitate the original's occasional sarcasm. Living through the war was grinding, and sometimes terrifying, but Pepys junior, like his predecessor, always had an eye for the entertaining, the intriguing, and the incongruous. As Freeman himself was living in south London, and frequently incorporated incidents from his own experiences, this was not just parody but life-writing.[42] His entry for 8 November 1940 shows how he reworked both Pepys's experiences and the terrors now unfortunately shared by many readers:

> Late last night, just before we went to bedd, we heard a weird piercing noise that I did instantly identify for a screaming bomb; my wife likewise. Whereat she hurriedly to dive under the bedd and I under the table. And there we lay holding our breaths and awaiting the explosioun, when lo! through the party wall the clearly audible voice of naybour Lee, saying, "Poor old Babbs!" (being the name of their catt) "Did I tread on him then?". Soe the laugh over the supposed screaming bomb, with which we did relieve our pent upp feelings, was all against ourselves. And in the circumstances I can honestly say that never did I enjoy a laugh against myself soe heartily. (p. 274)

This entry (which is complete for the day) makes more explicit than most the way in which Freeman's account of the war offered his readers amusement, heightened by the release of alarm and tension. More subtly, it drew on an incident in which Pepys similarly lay quaking in fear before discovering his mistake. On 29 November 1667, Pepys 'Waked about 7 a-clock this morning with a noise I supposed I heard near our chamber, of knocking.' As the noise grew louder, he and Elizabeth lay in bed, growing more terrified and wondering if it was murderous burglars. They also remembered the strange behaviour of 'our young gibb-cat' the previous night, that 'did leap down our stairs from top to bottom at two leaps and frighted us, that we could not tell well whether it was the cat or a spirit'. Perhaps the house was haunted? At last Pepys ventured tentatively downstairs to discover the noise was only next door cleaning their chimney. 'It is one of the most extraordinary accidents in my life, and gives ground to think of Don Quixot's adventures how people may be surprized', he concluded.[43] (Quixote, Cervantes's comic hero, had once spent a night preparing to battle whatever was causing terrifying noises nearby – only to find it was the sound of mills beating cloth.) Pepys evidently saw the funny side, turning terror into an entertaining anecdote. Two hundred and seventy-three years later, Freeman did the same, offering more amusing, cat-related terror – although this time the fear had all too real grounding in the now nightly air raids.

Many of the techniques that Freeman used in repurposing Pepys during the late 1930s and 40s were ones he had employed during the Great War. Then too he had drawn comedy from bombing raids, from the transformation of the city, and from the deprivations of war. A favourite tactic of his was to mimic Pepys's focus on (objectively) trivial personal matters, rather than graver national events. On 3 September 1665, as bodies piled up in the graveyards, Pepys had ventured to put on his periwig brought from an infected area and wondered 'what will be the fashion after the plague is done as to periwigs, for nobody will dare to buy any haire for fear of the infection – that it had been cut off of the heads of people dead of the plague'.[44] On 14 February 1916, Pepys junior worried about Scottish distilleries being used to manufacture munitions. This would drive up the cost of his whisky and lead to even greater problems in years to come when there would be no whisky ready to bottle: 'Which is a very sad example of the consequences of this warr, how they shall endure to our affliction long after peace restored.' The tragic loss of whisky notably troubled him more than the loss of a cruiser the same day and the deaths of its ten crew.[45] Pepys junior was far less macabre than his predecessor, but both were given to interpreting national disasters through the potential disruption to their habits of conspicuous consumption.

Judging by contemporary comments, the appeal of Freeman's parody – and of Pepys's diary – was similar for readers during both wars. In October 1916, an advert for Freeman and Bennett's *Diary of the Great Warr* in *The Times* quoted a letter from an 'artillery officer, Somewhere in France':

> I am camping out in a sea of mud and am always either soaked or very damp. I hope I shall be posted to a Battery soon. At present I carry ammunition up to the guns every night, and as it always rains and is pitch dark and a long way, and the Huns keep shelling the road, it isn't over gay.
>
> *However, there is always* S. PEPYS ON THE GREAT WARR *to come back to – a thousand thanks for sending it to me.*[46]

The marketing maintained that this book was amusing enough even to alleviate the ordeal of trench warfare. Tacitly, there was also a connection made between two kinds of life-writing in war: a soldier who, in letters home, summed up his life under fire with sardonic understatement ('it isn't over gay'), was a reader primed to appreciate Pepys junior's amusing accounts of zeppelin raids and whisky deprivation. Commentators in both 1916 and 1941 suggested that Freeman's rewriting of Pepys appealed to readers because it promoted a perspective on history that was ultimately comforting – a development of the appeal of *Punch*'s Victorian parody. The strong connections between the seventeenth-century original and the twentieth-century parody showed a pleasing and reassuring stability in Englishmen and English culture – one which was unaffected by geopolitical disasters. In 1916, the *Times Literary Supplement* (*TLS*) argued that Freeman revealed 'how little the character of our old families alters in the centuries', noting that his language carried the 'Pepysian flavour of the average Englishman'.[47] In 1941, Collin Brooks, Freeman's editor, took a similar line, but without reference to 'ancient' (implicitly aristocratic or genteel) families. To him, both the 'old Pepys' and 'the New Pepys', in their shared concern for national affairs and 'the normal habits of domesticity', showed 'the English unveiled'. Both diarists, he claimed were 'equally Everyman. Everyman does not change': Pepys as the typical Englishman and Pepys as the universal Everyman, in this account, were the same.[48] Peter Mandler has observed that ideas of the English character must be 'slippery and flexible' to function as a rallying point, altering to suit political needs while appearing timeless. In the first half of the twentieth century, he argues, representations of the English character shifted to cast the English as bourgeois, suburban, and domestic.[49] Pepys's protean life and afterlife made him peculiarly suited to reconfigurations of 'timeless' English traits.

While the relationship between Pepys and his descendant was seen to show the enduring nature of English culture, these two diarists also provided reassurance in another, contrasting way. They acknowledged the drastic changes brought about by war, and the ways that these encroached on every aspect of life. They did so by registering less dramatic – but keenly felt – changes and troubles. The *TLS* stated that Freeman had done a service in recording 'many events of the time which graver preoccupations have threatened to obliterate'.[50] Twenty-five years later Brooks, drawing on current discourse about the value of diaries and 'ordinary' life, argued that Freeman's volume would be a valuable record for future historians. While a parody, it nonetheless documented 'how the British behaved during the siege of Britain'. The new Pepys was not alone in being preoccupied by mundane disturbances such as 'the scarcity of mutton' and 'the "on-comingness" of the new girl who has replaced the milkman'. Brooks argued this revealed an enduring truth, for 'in the 1940's [sic] there are moments when a dropped piece of ash on the carpet seems for a moment to overshadow a world catastrophe', just as it did in Pepys's time 'where the future of Britain was in jeopardy'. Preoccupation with such trivial matters might seem reprehensible in wartime, but 'The New Pepys, by displaying with genial frankness the pettiness of one man, excuses the pettiness of us all.' This was an argument whose implications went beyond just excusing readers' own 'peccadilloes'.[51] For anyone who felt guilt at the pettiness of their own concerns, who failed to behave with heroic selflessness at all times, or who found themselves having a good deal of fun while others suffered, Pepys's diary and Freeman's parody provided precedents which suggested these were natural, pragmatic responses. And – if they were understood as maintaining the typical behaviour of 'the English' in dire straits – they were even commendable ones.

Trivial Stuff?

Brooks's position flipped the arguments made by Bryant and *Sam Pepys Joins the Navy*: rather than imitating Pepys's virtues of courage, diligence, foresightedness, and selfless service, readers should take heart if they shared his vices. Or, more accurately, they should be reassured that persisting in ordinary 'peccadilloes' was itself a kind of courage during war. To find out more about the approaches to Pepys's diary that readers did favour, we can look to the diary of Constance Miles (1881–1963) for clues. Miles, a journalist and housewife, lived in the village of Shere in Surrey.[52] She kept her diary between August 1939 and April 1943, and subsequently left it to the Imperial War Museum. She was fortunate in having easy access to books and plenty of time to read: 'this secret life of reading', she stressed, belonged in 'a war diary', because it had helped her cope with the anxiety caused by the conflict.[53] She especially enjoyed reading biographies and diaries. It was a common preference. Before the war, the Mass Observation project had begun documenting daily life in Britain through soliciting diary-like responses to questionnaires. The project's survey of wartime reading habits in 1942 found biography was the second most popular category of reading after fiction.[54] Studies of readers in the Second World War have investigated reading fiction as a form of escapism.[55] For Miles and her friends, escapism was one of the principal appeals of diaries and historical biographies. Miles was clear that these genres were therapeutic for her. Shane Leslie's *Mrs Fitzherbert, A Life* (1939), about eighteenth-century intrigue, was 'a good sedative in these anxious days'; a biography of Charlotte Brontë prompted the comment, 'I find all this sort of reading entirely consoling, and it helps me to take my mind off Singapore'; and a nineteenth-century diary provided escapism: 'I have been most successfully spirited away from this wretched war by re-reading Lord Esher's early diary.'[56] In October 1940, 'an American lady I greatly admire', wrote to Miles about using Pepys's diary in this way. Living alone in Sussex lodgings during the blitz, she had prescribed herself a sanative course of books:

> I am now reading 'The Mongol Empire in Transition' from the Russian. It's a good book as it takes me into an unknown world – and I am re-reading Pepys. I could not read Balzac, as you are doing, these days. He is, to me, too depressing, and I must keep on a strict <u>mental diet</u>; otherwise I find it takes my strength to keep cheerful.[57]

Her friend assumed that Miles needed no gloss on 'Pepys' and why his diary might fit the bill as historically escapist and uplifting reading. Miles indeed knew Pepys's diary well and here, in copying out the letter, she similarly assumed that her readers would need no explanation.

Miles was explicit that she *did* want her diary to have readers, including 'historians who may write in future' – she imagined it might eventually be published. At the same time, she frequently doubted that her diary writing was worthwhile: her life, she worried, was too 'mon[o]tonous' and 'such trivial stuff may not be worth keeping'.[58] In 1825, Braybrooke had jettisoned 'trifling occurrences' from Pepys's diary; Miles's concern about the historical value of her 'trivial stuff' was a twentieth-century version of this dilemma.[59] Reassurance came from diaries in print. Moran has proposed that many of the diaries published mid-century, 'served to validate and re-enchant the routines of everyday life in ways that may have encouraged the ordinary diarist'. He notes the words of one volunteer in the Mass Observation project who, explaining her interest in the project's work, remarked that 'the studies of daily lives with every little detail should be very interesting to posterity in the way the Samuel Pepys diary is'.[60] Miles's journal shows that she similarly took heart from advice in newspapers about diary keeping and from the examples of published journals (factual and fictional).[61] The minor events that shaped her daily experience would, to most of her contemporaries, be insignificant, but with time would acquire historical value: 'I persevere for it is in the nature of things I cannot judge <u>now</u> what will prove interesting to future generations.'[62] Reading diaries and fictional diaries helped her sense of self-worth, and encouraged her to imagine a future of sympathetic readers that gave her writing, and her daily routine, meaning.

It must have helped that the 'trivial stuff' that Miles was recording was the stuff she also enjoyed in other diarists, real and feigned. Among them was Freeman's *Pepys and Wife Go to It*, which Miles read in January 1942. Many episodes would have seemed very familiar. For example, like Pepys junior, her attention had been caught by the fate of Eros. She noted that he was still visible when she went shopping in September 1939, but no longer so in January 1940. Her style, dropping pronouns and articles as she dashes round the city, has a touch of Pepys himself:

> Entered London about eleven, sped to Piccadilly and dived into Swan and Edgars basement only to find it was empty and made into an Air Raid Shelter. Sandbags looked <u>very</u> ugly at shop doors. The statue of Eros is now wholly concealed by a wooden cone and sandbags.[63]

With these changes, London now seemed a bleaker place than it had a few months before. However, like Pepys junior, Miles had an eye for the absurdities of the war. Finding herself abruptly thwarted in her shopping by a department store's transformation into a communal shelter was just one instance. Freeman's darkly witty accounts of air-raid terror had parallels in her own diary. By the time Miles read *Pepys and Wife Go to It*, she had endured relentless raids and had leapt to the floor as bombs fell nearby – no laughing matter. She sometimes recorded her own experiences with a grim humour, and she documented how others turned their traumatic experiences to comedy: 'Heard that when the Hun was busy over Southampton our poor friend and ex-cook, Mrs. Smith, hid under a kitchen table and put a large saucepan on her head as a tin hat.'[64] This is a story that Mrs Smith had, apparently, told about herself. Freeman's comic tale of bombing was inspired, not just by Pepys's 300-year-old diary, but by a genre of anecdote current during the blitz. Ultimately, Miles was 'somewhat disappointed' by Freeman's book, which was not as funny as she had hoped – perhaps it was a little too close to her present to offer real enjoyment. She had, however, laughed at the bomb/cat scare, and she copied that passage into her diary in its entirety, to preserve both it and her response.[65]

Miles associated reading Pepys's diary and its imitator with therapeutic escapism and amusement; they also appear, along with other published diaries, to have encouraged a historical perspective that validated her writing. Less than a year into the war, an air raid meant that Pepys's diary acquired for her, and others, another set of connotations. The night of 29–30 December 1940 saw one of the most devastating air raids on London, killing hundreds of people and creating fires that stretched from Islington to St Paul's.[66] Almost immediately this became known as 'the second Great Fire of London'. It was a phrase Miles had adopted by 31 December, apparently prompted by a headline in the *News Chronicle* of that date. She was particularly pained by the destruction of the historic cityscape, with Samuel Johnson's home and many Wren churches gone. She was also indignant that the BBC's coverage failed to express sufficient anger at this 'vast, hateful fire' – it is a phrase that suggests she already had Pepys in mind.[67] Days later, on learning more about the devastation, it was Pepys she used to capture her disgust and rage: 'The "most horrid, malicious, bloody flame", as Pepys puts it, of the Great Fire of London resulted in literally millions of books being burned, many at the great binding stores as well as those in publishing houses.'[68] This was a quotation lifted from Pepys's entry for 2 September 1666, describing how, as darkness fell, the fire 'appeared more and more, and in Corners and upon steeples and between churches and houses, as far as we could see up the hill of the City, in a most horrid malicious bloody flame, not like the fine flame of an ordinary fire'.[69] Miles was referring to the destruction of publishers' warehouses in the 1940 raid, not to the burning of the booksellers' quarter around St Paul's in 1666, yet in her prose the ravages of 1666 and 1940 merged into one. The destruction of the capital's book trade was, for Miles, not just a devastating attack on the country's cultural and literary heritage, but on her personal history. Her late father, the editor William Robertson Nicoll, had worked in Paternoster Row near St Paul's, and in April 1941 she went to see the destroyed street. In her diary, evoking the Great Fire and Pepys was how she conveyed the threefold impact of the raid on London, on the nation's cultural heritage, and on herself.

Prime-Time TV

The diary's powerful associations with wartime endurance, humour, and disaster persisted for decades and inspired Pepys's further media adventures. The BBC was encouraged by the relevance the diary had acquired during the Second World War to invest its financial and cultural capital in Pepys. In 1958, the corporation produced *The Diary of Samuel Pepys*, an ambitious, fourteen-part drama that was broadcast live every Friday at 9 pm (Figure 6.2). In the 1950s, as Robert Dillon explains, the BBC sought to be 'the arbiter not only of taste and quality, but also of national identity'. However, in 1955, it lost its monopoly of TV broadcasting and in 1958 it was battling against ITV for the 50 per cent of UK households who now had televisions.[70] The BBC badly needed a ratings-grabbing hit. Pepys – as an entertaining, historically worthy, English everyman – seemed to fit the bill. The diary's wartime resonances were clearly regarded as an audience attraction because they featured heavily in advance publicity. In the run-up to the first broadcast, the screenwriter Arthur Rawlinson addressed a playful letter to Pepys in *Radio Times*, plugging the show under the guise of apologizing for adapting his secret diary. Among Rawlinson's justifications was 'the close parallel between so many of the circumstances of this day and age and yours. I, like you, have seen London engulfed in flames, have known the plague of epidemics and twice lived in apprehension of invasion by our enemies.'[71] The drama's producer, Chloe Gibson, told the *Children's Newspaper* that 'Some of the fire scenes are actual film from the London wartime blitz.'[72] Much time and money was spent on the Great Fire episode: as well as evocative blitz footage, there was an elaborate model of the city, smoke effects, showers of sparks, recorded explosions, and a huge cast of extras. It also featured multiple changes of scene, from the deliberations in Whitehall palace to Pepys's determination in Seething Lane to save his diary and his parmesan cheese.[73]

Rawlinson, Gibson, and their crew did their utmost to give viewers a comprehensive impression of the diary in an 'authentic seventeenth-century' setting.[74] Alongside staging major set pieces such as the fire, Rawlinson's script dealt with office politics, domestic woes, and London's delights. As he hinted to readers of *Radio Times*, fidelity to the record of a 'virile, lusty man' also had the advantage of excusing risqué content.[75] Over the course of the

Figure 6.2 *Radio Times*, 28 February 1958.

series, Pepys was seen 'comforting' Elizabeth behind the bedcurtains, 'fondling' Mercer (whom the script described as 'a pert and personable woman with excellent vital statistics'), and seducing Deb Willet, who was a willing, if naïve, participant in their 'secret happiness'.[76] The production trod the line expertly in prompting just enough controversy: the BBC's audience surveys noted some objections to the emphasis on 'Pepys' love affairs, sex and the bawdiness of the age', but (with one exception) no disgust. That exception was a teacher, who urged the BBC to '"Take it off"' after the first episode, for the corporation had '"touched rock bottom with this monstrosity"'.[77]

Rawlinson's adaptation of the diary took inspiration from Bryant, ensuring Pepys's naval contributions were emphasized. To impress Pepys's worthiness and the BBC's aims, the series commenced with an address by Sir John Lang, the current Secretary of the Admiralty. He appeared seated in the Admiralty Office next to a portrait of Pepys – the same scenario earlier used to sell war bonds. Namechecking Bryant, Lang reiterated his formula that Pepys was 'the father of naval administration and the forerunner of the Civil Service'. There was an air of pre-emptive defence about this address: 'Although himself willing to accept gifts for services rendered, [Pepys] had a complete honesty of purpose.'[78] Viewers had to take Lang's word for it, as Rawlinson's script invited a harsher view of Pepys's motives than Bryant's biography. An episode dealing with the scandal over Dutch prize goods saw Pepys repeatedly stress the desperate state of navy finances. Yet his eyes 'light up' at the prospect of personal profit and (unlike in the diary) he tacitly encourages Sandwich's plans. Later, as Pepys and Hewer discuss how Pepys's scheme for reforming the navy's victualling will bring him more gold, a starving sailor breaks in and collapses, dying. The drama invited viewers to draw their own conclusions about Pepys's behaviour, but it was bookended with scenes that emphasized Bryant's interpretation: an epilogue set in 1703 saw Hewer and Evelyn reflecting on Pepys's illustrious naval career.[79]

The BBC series made Pepys familiar to a new audience. Summarizing the responses of a sample of 220 viewers to the first episode, the compilers of the BBC's Audience Research Reports indicated some viewers already knew the diary well, while some knew it largely by reputation – others presumably had not come across it before.[80] Respondents reportedly enjoyed '"polishing up"' their knowledge of the past, 'without [it] seeming in any way "a history lesson"', indicating that the BBC was achieving its aim of education alongside entertainment. Peter Sallis was praised for playing Pepys with a winning combination of 'earnestness' and 'roguishness'.[81] By the final episode, viewers were 'sorry to say goodbye to "Master Pepys"', whom they liked, and to characters who had 'eventually become, it was said, as interesting as those of "real life friends"'.[82] This suggests the series had something of the appeal of later soap operas. Yet, it was not the hit the BBC had hoped. Some viewers felt the series was 'much too long, dull in parts' and that it was confusing '"with so many characters appearing at the same time"' – there were

162 speaking parts in all.[83] It is a testimony to the fidelity of the adaptation that many of the praises (engaging lead, intriguing characters, a vivid recreation of the past) and the criticisms (too long, too many people, not enough action) are also ones often voiced by readers of the source material. Although the production was judged a success, its audience figures were evidently lower than the BBC had hoped. The average audience share for the series proved to be 5 per cent below the preceding serial, *Pride and Prejudice*.[84] When it came to costume drama, Jane Austen would always lord it over Samuel Pepys – but notably he was now getting the full treatment alongside other literary classics.

Pepys's diary was not quite a hit as a Friday night classy drama. However, as a cheeky song, inspired by – and poking fun at – that drama, it did much better. *The Benny Hill Show*, broadcast on Saturday evenings, was one of the BBC's most successful programmes, with excellent approval ratings and reach.[85] On Saturday 26 April 1958, the evening after Sallis's Pepys faced the plague, Hill appeared in a resplendent wig and brandishing a large book labelled 'Diary'. Accompanied by a harpsichord, a seventeenth-century choir, and a fair amount of smirking, he sang about bantering with a lady in 'a very saucy tone'. The song climaxed with:

> A fair young maid has took a room down at the local inn.
> Her bedside light is oh so bright and the curtains oh so thin.
> At nine o'clock she enters her room; at ten o'clock she sleeps.
> Lord Clarendon he just walks on, but naughty Samuel peeps.
> Chorus: Oh we know it's right.
> It's in black and white
> And it's all written down in his diary.[86]

The chorus's solemn affirmation was all the wittier because the BBC were broadcasting their own monochrome, studiously authentic production. It is just about possible that Hill's lyrics are a profound commentary on the difference between Pepys's intimate, explicit journal and the Earl of Clarendon's *History of the Rebellion* (1702–4), which passed swiftly over domestic matters – but the chances are 'Clarendon' was selected more for the rhyme than the historiographical commentary.

Escaping its origins as a parody of a flagship drama, Benny Hill's skit was repeatedly performed throughout his long career. It featured as the B-side on a single of his that reached number twelve in the charts in 1961. The song was filmed again in 1971 and was performed for his final UK TV show in 1989. Over time, the lyrics strayed further from the diary, with new verses featuring willing shepherdesses, cuckolded squires, and chastity belts: this was Pepys as a conduit for an eclectic version of England's naughty heritage, one that combined the medieval, the pastoral, cod-seventeenth-century exploits, and settings that could be twentieth century (a butcher's shop, a hospital visit).[87] The 'saucy' Pepys propagated by Benny Hill's song was fun and required two minutes to grasp. Hill offered music hall humour (muted for prime-time TV), featuring innuendo and cheekiness, with Pepys slotted easily into the stereotype of the randy but often thwarted husband.[88] It was a tradition of humour that appeared subversive, while being an established source of national pride. For this reason, among others, efforts to quash the view of Pepys as an 'amorous buffoon' were doomed to failure: in this game of cultural whack-a-mole, Bryant was never going to be able to cosh the irrepressible version of Pepys offered by the likes of Benny Hill.

Everybody's Pepys

The twentieth century saw the development of a veritable cultural industry around Pepys and his diary. Scholarly works, biographies, and 'authentic' adaptations of the diary enjoyed a symbiotic relationship with parodies, skits, and fictions that were preoccupied with its disreputable aspects and with mocking its fame as the archetypal reliable, comprehensive source. The one fed off the other, and valuable historical commentary on the diary was not confined to scholarship. Although novelists' challenges to the perspectives of Pepys and his biographers were generally comic, this did not preclude their making points about the portrayal of women within the diary, and within historiography, that were decades ahead of trends in more esteemed genres of historical writing. At the same time, such irreverent treatments of Pepys and his diary drove interest in him and the demand for more works. Collin Brooks was not wrong when, in 1941, he suspected that many people's knowledge of Pepys came at least partly from comic riffs on his diary – Freeman's diaries and, later, Benny Hill's parody being two extremely successful examples.

Pepys's inconsistent character had always intrigued readers, and during the First and Second World Wars those seeming contradictions became particularly valuable. Among other benefits, they allowed him to be adapted to whichever version of 'the English' best suited present need. Depictions of him as a 'great Englishman' certainly had their uses in wartime, and he was held up as an example of non-martial courage and as a reminder of Britain's enduring naval greatness. His vivid, emotional writing could offer readers such as Miles parallels for responding to disaster and expressing their own pain and indignation. However, rather than a narrative of stirring patriotism, the diary's usual appeal seems to have been as a source of amusement and of escapist distraction. This, it should be stressed, was not an 'English' phenomenon: in Nazi-occupied Paris, a dramatization of the diary in the style of a 'vaudeville comedy' proved a smash hit, running for over three hundred performances.[89] For readers on the British home front the support that the diary offered to morale came less from its documentation of Pepys's noble qualities, than from his flaws. Nineteenth-century discussions of Pepys's diary had often implied that readers should look generously on the diarist's parsimony, selfishness, vanity, and other shortcomings. Pepys's documentation of these was presented as evidence of his honesty, it was amusing and, in recognizing his lapses, readers might rise above them. In the twentieth century, Pepys's 'bourgeois' attitudes and domestic preoccupations were less likely to count as demerits which readers should excuse, and more likely to be cited as instances of his representativeness. When war reduced the historical and experiential distance between Pepys and many of his readers, the emphasis in responses to the diary shifted from the idea that readers should excuse Pepys, to the idea that Pepys excused readers. What Walter Scott had once called Pepys's 'petty vanity' and 'odd littlenesses' were not signs of failure at a time of national crisis.[90] Rather, they were enduring, natural traits and evidence of his personal resilience. If readers shared those traits, this was no cause for self-recrimination. Pepys's failure to live up to the ideals of virtue, nobility, and heroism, in other words, was psychologically comforting. Also comforting was the fact that this detailed account of mundane matters was now prized as fascinating and important. If your own experiences seemed trivial, tedious, or absurd, this did not mean that they were unimportant, and they might have a historical value that you could not yet discern. This was a message conveyed by the diary and by Freeman's parodies, and it was one that Miles took to heart.

By the 1950s, the experience of living under the immediate threat of invasion and, especially, witnessing the Second Great Fire of London, had lent the diary a new relevance for many of its readers and given it a new cultural status in Britain. Some things, however, had not changed – such as its publishers' economical way with the truth. While the BBC was airing *The Diary of Samuel Pepys*, Bell's seized the opportunity to win new readers via the BBC's magazine, *The Listener*. The firm advertised both 'the delightful abridgment *Everybody's Pepys*' and, for the more committed reader, Wheatley's 'complete edition'.[91] The diary might be firmly ensconced as a classic text of British history and English literature, celebrated as exemplifying the national character, and feted for its contemporary relevance but – despite Bell's misleading advertising – no one could yet read a 'complete edition' of that diary. Pepys might be everyman, but everybody's Pepys was still an abridgement. That was about to change.

CHAPTER 7

'Every Last Obscenity': Complete and Online

The story of how a complete edition of Pepys's diary finally made it into print is one of legal guile and editorial ingenuity. The first volumes of the 'new and complete transcription', edited by Robert Latham and William Matthews, were published in 1970 to great acclaim: here, finally, was a reliable text of the diary.[1] It was not until 1976, when the last volume of the main text appeared, that the public could access the whole diary. To reach that point, a series of obstacles had to be overcome. First, there was the law to contend with: was Pepys's diary an obscene text and therefore illegal to publish in full? Until the sixth decade of the twentieth century, the expert answer to that question was 'yes'. Then, in 1959, a new Obscene Publications Act held out the prospect that printing the diary's 'every last obscenity', in Matthews's words, might be legally defensible. (It's a measure of the caution required that Matthews subsequently thought better of using this incriminating phrase publicly and instead spoke of publishing 'every last naughtiness'.)[2] Meanwhile, the process of exploring the legal possibilities changed how the diary was discussed in ways that alarmed its guardians, Magdalene College. It was conventional to draw parallels between Pepys's diary and Evelyn's, or to compare the diary with the Earl of Clarendon's *History*. Now, the pertinent parallels were with D. H. Lawrence's *Lady Chatterley's Lover* or Nabokov's *Lolita*: twentieth-century novels that infamously served as tests for what was judged obscene. Pepys was keeping dubious company. The reputational risks – to Pepys and to the college – were almost as significant as the legal ones in deterring full publication, and these too had to be dealt with. Then there was just the small matter of the actual work of publication. Pepys's diary had form when it came to causing trouble for editors and 'decipherers', and the Latham and Matthews edition proved no exception. The fallout – from the legal, reputational, and editorial controversies – has left a vivid and unusually comprehensive record of the people who worked to bring

Pepys's complete diary to the public, along with the methods and tactics they employed to do so.

Latham and Matthews's eleven-volume complete text is the most valuable edition of the diary to date: it has energized scholarship and been widely read in abridgements and anthologies.[3] But this text now has a twenty-first-century rival when it comes to promoting access to the diary and interest in it. In 2003, Phil Gyford, a web developer, began publishing an entry from Wheatley's edition online every day, with readers able to annotate the entries. Over twenty years later, his pepysdiary.com is still going strong, attracting a community of readers and commenters. It is an international effort that has brought new ways of reading to bear on tackling now familiar puzzles. With echoes of readers during the First and Second World Wars, this project has also seen Pepys's diary used to make sense of a deeply unfamiliar present when, in 2020, the COVID-19 pandemic took hold. While the Latham and Matthews text is the product of extraordinary legal and editorial stratagems, pepysdiary.com shows the extraordinary results of a host of readers engaging with the diary.

An Obscene Publication

In the first half of the twentieth century what could be legally published was governed by the Obscene Publications Act of 1857 and by a piece of case law from 1868 known as the Hicklin test. Together these determined that a work could be seized and destroyed if any bit of it was obscene, and that the test for obscenity was whether the material tended 'to deprave and corrupt those whose minds are open to such immoral influences, and into whose hands a publication [...] may fall'.[4] This meant both the content and the potential readership of a work were relevant to judgements on its obscenity. In the 1930s, with the publicity around the tercentenary of Pepys's birth, demand for a complete edition of the diary was again making itself felt. Both the Pepys librarian Francis Turner and Pepys's biographer Arthur Bryant had come to believe that expurgated diary texts, by provoking rampant speculation, were doing Pepys's reputation more harm than good. Putting the case for greater openness to Magdalene College's governing body, Turner instanced Wheatley's ellipsis at the point where Elizabeth Pepys caught her husband with Deb Willet. This silence, he argued, caused 'the reader to put a worse construction on Pepys's famous affair with Deb than the full account justified'.[5] (Presumably he thought that readers imagined Pepys and Deb were engaging in something more spectacular and athletic than was actually the case.) Turner was planning his own expanded edition. This never materialized, but the discussions of it are revealing about the law, the diary's reputation, and the assumptions about its readership in the early twentieth century.

In 1936 Turner's would-be publishers, George Bell and Sons, took legal advice and resolved that printing a full text remained too dangerous. They were prepared to risk publishing previously omitted 'coarse' words, references to Pepys's 'marital relations', and any descriptions of his extramarital relations that did not 'raise an image of a lewd nature'. Yet about half the still unpublished material (such as lewdly descriptive extramarital encounters) was likely to fall foul of the law. The publisher's managing director, Guy Bickers, was the third generation of his family to have dealt with the challenges of Pepys's diary: his grandfather and father were the 'Bickers and Son' who had published Bright's edition in the 1870s. He now explained to Turner that Bell and Sons had weighed up the situation and thought they saw a potential loophole. Pepys's journal, Bickers wrote, was 'an important historical document which historical scholars naturally wish to be able to consult in its original form'. However, it was also 'a popular work which appeals to, and is circulated amongst, all classes of the community'. This public enthusiasm was both the commercial incentive to publish and the legal problem, for the obscenity law considered anyone who might encounter the work. A judge might be persuaded to regard 'historical scholars' as immune to the diary's immoral content, but the same could not be said for readers 'of all classes' into whose hands the diary might fall (children, women, and the working class were among the groups thought to need the law's protection). Bickers believed the diary might not legally be obscene if it was sold only to historical scholars, yet checking the 'bona fides of "historical students"' was beyond the book trade.[6] Notably, historical research was the only potentially defensible study of the diary mentioned here: the diary's value as history was considered more self-evident than its literary status and, anyway, offering literary merit as a defence had failed to deter prosecutions and convictions under the 1857 law.[7] The best way of dodging legal trouble, Bickers ultimately concluded, would be to publish an expurgated text for a general readership, while also creating a small number of bespoke copies for university libraries, into which the passages most likely to deprave readers would be interleaved.[8] In this scheme, the full publication of the diary depended on preventing the majority of readers from accessing it. University libraries would act as gatekeepers when it came to determining scholarly credentials, class membership, and resistance to Pepys's immoral influence.

Bickers's plan was adopted as the policy for a new edition, but never put into practice.[9] Indeed Magdalene's authorities remained reluctant to give access to the full diary even to researchers who could show their 'bona fides'. In 1952, Professor Alfred Kinsey, who had already issued the first of his two famous reports on human sexual behaviour, wrote to the master and the current Pepys librarian to ask how much of the diary's 'sexual material' was in print. He hinted that his researchers would like to consult the manuscript, should the printed editions 'not serve our purpose'. The master, Henry Willink, gave him a polite but emphatic brush-off: the college 'was not prepared to make any of the excluded passages available'.[10] Samuel Pepys was not going to be a source for sexology any time soon.

The Public Good

For Pepys's diary to be available in full, the law needed to change and the college and publisher would have to screw their courage to the sticking place to publish the screwing. In these terms, the Obscene Publications Act of 1959 was both an opportunity and an obstacle. It redefined 'obscene' in ways that could, perhaps, exclude the diary, but the publicity around test cases unnerved the college authorities, who did not want Magdalene associated with smut-peddling. The deliberations about a new edition resumed in 1960, during the run-up to the infamous trial of Penguin Books for publishing D. H. Lawrence's *Lady Chatterley's Lover* – this was the case that ultimately demonstrated how a 'public good' defence would operate. Some of the people involved in the consultations about the diary's publication were clearly enjoying themselves, among them Gerald Gardiner the counsel appointed by Bell's to give his expert advice. A few months after advising on Pepys, Gardiner would be the defending counsel in the Lady Chatterley trial. The witty 'Opinion' he produced for Bell's in March 1960 evaluated the risks of publishing the diary in full and how these might be mitigated. This document materially shaped the text of the full edition in ways that went unacknowledged, and it continues to affect the ways the diary is understood now.

Gardiner began his report by highlighting changes in the new act that made a complete edition of the diary more easily defensible. For the first time, the law specified that a publication could be 'justified as being for the public good on the ground that it is in the interests of science, literature, art or learning, or of other objects of general concern'.[11] Thus, Gardiner reasoned, the diary would be defensible as 'an historical and literary work of an outstanding character which should be given to the world as it is'. It was not for 'the owners of such a manuscript' to decide which parts were of use to 'historians, literary critics, sociologists, philologists or doctors' (or, we might add, sexologists).[12] In contrast to the 1930s, the diary's literary standing was now made crucial to its full publication. Thanks to the change in the law, its usefulness to disciplines other than history was likewise acknowledged. Also significant was that the 1959 act reversed the requirement to judge a work's obscenity by its most outrageous parts: the publication had to be judged 'as a whole'. This was advantageous because, as Gardiner dryly explained:

> The passages hitherto excluded are very small in relation to the work read as a whole. It would take the prurient-minded man a week to find out which the hitherto excluded passages are. He would be very disappointed when he got there.

It helped too that 'Pepys was his own censor', using polyglot for 'statements which might have offended the young if they had come across them'. The diary could not have been written as pornography as 'it was never intended to be seen by anyone', putting its author 'in a better position than any author ever was'. This line of argument meant imagining how Pepys might have defended himself had he appeared in the witness box. It was (Gardiner implied) rather convenient that he was dead and so, unlike contemporary authors, not available to be humiliatingly cross-examined on his word choice.[13] Yet – and this was a vital point – if the editors opted to publish more than Wheatley's text, but not the whole diary, they were likely to find themselves in the dock in Pepys's place, defending each new inclusion. This advice effectively ruled out following the 1930s plan for a public edition that would include only some additional passages: it was all, or Wheatley.

Gardiner believed publishing the whole was desirable and defensible, but only with certain safeguards. Once again, readership was legally significant. The new act no longer judged obscenity on the need to protect anyone susceptible to 'immoral influences' who might happen on the text. Instead, the test was whether it would 'deprave and corrupt persons who [were] likely, having regard to all relevant circumstances' to read a publication.[14] The loophole that Guy Bickers had been trying to fashion was now part of the law: factors such as the price of the new edition and where it was sold could determine whether it was judged obscene. Pepys's diary should be safe if care was taken to distinguish it commercially and materially from pornography. As Gardiner remarked, 'A 20 guinea [£21] edition of Pepys is not the sort of book which would be likely to form part of the stock of bookshops in which the police take an interest.'[15] The bookshops that interested the police sold pornographic works with titles such as *The Biggest Ever* and *The Perversions of Aphrodite*. Their stock ranged from magazines for a few shillings to 'privately published' novels at seven pounds.[16] In contrast, Gardiner believed that the Director of Public Prosecutions was now minded to leave 'serious literary work alone': Nabokov's *Lolita*, he noted, had recently been published in England without action by the director or the police.[17] Gardiner's sense that the policy on prosecuting 'literary work' had changed proved optimistic. The Lady Chatterley prosecution was announced in August 1960, five months after he produced his opinion and while deliberations were still underway about the risks of a new diary edition.

Recognizing that arguments based on readership offered limited protection, Gardiner gave advice on the content of a complete edition. In editorial policy, discretion would be the better part of valour. Gardiner understood the plan was 'merely to transcribe and not to translate' Pepys's polyglot, and he encouraged that course: 'there ought not to be, e.g. footnotes, translating the passages in question'. Although the main selling point of a new edition would be its completeness, no statement should be made 'as to which were the particular passages being published for the first time'.[18] Prurient readers seeking excitement, or enthusiastic guardians of morality looking for evidence to prosecute, would have to work for it. This legal advice directly affected the edition that was eventually published in the 1970s: there was no explanation of Pepys's polyglot and, across the edition, sexual content was consistently downplayed. Since legal cases testing the interpretation of the Obscene Publications Act continued throughout the 1960s, while the edition was being prepared, discretion remained a sensible precaution. However, even the 'Companion' and 'Index' volumes that were published in 1983 avoided drawing attention to the sexual content. As one eagle-eyed reviewer noted, there was no article on 'Sex' in the Companion's encyclopaedic coverage of the diary's contexts. The topic had instead been 'smuggled in' under the heading 'HEALTH (A Psychoanalyst's view)'.[19]

Supported by Gardiner's legal advice, Bell's was keen to proceed with an unexpurgated text. First, the company asked the college to procure an opinion 'from one or two senior Cambridge historians' on the issue of whether an unexpurgated text was in the public good, for experts were now allowed to testify on this point. Interestingly, Magdalene's preferred experts were not 'senior Cambridge historians' but more strategic choices: Arthur Bryant and C. S. Lewis.[20] Bryant was, of course, a famous Pepys expert and popular historian (while not officially attached to the university, he had strong academic credentials). C. S. Lewis was a fellow of Magdalene, an expert in medieval literature, and – like Bryant – known to the public. He broadcast on Christian topics and had recently secured his popular fame with the Narnia series of children's books. While scholarly repute was clearly a factor in these choices, the college had cannily opted for trusted media personalities, seeking to cover its bases in terms of both 'historical' and 'literary' defences. Lewis, giving his advice, directly addressed the governing body's concerns about reputation. The publication of the '"curious" passages', he said, entailed a 'prudential' problem (which was the risk of 'dispute and ridicule') and a moral one. For Magdalene to act from fear of ridicule would be 'pusillanimous and unscholarly' since a couple of weeks of mockery in the press were nothing in the life of a noble college. The essence of the moral problem was whether publishing the diary in full might lead someone to commit an immoral act. That was incalculable and, Lewis thought, also at bottom a poor excuse:

> To suggest that in a society where the most potent aphrodisiacs are daily put forward by the advertisers, the newspapers, and the films, any perceptible increment of lechery will be caused by printing a few, obscure, and widely separated passages in a very long and expensive book, seems to me unrealistic or even hypocritical.[21]

Having dispensed with the moral argument on the grounds that society had sunk so low that exposure to Pepys's activities was unlikely to sink it lower, Lewis gave his verdict in favour. Bryant was asked for his view just as Penguin were mustering their battalion of witnesses for the Lady Chatterley trial. He had received a 'round Robin' from Penguin's solicitors seeking volunteers but told Turner he would be delighted to deny Lawrence in favour of Pepys: the diary was 'an infinitely more important publication'. Also, he cheerfully admitted, he seldom read a novel, so his ability to speak for Pepys might be dinted 'if I set myself up as a bogus authority on D.H. Lawrence's novels!'[22] Bryant's response was the final piece of the puzzle, confirming an earlier majority vote by the governing body to allow full publication. The college, which had dragged its feet for decades over sanctioning a full edition for public sale, significantly did not wait for the verdict of the Lady Chatterley trial. Two days before Penguin Books was found not guilty of obscenity, the college's bursar wrote to Bell's to announce that work on a complete edition could proceed.[23]

Latham and Matthews

The complete edition proved far more trouble than anyone had imagined, as was by now traditional in Pepys editing. As in the nineteenth-century, arguments over labour, credit, and copyright all reared their head.[24] The work began promisingly. Robert Latham, a Restoration historian, was appointed to run the project: he had in fact begun work back in the early 1950s, when he was engaged by Bell's to assist Francis Turner with his still-theoretically-forthcoming edition. Latham was to provide most of the commentary and manage the work of other specialist editors. William Matthews, an expert on shorthand and British diaries, was recruited by Latham in 1962 to carry out the transcription and to author some of the introduction.[25] Latham hoped that the new edition would encourage investigation of the diary itself, rather than simply further its use as a source on other topics. 'Historians have not been in the habit of going to Pepys with serious questions. They have been content to plunder the diary piecemeal for quotations rather than to study it', he wrote.[26]

Both the commentary and the transcription proved herculean tasks. Latham embarked on a decades-long piece of detective work, pursuing thousands of investigations into the people, places, events, and customs mentioned by Pepys. The trickiest people to track, he wryly noted, included 'solicitors, merchant captains, foreigners who don't take out denization or naturalization; Roman Catholic priests, and women' (over 50 per cent of the population of Restoration England therefore proving elusive).[27] The transcription was also an epic labour. Matthews judged the 1890s text a complete mess: Wheatley's 'is the fullest edition of Pepys's text, but it is otherwise much the worst', he concluded. Aside from Wheatley's deliberate omissions and bowdlerizations, there were phrases, passages, and whole days accidentally missing. There was also no apparent rationale behind whether the shorthand was modernized or rendered in "olde" spelling.[28] The new transcript would be based on researching Pepys's usual longhand spelling but, for readability, would err on the side of modernization.[29] This new edition would have been a formidable job under any circumstances, but it was to be a transatlantic collaboration, conducted mostly by post. Latham was based in England, eventually taking up a post at Magdalene where he became the Pepys librarian. Meanwhile, Matthews was at the University of California, thousands of miles from the manuscript he was transcribing.

That the project produced a reliable transcript of the diary is, frankly, astonishing. Much of the transliteration was done in California using 'xerographs' (photocopies) of the manuscript. Transcribing shorthand from photocopies – which add random marks and make pen-strokes hard to discern – is not ideal, to put it mildly. In 1964, Matthews explained the process of trying to ensure the text was accurate – a process involving multiple people, technologies, and journeys on the high seas. He had first made a handwritten transcript of the diary using Wheatley's edition and the photocopy. This had been typed up by 'an Oxford Lady' (whom he praised for her 'accuracy and complaisance with professorial punctilio').[30] Next, the typescript was checked by William and his wife Lois. William read aloud

> spelling, stops and all – from the xerographs, and Lois my wife – poor wretch, poor soul – following the typescript with eye and forefinger. Part of this stage was done during a freighter trip round the world [...]. As the Danish captain put it, we peeped every morning.

Later, on an extended visit to Cambridge, Lois checked the galley proofs of the edition while William read aloud from the diary manuscript. They did this nine hours a day, six days a week, for fourteen weeks.[31]

In creating the edition, huge quantities of letters, drafts, and proofs were sent back and forth across the Atlantic with layer upon layer of corrections and re-corrections. What was supposed to be a project of a few years turned into decades. Amid all this, the editorial relationship between Latham and Matthews was increasingly strained, and ultimately threatened to collapse spectacularly. Tensions grew over credit. Matthews wanted, and got, equal editorial billing with Latham – who gave way to keep the peace, despite taking on tasks that had originally been assigned to Matthews. This included correcting the transcript, for Latham had been learning shorthand on the job. 'From the reading public I shall get no adequate recognition since the extent of my revisions have to be kept in the dark', he told the publisher.[32] Meanwhile, Matthews had discovered that Magdalene was due to get a cut of the edition's sales, although he and Latham had been denied any royalties by Bell's. Rightfully annoyed, he decided to copy his correspondence with Magdalene's master around Cambridge circles (the 1970s equivalent of a mass institutional email). The college and publisher's behaviour, he informed the master, was part of a long history of undervaluing and exploiting the diary's transcribers (Smith, Bright, and now himself). He demanded royalties for both him and Latham – and that his be the greater share. If forced, he said, he would go to the press to raise 'a stink' or withdraw from the edition. Latham agreed with Matthews that they were underpaid but sharply disagreed with Matthews's methods (this was his employer Matthews was attacking, and his private business that was being vented around town).[33] Further disputes followed, and lawyers became involved. Just as the first three volumes were being celebrated in the press, Latham decided the relationship was unsalvageable and asked the publishers to remove Matthews from future work on the project.[34] In response, Matthews wrote to the college's lawyer warning he would bring down the edition by using his knowledge of the diary's history. As in the copyright disputes between Bell and Bickers in the 1870s, Matthews now challenged what constituted 'Pepys's diary' and who owned it. The new edition, Matthews wrote, was 'not Pepys's diary at all', but his own transcription 'into longhand, typewriting and print', on which he believed Bell's and Magdalene had no valid legal claim. Indeed, Matthews said, the college had no rights to the manuscript of the diary either, for Magdalene had repeatedly broken the conditions in Pepys's will that entitled them to retain it. Pepys's stipulation not to remove books further than the master's lodge had, for example, been broken at least five times. (Matthews did not say so, but this included for his own work, when the diary was taken to be photocopied in Cambridge University Library.)[35] Matthews was threatening to turn the triumph of the diary's full publication into a very different kind of scandal than the college had feared in 1960. Instead of ridicule for publishing obscenity, they would be faced with a principal editor suing the publisher, while publicly accusing the college of illegally claiming ownership of Pepys's library.

This was a scenario that, ultimately, no one wanted. An uneasy peace was brokered.[36] Although the editorial strife was kept out of the headlines, its effects have made the editors' unpublished papers and the edition itself unusually revealing about the variety of work required and who was responsible. Many of these workers – paid and unpaid – were women. In 2017, the satirical hashtag 'thanks for typing' was coined to capture the scant acknowledgement given to what were often major contributions by male writers' female kin.[37] The Latham and Matthews edition was published when it was routine for the wives of academics to work at length and unpaid on their projects, but also when second-wave feminism was drawing attention to such inequalities. The sheer amount of textual labour needed on the diary also seemed to require recognition. A publication's 'Acknowledgements' was the usual place for recognizing unpaid assistance, along with transcription work and proofreading. Latham and Matthews's acknowledgements unusually contained a whole paragraph thanking 'secretaries and assistants', all of whom were female. These included 'Mrs D. Hopkins' (evidently the skilled typist mentioned by Matthews) and

William Matthews's research assistant, Ruth Pryor, who had worked unpaid on the diary.[38] References to family traditionally go at the end of 'acknowledgements'. It was here that Latham thanked his wife, Eileen, who had died in 1969: 'The late Mrs Robert Latham read many of the proofs. Beyond that, she gave help which can never be measured.'[39]

As William Matthews's account of 'peeping' round the world shows, Lois Matthews had also done considerable work on the diary – her husband estimated it amounted to two years of part-time labour.[40] Instead of appearing in the acknowledgements, she was credited as a 'text assistant' after the list of the work's editors that followed the title page. Writing to Matthews when relations had soured, Latham described this as unorthodox: he had understood Lois Matthews's contribution was 'of the sort which scholars' wives do free, as helpmeets', but had bowed to William's argument that the amount of work merited her being named on 'the title page'.[41] This was in 1970. Thirteen years later, when the final volumes of the edition appeared, scholarly and commercial expectations still meant the default place for married women was in the acknowledgements, although this looked increasingly awkward. Robert Latham worked on the edition's index with his second wife, Linnet. The Index became an award-winning publication in its own right and was much praised as an artfully constructed guide to the diary.[42] In the volume's acknowledgements, Robert explained how Linnet had 'involved herself in every process' of the index's construction: she had shared decisions on its structure and terms, conducted her own investigations into details, and checked it for accuracy. This was considerable editorial work, but it did not merit joint editorship of the Index volume, which appeared as 'compiled by Robert Latham'.[43] Linnet Latham did, however, appear as a joint editor of the diary *Anthology* that she and her husband produced in 1987.[44] In sum, being female and being married generally decreased your odds of moving out of the acknowledgements of a work, but so too did performing editorial tasks that seemed 'textual' rather than intellectual. The text (mechanical) and commentary (intellectual) division had always been a false one, and the divisions between 'scholars', 'assistants', and 'helpmeets' were also clearly tenuous. This was true of editing work generally, with the nature of Pepys's diary bringing such tensions to the fore.

The acknowledgements to the complete edition of Pepys ended with tacit acknowledgement of the trials it had involved: the publishers were thanked for 'their quite extraordinary patience'.[45] Bell's had, by 1970, been waiting for the edition for over thirty-five years. The enthusiasm with which it was received helped the company and its US partner, the

University of California Press, recoup their investments. Reviewers praised the work of both Latham and Matthews, but above all celebrated Pepys. In line with Gardiner's advice, there was no specific publicity on what had been added to this text, so few reviewers were equipped to discuss whether having a full text changed their views of the diary and its writer. However, the publication of the last volume of the main text in 1976 did prompt a couple of reviewers to remark that this instalment had lowered their impression of Samuel and raised their view of Elizabeth – although it was not always clear this was down to the presence of new passages. For example, Michael Ratcliffe in *The Times* commented that 'the editors have done Elizabeth Pepys a noble service. It is quite clear now that [her husband] was, as she suspected all along, unfaithful to her in body whenever the chance came, and in mind every day of his life.'[46]

Scholarship that employed the diary as a source grew as a result of this new text. By producing a complete transcript, with a detailed commentary and index, the team behind the Latham and Matthews edition enabled research on subjects that it would have been either extremely time-consuming or foolhardy to attempt with earlier editions. Among these topics were social networks, clothing, public duty, and, of course, studies of sex (whether political, psychological, economic, or artistic).[47] Ironically, the seeming comprehensiveness of the index also facilitated the kind of historical 'plundering' which Latham had hoped to discourage – it is easy to dip into the diary for an episode on a particular subject, and easy to miss an episode not listed. The ways in which this index categorized Pepys's activities has likewise made it harder to break certain patterns of thought.[48] The decades of work by the production team profoundly influenced subsequent work about Pepys and his time, with much of this influence subtle enough that it goes unnoticed.

Pepysdiary.com

Latham and Matthews's 'complete transcription' quickly became the most respected edition of Pepys's diary. Yet despite the success of this text and its spin-off selections, Wheatley's 1890s text remains the most widely used – even though readers rarely realize it. If Wheatley's edition is, as Matthews claimed, 'much the worst edition' in certain respects, it has the virtue of having been out of copyright since 1968.[49] As a result, many diary editions and selections available today, including online texts and free ebooks, use this text. Pre-eminent among them is pepysdiary.com – it tops search results, is easily navigable, and much quoted. Unlike many e-texts of the diary, pepysdiary.com is explicit that it is based on Wheatley's censored edition.[50] What makes this site distinctive is not the text itself but the method of publication. Starting on 1 January 2003, a diary entry was released every day, spreading reading the diary across nine years and five months, the timespan that Pepys was writing the original. Below each entry, readers of the site were free to add comments or ask questions. This crowdsourcing of knowledge to annotate a Victorian text in fact has a Victorian precedent: in 1893 Wheatley had asked 'the kind assistance of any reader' who could help with his 'unnoted' passages.[51] Combined with the daily publishing schedule, these public contributions have enabled new ways of reading. Readers take on tasks normally done by editors, glossing passages and adding reflections.

Pepysdiary.com puts regular visitors in a novel set of temporal relationships. It has always been possible to make print editions part of a daily routine – in 1918 Virginia Woolf believed that many people 'read themselves asleep at night with Pepys and awake at day' with him.[52] However, readers of pepysdiary.com saw Pepys's life unfurl before them together, day by day, in a pattern that mimicked the writing of the diary. This was compelling, and seemed to contract the historical distance between writer and reader. Reflecting on the final lines of the diary, on 31 May 2012, one reader commented that 'Sam has been truly alive for us in "real time".' This, he thought, heightened the sense of a connection to Pepys, and so the sense of loss when the publication ended, and Pepys returned to being long dead.[53] Back in 1958, the BBC's weekly *Diary of Samuel Pepys* drama had fostered in some viewers the sense of becoming acquainted with 'real life friends'.[54] In the early 2000s, serial publication of the diary had a comparable effect, with the addition that frequent commenters became part of the familiar 'cast of characters' readers came to know.[55] By popular demand, the cycle of daily publishing began again in 2013 and once more in 2023, this time with excerpts from the Latham and Matthews text added to supply Wheatley's omissions. These cycles added other timeframes to the experience of reading for, as well as following Pepys's 1660s entries in relation to their own daily lives, readers could now also see the comments of two sets of readers before them, going back twenty years. The result is an edition that is an ongoing accumulation of public knowledge about the diary, an evolving account of reading experience, and – as the commenters have begun to recognize – itself a valuable historical record.

It is a strength of pepysdiary.com that it allows for a variety of contributions, but the comments can be usefully divided into two types. There are explanatory posts which, much like annotations in conventional editions, are designed to gloss the text. Posts of this type include explaining a tricky phrase, or posting a link to a relevant portrait, map, or podcast. The other type of post can best be described as 'responsive': these posts can have an explanatory element, but the focus is the commenter's reaction rather than the entry itself. This type of note is very unusual (though not without precedent) in conventional print editions.[56] On pepysdiary.com a responsive comment might discuss a reader's view of a character, offer a personal anecdote, or even present a piece of creative writing inspired by the day's entry. Soon after creating pepysdiary.com, Gyford described it as a worldwide bookclub, a characterization which fits much of the activity.[57] Research on book groups has shown that members often interpret texts 'through the lens of character' and describe personal experiences in assessing them.[58] On pepysdiary.com, bringing personal experience to bear on Restoration history has developed in some sophisticated ways as readers deal with the enduring puzzles raised by the diary.

Pondering the possible motivations of Pepys and other figures in his journal sometimes expands into debates about the ethics of judging Pepys's behaviour. In 2010, Pepys's entry for 29 March 1667 began an unexpectedly fierce discussion. The matter at hand was Pepys's concern to avoid responsibility for supporting his sister-in-law while her husband was at sea. This led some readers to observe they were becoming more critical of Pepys. As 'Phoenix' put it, 'there is very little beyond his ambition, work ethic and – thank you, Sam – a confessional diary, to admire. He is in many ways a nasty piece of work.' Others promptly came to Sam's defence. 'Nix' pointed to Pepys's frankness, his representative nature, and to the society in which the diary was written: 'He is a man of his class and time, with the mores of his class and time [. . .] I can't speak for anyone else, but were I to keep a diary as unguarded as Samuel's, I'm sure that many folks 350 years hence would think me a nasty piece of work as well.' Historically, the call to appreciate changing mores and to recognize that we are all flawed (but lack Pepys's frankness) have often been editors' and reviewers' last words on Pepys's character. 'Language hat', however, was not persuaded. Although standards changed, 'faithful husbands and honest, generous people' had existed in the Restoration. The objections to criticizing Pepys seemed to boil down to the idea that 'we're all corrupt and selfish, it's just that some of us hide it better. That's an attitude that [. . .] satisfies our desire not to be too smug, but it's wrong, and it does a disservice to honest people. Sam was far from the worst guy around, and I'm not saying we should stone him, but it's reasonable to judge him by the evidence he presents.'[59] There the matter rested until the second cycle of reading, in March 2020, when readers during that phase encountered the earlier responses and were prompted to comment in turn. Now the topic was not Pepys's character, but that of his readers. 'John' remarked 'Some diary entries tell us more about the readers than about Pepys.' Others seconded this, finding previous commenters 'smug and complacent'. 'Timo', agreeing, added: 'There is little point morally judging Pepys['s] actions and character 350 years later – just sit back and enjoy the entertainment. It's far more interesting than any modern soap opera.'[60] The parallel between pepysdiary.com and soap operas is fitting: both are narratives in which episodes from the lives of a 'cast of characters' are serially released. Timo suggested it is both ethically unsound and fruitless to judge Pepys, and that this obstructs appreciation of the diary. Neither his comparison with soap operas nor the lively debate on the site quite support that argument. For soap opera fans, like readers of Pepys's diary, the opportunities to judge character and actions are often part of the narrative's appeal.[61] Scholarly editions are expected to develop a consistent stance on such difficult questions or stay silent. The commentary at pepysdiary.com, which is multi-vocal and evolving, is under no such obligation and, in the process, prods readers to reflect repeatedly on these points.

In publishing their own reading experiences as guidance, commenters also draw directly on their personal history of comparable circumstances. This can be a means of establishing authority to speak on the matter at hand – it is a technique called 'category entitlement' that is common in book groups.[62] On pepysdiary.com, as well as offering an interpretation of the text, this technique can serve to memorialize an experience. The experience becomes worth sharing and recording because of Pepys's example, a phenomenon also seen among readers during the Second World War. In 2009, Pepys's account of the Great Fire encouraged commenters to offer their own knowledge of dangerous fires. 'Nate', who had experience of researching brush fires, suggested that Pepys's burying of his cheese and wine, contrary to popular belief, was a smart decision ('If it's buried [with] more than 20 cm of soil on it away from a burning building it should be all right').[63] 'Doug', responded to Pepys's descriptions on a more emotional level, seeing parallels between his recent past and the diary:

> Living in San Diego, I can't help but remember my own experience one morning almost 2 years ago that was very similar to Sam's experience here ... Being awakened by phone & being told to evacuate; Sam being awakened by a servant & looking out at the fire ... [...] Packing the car with what we thought were the things we really needed and/or wanted; Sam

taking the money, plate and 'best things' ... Watching my neighbor's house burn down on TV with the same surreal sense of 'this can't really be happening' that Sam must have felt when he saw the pigeons fall ...[64]

This set out common responses to disasters that spanned the centuries, and used this shared experience to deduce what Pepys 'must have felt' (but did not write), when he saw 'the poor pigeons [...] were loath to leave their houses, but hovered about the windows and balconies till they were some of them burned, their wings, and fell down'.[65] As with Doug's example, commenters' motivation for publishing a piece of personal history was often because it offered others emotional insight into what Pepys had described or why he had chosen to describe it.

Living through History

Using personal experience to interpret Pepys's diary became abruptly more significant when, in mid-March 2020, contributors realized that they were experiencing a pandemic. An early effect of COVID, was that new readers flocked to the site. On 23 March, when the first lockdown was declared in the UK, traffic to pepysdiary.com more than tripled. Many were likely coming to the diary on their own initiative to read about the plague-hit London of 1665, with its deserted streets and quarantined households. However, Gyford suspected many visitors were following up on a tweet which had gone viral:

> On hearing ill rumour that Londoners may soon be urged into their lodgings by Her Majesty's men, I looked upon the street to see a gaggle of striplings making fair merry, and no doubt spreading the plague well about. Not a care had these rogues for the health of their elders![66]

Pepysdiary.com had its own very popular Twitter account for diary excerpts, but this was not a passage from the diary. It was one of the first tweets of an anonymous parody account @Pepys_Diaries that had been set up as a response to the pandemic. This tweet had rapidly escaped its original framing as a joke and, by 23 March, was being widely credited on Twitter and Facebook to 'Samuel Pepys Diaries 1664'.[67] The enthusiasm for the tweet speaks to the public's readiness to believe in the diary's contemporaneousness, as well as to widespread worries about other people's irresponsibility. Both the worry and irresponsibility were here being reworked, amusingly, as enduring behaviours. Freeman's parody had done similar work during the world wars. Like Freeman, this new spoof excluded the more disturbing aspects of Pepys's journal. It is notable that in spring 2020 there was no viral circulation of the original Pepys's tales of irresponsibility, which were far bleaker about human nature: he had heard how at Westminster 'bold people there were to go in sport to one another's burials. And in spite to well people, would breathe in the faces (out of their windows) of well people going by.' Across the world, only two accounts tweeted that passage in March and April 2020, and it got exactly one 'like'.[68]

When the pandemic hit, pepysdiary.com's publishing cycle had reached March 1667 – it was not in the plague year of 1665. Commenting on the current plague was therefore technically off topic, but the similarities were too striking to ignore. On 24 March 2020, 'Tonyel' from Somerset, England, wrote:

> I'm surprised that no-one so far has referred to our present world-wide plague which is beginning to make Sam's world sound even more familiar – shops shutting, folk out of work, unreliable cures and nostrums being offered and an air of panic coupled with mistrust of politicians . . . . . .
>
> A plane flew over yesterday leaving a contrail in a clear blue sky, the first for about a week. I found myself watching it until it disappeared – not quite open–mouthed but with a vague sense of wonder.
>
> Good luck to all of us.[69]

Having drawn historical parallels, Tonyel chose to pick out one personal moment to represent his experience of this strange new reality. This was a characteristically Pepysian response, both in choosing a significant detail (such as 'the poor pigeons') to capture a previously unimaginable situation and in relishing a pleasurable experience in the context of a larger disaster. Tonyel was also surprised that others were not commenting on the present. That may have stemmed from a determination to maintain normal routines of reading and responding while normality was vanishing in other areas of life. The debates about readers' reactions to Pepys's character, which ended with Timo advising everyone to 'Just sit back and enjoy the entertainment' happened around this time, on 30 and 31 March. Entertainment was in short supply, but pepysdiary.com could supply it. Six weeks later, on 11 May 2020, Timo used the comments section to draw his own parallels and record a historic moment that might otherwise have slipped by:

> When I first began to read this diary 7 years ago the part I most looked forward to was the Great Plague. To get an insight into what it might be like to live through a pandemic was fascinating to me, little knowing that we would one day live to experience anything similar. Yet here we are . . . Today

marks an important turning point – after 8 weeks of solid lockdown in Spain (and I mean solid, unlike most other countries), constantly checking the local parish records of infections and deaths, we have finally been allowed out to enjoy a beer in the sunshine.[70]

Rather than using their past to explicate Pepys, some readers were clearly turning to the diary to help understand their present. The 1660s diary became a tool to help 'to live through a pandemic'. Readers were 'living through' history in more than one sense – experiencing what was recognizably an important historical moment, while using history to interpret those experiences. On 15 March 2020, for example, 'San Diego Sarah' noted that she was coping better with the pandemic because she had read Pepys's account. It made her 'better prepared to talk about the realities of quarantine' and the fact that Pepys and his family had got through their plague also gave her hope. However, looking back in February 2022, she felt she had not taken the right lessons from the journal. She had failed to see a connection between seventeenth-century Londoners' 'state of denial that the plague could happen here' and her own expectation that the COVID crisis would pass in weeks: 'Now we're going into year three, I wonder how I could have been so naive having read the Diary.'[71] The diary contained clues to personal understanding and to understanding societal inertia that she felt she had missed – but which were now on record for everyone to recognize. As these entries suggest, pepysdiary.com was being used to cope with COVID-19 in multiple ways, and one of these ways was the creation of a communal historical record of personally significant moments. There are clear correspondences here with how Pepys's diary was employed during the 1940s in Britain, especially in the way that Pepys's record valorized recording episodes that might seem trivial but are far from it (admiring a contrail; having a beer in the sunshine). In this period of disaster, the diary was being used to try and anticipate what might come, for reassurance that it would end, for distraction, and for companionship in isolation – via a developing sense of fellowship with Pepys and with a community of other readers. Pepysdiary.com has not yet been going on as long as Latham and Matthews's editorial project, but it is a collaboration as remarkable.

Innovations

The diary's history since the early twentieth century could be told as a story of increasing openness and democratization. The full text of the diary is now public, with editorial commentary being carried out and published by readers around the world, not just by academics. Yet an emphasis on readers' more direct relationship with Pepys would miss the ways in which his published diary is not just a record of the Restoration. We naturally expect Pepys's journal to document the morals and practices of the 1660s; less apparent is that the texts of the diary most read today also reflect the laws and mores of the 1890s and 1960s. Pepysdiary.com and all freely available diary e-texts rely on nineteenth-century texts. Back in the 1960s, lawyers, editors, and publishers shaped the complete edition to fit current legislation and avoid reputational damage (to Pepys, to Magdalene College, and to themselves). Publishing 'every last obscenity' was confirmed as the policy because, ironically, it made a conviction for obscene publication less likely. The risks of prosecution and mockery were also minimized through measures such as calculatedly not offering explanations of the polyglot. When it came to these particular passages, the devisers of the complete transcript shared Pepys's concern to hinder readers' too easy comprehension.

Until 1960, arguments for publishing the full text had largely been based on its status as a 'historical document' – this was the position taken by Scott in 1826, Stevenson in 1881, and Bickers in 1936.[72] When the law changed, making obscenity in the interests of 'literature' a public interest defence, Pepys's diary was excellently positioned to take advantage of the shift, and a defence based on both historical and literary merit was planned. While these manoeuvrings put the diary in the same disreputable category as *Lady Chatterley's Lover* and *Lolita*, they also attracted some more righteous literary allies. There is something very pleasing in the fact that to get Pepys's 'curious' passages into print required having the moral clout of Narnia's Peter the Magnificent, Susan the Gentle, Edmund the Just, and Lucy the Valiant ready to marshal to his defence.

The achievements of Latham, Matthews, and their team in finally getting a reliable text of the diary published are the more impressive when we recognize the legal, editorial, and personal tribulations involved, and the sheer number of men and women who contributed, whether paid, underpaid, or unpaid. There is no such extensive documentation or detailed acknowledgements for earlier diary editions to record the work of researchers, 'assistants', or 'helpmeets'.[73] Pepys's diary brings to the surface the tensions that lurk in publishing and editing: whether work is done for love of scholarship, kin, payment, or glory; the status of textual work versus commentary; and the distance between a manuscript and print. The internet can make such work available at little or no cost to readers, but online that work is easily severed from its origins and its creators: texts appear without the kind of cues that help us discern sources and intentions. On social media, day-old parodies look like prescient observations from three hundred and fifty years ago, while nineteenth-century editions of Pepys circulate online without acknowledgement that they are censored and superseded texts.[74]

The prevalence of nineteenth-century editions of Pepys shows that what are exciting innovations in publication and in reading practices, are often not quite as new as we might think. The surge of interest in Pepys during the pandemic mirrors the popularity of the diary during the Second World War. Even the enthusiasm for Pepys parody during an international crisis was not new. What remains significantly novel about pepysdiary.com is the serial, daily form of reading it encourages and the ongoing reflection on that experience which contributors have publicly documented, creating a singular historical record. More generally, their comments highlight the perennial challenges of reading the diary: understanding the language; recognizing and tracing the figures in it; how or whether to judge Pepys's character – and so on. My final chapter tackles some of those perennial challenges. We can now read all the diary 'for the public good'. In realizing that 'good' or (to put it in less grand terms) to get the most from Pepys's diary, we can learn from the experiences of readers over the last two hundred years.

CHAPTER 8

Reading against the Grain

The ways that we understand Pepys's diary today are shaped by the versions that we encounter and by popular traditions of reception, especially since many people know about Pepys largely by reputation rather than by reading his diary themselves. Pepys is famous as an unusually frank and detailed diarist, and as a quirky, naughty one. These reputations have historically been used to win him readers and sell books. In 1876, a reviewer in *The Athenaeum* wryly claimed that everyone curious about 'social history' scrutinized new versions of the diary for 'traits of [...] naughtiness' removed by editors. When, in 1964, William Matthews thought better of referring to the diary's 'every last obscenity' and instead spoke of its 'every last naughtiness', he was presenting the diary, and Pepys himself, as legally unobjectionable, entertaining, and inoffensive.[1] Naughtiness gains Pepys admirers, but even more widespread is celebration of his frankness. It is hard to get near a text of the diary without being told by adverts, blurbs, and editors (myself included) that this is a remarkably candid account. Editors have routinely praised Pepys's 'unselfconscious charm' and his 'garrulous frankness'. Some writers go further, crediting him with 'full objective reporting' or 'objective, almost omniscient narration', notably in relation to his sex life.[2]

While Pepys's diary certainly is inadvertently funny, at times naughty, and often startlingly frank, reading it with these expectations can prevent us from fully recognizing the kind of information and insights that it offers. If we, like generations of readers, want to get more from the diary, we can take some cautions and cues from them about productive approaches. Like *The Athenaeum* reviewer, readers have had an abiding fascination with what the diary does not contain – with silences that are the result of editorial choices or Pepys's own omissions. Following that curiosity can lead to a deeper understanding of the history that the diary offers. Scholarship on gender and race has shown the benefits of reading archival sources 'against the grain', that is, perceiving the assumptions that shape records, noting what goes unspoken and why. This involves focusing on silences and ambiguities to discern people and experiences that archives often exclude.[3] It means giving attention to what Pepys's diary does not say: what he leaves out, misrepresents, or covers up – and how readers have dealt, or failed to deal, with those omissions. Readers today are better placed than many before us to examine his silences, since we now have a full transcription of the diary and – thanks to the internet – easier access to the kinds of historical information that it would previously have taken teams of editors, research assistants, and wives years to assemble. I am concerned here with the experiences of people whose lives are sparsely documented in historical records and whom Pepys himself often treats dismissively or mentions only briefly: Elizabeth Pepys; the women and girls in whom he took a sexual interest; and the Black Britons whom he refers to in passing.[4]

Elizabeth Pepys excited readers' interest from early in the diary's publication history, acting as a counter to her husband's dominant perspective. There is a long tradition of imagining Elizabeth's views through historical fiction, sometimes inspired by close reading passages from the diary.[5] A similar reading strategy can produce an account which, while remaining grounded in the evidence, reveals more than Pepys intended to record. Meanwhile, other women and girls in whom Pepys took a sexual interest have had far less attention from writers. In 2002, Claire Tomalin's biography of Pepys was the first to contain a balanced, detailed portrayal of Elizabeth; it also proved distinctive in giving sustained attention to two servants he lusted after, Jane Birch and Jane Welsh.[6] More often commentators have alluded to these girls and women as a homogeneous group of lower-class females, or sometimes just undergarments. As one review of the complete edition put it, Pepys is 'forever delving under the petticoats of pub-keepers' and book-sellers' wives'.[7] While feminist social history has encouraged interest in these women as representatives of London life, efforts to distinguish their experiences from Pepys's accounts of them remain rare.

Work on women's experiences encounters some of the same challenges faced by researchers seeking to use Pepys as a source on Black Britons. From the 1970s in particular, the diary has been employed to trace the history of Black presence in London, with twenty-first-century historians further developing these insights.[8] To use the diary as a source on women and Black people in London requires reading against the grain in at least two ways: attending to experiences that were not Pepys's, and focusing on aspects of his life that readers have often preferred not to acknowledge, specifically Pepys as a sexual predator and an enslaver. These aspects are, however, part of what makes his records valuable. Indeed, acknowledging them is a logical extension of following the calls by early twentieth-century historians to appreciate Pepys's power and influence, for Pepys's power had casualties.[9] To take Pepys seriously means taking others' lives seriously, and in the process recognizing other histories as meaningful and intriguing as his.

Elizabeth Pepys

Samuel Pepys often had difficulty crediting his family members with astuteness: he saw himself as managing their behaviour, rather than vice versa. Elizabeth, who was the most subject to her husband's surveillance, had the most need to employ subtlety with him – although confrontation worked too. During the quarrels over her desire for 'money and liberty', Pepys occasionally became aware that he had misjudged his wife's intelligence and resourcefulness. One such occasion was when he discovered that Elizabeth had kept a copy of her protest to him about the enforced 'retirednesse of her life' – a discovery which led him to destroy this and most of the rest of her archive out of fear of the 'dishonour' it might bring to him. On another occasion, they fell out over a discrepancy in her kitchen accounts: 'I find she is very cunning, and when she least shows it, hath her wit at work', he concluded.[10]

Pepys's jealousy about his wife runs through his diary. As Tomalin has remarked, knowledge that other men had made passes at Elizabeth did not immediately trigger his anxiety; what troubled him were the moments when he feared she might reciprocate.[11] There were also times that he failed to spot or chose to ignore her warnings, which only become apparent when we closely re-read his account. In 1664, Elizabeth repeatedly told Samuel over several months that his Uncle Wight was showing unusual 'kindness' to her and relayed 'mighty stories of my uncles fond and kind discourses'. Samuel, despite some misgivings, chose to interpret this as meaning that the childless Wight might make him his heir. Elizabeth had evidently realized much earlier than her husband that something untoward was afoot. Uncle Wight's kindness culminated in his proposing that the solution to her childlessness and his lack of an heir was 'to have one between them'; whereupon Elizabeth gave him 'a very warm answer' (an angry one), and told her husband, explicitly, about that affront. Samuel feared that 'all [Wight's] kindness is but only his lust to her'. However, his response was to carry on as normal with Wight, stating in his diary that he would wait to 'make my use of' the information (this may just have been his way of explaining to himself why inaction was acceptable, since he showed no sign of ever using his knowledge).[12] The families continued to socialize and Elizabeth was left to manage the situation, which she apparently did without assistance from her husband.

Given Samuel's jealousy and his willingness to prioritize financial gain over what might suit his wife, it is not surprising that Elizabeth generally chose not to alert him to other men's interest in her. She too knew how to hold back information until it would prove most useful. Four years later, after discovering her husband's sexual relationship with Deb Willet, Elizabeth suddenly revealed that she had had 'many' approaches herself, and tempting ones at that. Samuel reports she upbraided him with:

> the many temptations she hath refused out of faithfulness to me, whereof several she ~~confessed and pert~~ was perticular in, and especially from my Lord **Sandwich** by the solicitation of **Capt. Ferrer**, and then afterward the courtship of my Lord **Hinchingbrooke**, even to the trouble of his lady. All which I did acknowledge and was troubled for and wept.[13]

Pepys was clearly trying hard not to see this as a "confession" by her (hence his deletion). The fact he acknowledged the advances does not mean that he knew about them, but that he believed they had happened. Elizabeth had, it transpired, confided in Will Hewer at various points and Hewer now confirmed her account.[14] The two temptations that she named (or at least that struck Pepys forcibly) were from his patron the Earl of Sandwich and from Viscount Hinchingbrooke, Sandwich's married twenty-year-old son. When Elizabeth instanced her constancy, she appears to have selected her examples for maximum rhetorical effect: she chose one approach that must have been very recent and one from six years before. Pepys was unaware of these at the time but there are, in retrospect, details that allow us to work out when these occurred. 'The courtship of my Lord Hinchingbrooke [...] to the trouble of his lady' was recent, for Hinchingbrooke had become engaged and married in the last year. He had not spent much time around Elizabeth, suggesting his attempt was made in spring 1668 when Elizabeth was visiting her father-in-law at Brampton, while the viscount and his new wife were staying nearby at the family's country seat.[15] As Tomalin suggests, Sandwich's approach to Elizabeth must have happened in Brampton in the summer of 1662. On the day of Elizabeth's return, Pepys observed, 'I perceive my Lord and Lady have been very kind to her. And Captain Ferrers, so kind that I perceive [I] have some jealousy of him; but I know what is the Captain's manner of carriage, and therefore it is nothing to me.'[16] Significantly, after Elizabeth had revealed the men's advances and Hewer had confirmed them, Samuel never mentioned this directly again and only once alluded tacitly to it. This silence is striking, coming from a man who had been repeatedly and obsessively jealous of Elizabeth – even going so far as to check the bed sheets after her dancing master visited.[17] It is possible that he saw powerful, aristocratic men propositioning his attractive wife as literally unremarkable, which would be telling about what passed for normal behaviour in his circles. Another explanation, which does not exclude the first, is that Pepys did not want to think about that element of his wife's experience: it was painful to him and, in terms of his relationships with potential benefactors, inconvenient to acknowledge.

Even though Pepys rapidly closed off his reflection on Elizabeth's experiences, he provided enough explicit and implicit detail to allow us to understand how she dealt with sexual advances and managed her husband. When she thought it prudent, she would intimate to Samuel that a man had been unusually 'kind', leaving him to interpret what that meant. 'Kind' and 'kindness' were how Pepys initially reported Elizabeth's account of men's attitudes to her in both Wight's and Sandwich's cases. Elizabeth also sometimes told Hewer. Both these measures appear to have been ways to test the emotional and practical support she could call on, and to alibi herself if required. Hewer was an ally who could intervene, if necessary, to obstruct an admirer or (as he did) to vouch for her with Samuel. If the advances were subsequently uncovered, Elizabeth would have been able to argue that she had behaved honourably: she had tactfully cautioned her husband and, far from hiding the situation, she had told a trusted servant. By piecing together entries, we can see the pervasiveness and the normality of experiences that Pepys failed for much of the time to register. This included the tactics that women such as Elizabeth used to protect their bodies and their reputations, along with the rhetorical tactics available to them to make their views heard. Pepys does not always recognize these strategies, but they are there if we choose to look.

Girls and Women

If it requires careful reading to try and construct Elizabeth's experiences from her husband's record, the challenges are all the greater for other women. These are people who were often entirely cut from the first edition of the diary, for they were not considered 'of public interest'.[18] Pepys's sexual relationships subsequently became one of the most talked about aspects of the diary. However, with the exception of the actress Mrs Knepp, this fascination did not extend to interest in the women and girls with whom he was involved.[19] This cannot be attributed to censorship. Most of the encounters I discuss in this chapter, including Pepys's sexual contact with his maid Susan, with Frances Tooker, and with Mrs Bagwell, have been in print since the 1890s.[20] What led to sexual content being censored in Wheatley's edition was not the age of Pepys's targets, nor signs of coercion, but explicit references to the lower body. Since most encounters were sufficiently vague on that score, they made it into Wheatley's text and became, in legal terms and apparently in the eyes of readers, uncontroversial.

Even with the full text in print, there are still multiple obstacles to distinguishing the very different types of relationships that Pepys records, and to disentangling the perspectives of women and girls from his own. The Latham and Matthews edition provides almost no help with translating Pepys's sexual polyglot.[21] The limited references to sex in its editorial apparatus also do little to encourage readers to distinguish coercion from consent. The Index, for example, will usually name a woman and then deploy the headings 'amorous encounters' or 'kisses/caresses' to cover all manner of sexual contact, including that which Pepys got by force.[22] Other obstacles to attentive reading are extra-textual, and come from firmly established attitudes to the diary and to women. Some of the earliest reviews of Latham and Matthews's edition make these especially clear. Here are a few samples:

> He was a worldly, vivacious, unfeigning man, interested in music and money and the latest play as well as the pinchable character of the new maid's bottom.   (Robert Nye, *The Scotsman*)

> Being Pepys, he somehow only slipped [Deb Willet] half as much money as he first thought of doing – while managing to slip his hand where it shouldn't have been, as part of the same transaction.
>   Mercy! What a shocker! And how close one feels to him. How sadly one reads that last sentence when he thought (wrongly) that his sight was failing.   (Peter Lewis, *The Daily Mail*)

> Randy he was, but innocent, almost adolescent, in a violent and vicious age – impossible to imagine Pepys guilty of rape.
>   (Michael Ratcliffe, *The Times*)[23]

These show reviewers reading the diary's sexual content imaginatively, in ways that have a great deal to do with Pepys's charm, the diary's reputation, and patriarchal attitudes to sex, but only tenuous links to what is described in the shorthand. At no point does Pepys ruminate on 'the pinchable character of the new maid's bottom' – that phrase reflects a comic, Benny-Hillesque tradition rather than the journal's content. Peter Lewis urged his readers to share his amusement and admiration at Pepys's sly behaviour – standard responses to the diary. However, the passage which he found enjoyably shocking, and which precedes his statement of feeling close to Pepys, describes how Pepys 'did besar [Deb] and tocar her thing, but ella was against it and laboured with much earnestness, such as I believed to be real; and yet at last yo did make her tener mi cosa in her mano' ('did kiss her and touch her thing, but she was against it [. . .] and yet at last I did make her hold my thing in her hand').[24] Lewis's response was an unthinking invitation to identify with Pepys during a sexual assault. Michael Ratcliffe's more considered reading of the complete edition encouraged him to reflect on Elizabeth's perspective, and apparently to consider that Pepys might be 'guilty of rape' (or else why mention it?). However, that possibility is quickly rejected: Pepys is declared an innocent in sexual terms and (with resort to a familiar exculpatory argument) less guilty than many men would have been during the famously depraved Restoration.

Nearly fifty years after its publication, access to the complete text has done little to alter what are entrenched approaches to the diary, bound up with fondness for Pepys and casually sexist, classist assessments of the women and girls who became sexually involved with him. This is despite challenges being raised. In 1983, E. Pearlman identified a 'traditional' view which celebrated Pepys as '"a man who truly loved a pretty wench"' or which saw him as, at worst, '"unheroic"' towards women. Pearlman argued that, with the recent publication of the full diary, these could only be seen as 'immensely euphemistic' descriptions of 'casually exploitative and occasionally brutal' relationships.[25] Nonetheless, the usual language for discussing Pepys's sex life remains playful and celebratory. Commentators describe Pepys having 'sexual adventures', 'sexual frolics', 'extramarital pursuits', 'extra-marital exploits', 'love affairs', 'romance', and 'romantic liaisons'.[26] These are used as catch-all terms to cover a range of sexual contact: some of it mutually enjoyed but much of it, by Pepys's own account, with girls and women who were upset or angered by his behaviour. Twenty-first-century scholarship on the diary is much more likely to acknowledge the exploitation in many of Pepys's relationships, but there remains hesitancy in registering coercion, abuse or, indeed, violence.[27] To understand these passages requires contending with euphemisms, silences, and a range of unfounded assumptions about women's behaviour (Pepys's assumptions, the law's and, perhaps, our own).

Timothy Meldrum identifies 1665 as the first time that Pepys 'fondled and kissed' one of his servants (the verbs, often used by commentators, echo those used in the Lathams' Index).[28] The servant was Susan. Her age and status suggest why Pepys chose her as his first recorded target among his servants, for they made her vulnerable. She was 'Susan, a little girl' when she was employed in 1663 to replace a 'parish-child'. With no surname recorded, her age cannot be established, but the evidence points to her being younger than fourteen when she was hired: fourteen was an age commonly associated with adulthood, first employment, and sexual maturity. She was probably several years younger, since her promotion to cookmaid was later delayed, apparently on the grounds of her smallness.[29] She was still the 'little girle' in August 1665 when Pepys wrote:

> dressed and had my head combed by my little girle, to whom I confess que je sum demasiado kind, nuper ponendo sæpe mes mains in su dos choses de son breast. Mais il faut que je leave it, lest it bring me to alguno major inconvenience.[30]

> (dressed and had my head combed by my little girl, to whom I confess that I am too kind, lately often putting my hands on her two things of her breast. But it is necessary that I leave it, lest it bring me to some major inconvenience.)

Note that 'lately often'; this is only the first time he has referred to groping Susan, not the first time it has happened. The diary under-records Pepys's sexual activity, including his attempts on servants. If this 'combing' scenario was not already established as a predatory strategy, it soon was. Early in 1666, Pepys targeted another 'little girl' by getting her to comb his hair. Frances Tooker, a family friend, was, like Susan, repeatedly called 'little' and was prepubescent: fourteen months after this episode Pepys would note that she was 'grown a little woman'. In January 1666, Pepys kept 'little Mrs. Tooker' up late, 'talking and making her comb my head; and did what I will with her et tena grande plaisir con ella, tocando sa cosa con mi cosa, and hazendo la cosa par cette moyen' ('... and had great pleasure with/by her, touching her thing with my thing and doing the thing [orgasm] by this means'). Pepys's polyglot means it takes effort to interpret the exact nature of what he does, while it is easy to not register the circumstances, including the ages, of those he targeted. 'Mrs' (mistress) was used of both married and unmarried women, and this particular 'Mrs' was a 'child'.[31] In Susan's case, Pepys recognized his behaviour was wrong and shameful, but described it as an error of overindulgence, of being 'demasiado kind' to Susan. 'Kind' had also been Elizabeth's choice of word (or Pepys's gloss for her account) when judicious impreciseness about the nature of a man's attentions was needed. Here 'kind' served Pepys as a polite synonym for 'lustful'. Since Pepys was putting at risk Susan's emotional wellbeing, her job, and her reputation, an antonym of kind – 'cruel' – would be more accurate.

This example is a clear instance of Pepys's mitigating language – although not so clear that commentators on the diary have previously noted it. Further evidence of how this mitigation operates comes when Pepys met with strong resistance – that is, when he encountered resistance from women and girls that he felt was significant enough to merit registering. In 1667, Frances Udall was working at her uncle's tavern and repeatedly having to fend off Pepys. On 9 April 1667 'la little mosa [the little girl/maid]' was 'enojado [angry]' when Pepys made her 'tocar [touch]' his penis, but he gave her money 'and so', he said, 'all well'. On 20 May, he tried 'tumbling of la little fille [girl/maid]', which led her uncle to notice she was missing her neck-cloth. On 30 September, he tried again: 'to the Swan; and there I did fling down the fille there upon the chair and did tocar [touch] her thigh with my hand; at which she begin to cry out, so I left off and drank, and away to the Hall'.[32] Udall's crying out, with people within earshot, was the kind of resistance that Pepys could not dismiss as token. It was an emphatic form of dissent and a legally recognized one, for 'crying out' was a criterion that the courts used to determine whether a rape had occurred.[33] Pepys's "flinging down" of Udall and his "touching" of her thigh are high-spirited or gentle words for what she evidently perceived as threatening and violent – a perception Pepys recognized others might share. When Pepys wrote of 'tumbling' Udall in May, this was a word he later used to dismiss a violent sexual assault. On 6 July 1667, Doll Lane (a shopkeeper and one of Pepys's willing partners) came to Pepys and her sister 'blubbering and swearing' against Captain van den Anker who had 'pulled her into a stable by the Dog tavern and there did tumble her and toss her; calling him all the rogues and toads in the world'. Pepys felt Lane's objections were hollow since 'ella [she] hath suffered me to do anything with her a hundred times'.[34] Her claims of assault he regarded as exemplifying a woman's 'falseness', not because he thought there had been no violence, but because she had no moral right to protest. Pepys's sexual language of being 'kind', 'touching', and 'tumbling' emphasized his indulgence and playfulness, while masking coercion and violence.

Consent and Force

The entries concerning Frances Udall on 30 September 1667 and Doll Lane on 6 July 1667 offer two clear examples of women who experienced sexual assaults, one of them at Pepys's hands. Gauging what happened in other encounters can be complicated because Pepys often says little about the woman's reactions. It is also the case that, in the seventeenth century, the language used to describe consensual sex routinely included the language of force or violence. Conventions of courtship and seduction meant that willing women were expected to evince initial unwillingness, while – as historians have discussed – representations of sex were dominated by men besieging, conquering, or occupying women.[35] Pepys's language, as with his talk of 'flinging down', follows these patterns. His favourite phrase for describing his satisfactory sexual encounters was 'I did what I would': it was the phrase used for abuse, as when he 'did what I would' with Frances Tooker, and for consensual relations, such as doing 'what I would with' the linen-draper Betty Martin.[36] Although this phrase was vague enough to evade censorship after 1890, 'I did what I would' did sometimes mean penetrative sex when Pepys referred to married women. Pepys preferred to keep penetrative sex within marriage (just not within his own marriage), since any pregnancy could be attributed to the husband. One episode of 'haze what jo would' with Betty Martin in early June 1667 led to a pregnancy scare in July when her period was late, and her husband was hurriedly called back from sea.[37] Pepys's focus on whether he achieved his will, rather than on his actions or a woman's actions, often makes his diary less explicit than its reputation would suggest.

This lack of explicitness has made it easier for commentators to avoid considering Pepys as a 'rapist'.[38] It is a reluctance that stems from Pepys's appeal as an engaging narrator and our own society's attitudes towards rape, rather than any close assessment of what he writes and of his society's attitudes to sexual violence, because that assessment has not been done. In the early modern period rape was a felony, but there was no specific definition of the act in statutes. In the late seventeenth century, an average of just two rape cases per year were heard at London's main criminal court. Obtaining a conviction normally required proving lack of consent, and that both penetration *and* ejaculation had taken place – criteria that were extremely difficult to meet.[39] Rape was regarded seriously enough to merit the death penalty, but rapists were at no serious risk of prosecution, let alone conviction. This legal context was not, however, the sole standard for judging sexual violence: after all, most Britons today do not have section 1 of the Sexual Offences Act 2003 memorized as their standard for understanding rape. Laura Gowing's investigation of non-capital trials for sexual crimes leads her to argue that seventeenth-century women were clear both about men's use of physical force and about consent. There was 'a substantial gulf between legal and popular understandings of rape', for 'the violations of sexual assault and forced sex were familiar social facts, as well as personal experiences'.[40] The frequency with which Pepys sought gratification from women and girls who had to either physically defend themselves or who were not in a position to resist coercion bears out that view.

It is with a married woman, Mrs Bagwell, that Pepys most clearly records the extent of his physical force in terms that mirror those used in the seventeenth century to describe rape. His account of this relationship is also a sharp caution against overestimating the frankness and explicitness of the diary. Mrs Bagwell was the wife of a ship's carpenter. Her first name is not mentioned by Pepys, but she was called Elizabeth.[41] In 1663, Pepys had designs on her. She and her husband approached Pepys seeking his patronage, and Pepys subsequently approached her seeking sexual gratification as advance payment. Elizabeth Bagwell's behaviour indicates she was prepared to offer some sexual contact to gain her husband's promotion.[42] There were, however, limits to what she would allow, limits which Pepys disregarded. In December 1664 he dined with the Bagwells, found an excuse to send William out, and 'alone avec elle je tentoy à faire ce que je voudrais, et contre sa force je le faisoy, bien que pas à mon contentment' ('alone with her I tried to do what I would, and against her will I did it, though not to my satisfaction').[43] The French word 'force' (here translated as 'will') literally means 'strength': Mrs Bagwell tried to fight him off. Over the next few months Elizabeth Bagwell continued to seek Pepys out at his office, requiring the assistance he had promised but had yet to deliver. On 20 February 1665, Pepys told her:

> to go home and I would do her business; which was to write a letter to my Lord Sandwich for her husband's advance into a better ship as there should be occasion – which I did; and by and by did go down by water to Deptford-yard [...] and it being dark, did privately entrer en la maison de la femme de Bagwell, and there I had sa compagnie, though with a great deal of difficulty; néanmoins, enfin je avais ma volonté d'elle. And being sated therewith, I walked home to Redriffe, it being now near 9 a-clock; and there I did drink some strong waters and eat some bread and cheese, and so home –

Or translated, 'it being dark, did privately enter Bagwell's wife's house, and there I had her company, though with a great deal of difficulty;

nevertheless, finally I had my will of her'. The next day's entry shows Pepys's success in the face of 'a great deal of difficulty' came not via persuasion, but via force: 'Up, and to the office (having a mighty pain in my forefinger of my left hand, from a strain that it received last night in struggling avec la femme que je [with the woman that I] mentioned yesterday), where busy till noon ... '.[44] Pepys bore the marks of this violence, and it is more than likely that Elizabeth Bagwell did too. The phrase Pepys uses to describe his triumph, 'je avais ma volonté d'elle' ('I had my will of her'), could be used of seduction, but in a range of literature from scriptural exegesis to ballads, and in the courts, 'to have one's will' of or on someone also meant 'rape'.[45]

Pepys was not an opportunistic assailant and there are signs of planning which he does not make explicit. When Mrs Bagwell had arrived at the Navy Office on 20 February, the timing was significant. She had last attended on 14 February, saying she hoped to claim Pepys as her valentine. This was both an encouragement to continue the relationship and a reminder that he was obligated to her following previous sexual encounters: a man was expected to give his valentine a gift. However, on 23 January Pepys had sworn off women 'for a month' and so, he says, 'my oath preserved me from losing any time with her'.[46] That Mrs Bagwell just happened to return on 20 February indicates he had told her when she should come and that he did so with the oath's expiry in mind. He was given to retrospectively interpreting the letter of his oaths as best suited his passions and in this case a month seems to have meant exactly four weeks.[47] When Pepys arrived at Elizabeth Bagwell's home later that day and coerced her into sex – an encounter he describes as involving struggle and injury, and of which he uses the language often used of rape – it was carefully timed to avoid breaking his vow.

Pepys did not describe his attack on Elizabeth Bagwell as a rape. What she would have called it we do not know – though the fact that she did not see Pepys for nearly five months afterwards is suggestive.[48] It has proved easy for readers to make light of Pepys's assaults on Mrs Bagwell, including dismissing her resistance as 'a token struggle' or (when judged via the Index's summary) a 'little comic narrative'.[49] Along with other women and girls who continued contact with Pepys after he assaulted them, Elizabeth Bagwell's behaviour does not comply with rape 'myths': mistaken ideas about how survivors of attacks behave that (in the Restoration and today), are used to judge whether or not an attack happened. A woman who is sexually assaulted, for example, is supposed to immediately protest, to report the incident, and to take every step to avoid her attacker thereafter;

if she cannot demonstrate that she followed these steps impeccably then doubts are raised about whether there was any such assault. The idea that a rape can occur within a relationship and yet that relationship continue is one with which British juries continue to struggle.[50] Another factor in the trivializing of these episodes, as will now be manifest, is that Pepys himself minimizes them, seeing coercion as unremarkable or, indeed, as an achievement. In writing, he is brief, moving quickly to his next point. He does not need to make explicit to himself the extent of the strategizing involved. Recognizing the evidence for interpretations other than Pepys's own therefore requires treating Pepys as an unreliable narrator, rather than as a frank, explicit authority. It also requires resisting cultural assumptions that make it easy to disregard the experiences of non-elite women or even to treat sexual assault as comedy.

Black Londoners

From the late 1940s, indeed before, Pepys's diary has been employed as a source on another group of Londoners whose histories rarely ranked as of 'public interest': people of colour. Twentieth-century work on Black history cited Pepys's diary to show that, by the 1660s, Black people were 'everyday sights' on the city's streets, active in a range of occupations.[51] In 2008, Imtiaz Habib, in an important study, argued that the fleetingness of Pepys's attention was itself revealing: the 'background figures deeply buried in the narrative fabric of Pepys's diary entries are examples of the extent of the English normalization of African domestication'.[52] By understanding such references as part of wider patterns in the diary, we can glean more information from them – and sometimes more still when other records can be traced. This involves examining Pepys as an enslaver. Since his references to enslaved people in the diary are brief and, in terms of his own use of their labour, elliptical, his involvement in slavery has had little attention. Pepys's most explicit discussions of slavery are found in his later naval records. Those records are dispersed over several archives and, unlike his strictly personal papers, are unpublished. As a result, twenty-first-century researchers' efforts to use Pepys's papers as a source on Black Londoners' lives, or to trace his involvement in the slave trade, ironically face the same challenges that impeded efforts to write Pepys more firmly into imperial history in the early twentieth century: the division between the study of the diary and the study of Pepys as a naval administrator. As I write this chapter, the most comprehensive – if egregiously distorted – account of the Black people who worked for Pepys remains Arthur Bryant's biographies from the 1930s, for these drew on both Pepys's professional and personal archives.[53] The upshot is that, in order to contextualize the insights the diary provides, we have to first get a clear overview of the information in Pepys's papers. In doing so, the trajectory of Pepys's ownership of enslaved people emerges, but so too does the trajectory of one enslaved young man, known in the diary as Mingo. Like Pepys, but with none of Pepys's advantages, he was working naval patronage networks with skill.

London in the 1660s had a growing population of people of colour. Pepys's home parish of St Olave's, in the east of the City, had numerous mercantile and naval households and was close to parishes full of sailors and dockers. These were multinational areas, where people of colour, enslaved and free, lived.[54] Among Pepys's patrons, colleagues, and wealthy neighbours were many who had enslaved people working for them and who were directly involved in running and financing the slave trade.[55] Pepys's chief patron, James, duke of York, headed the Company of Royal Adventurers into Africa from 1660; another of his patrons, Lord Sandwich, was a founding member. In 1663, the Company's new charter specified that its monopoly on West African trade included the trade in people. After financial troubles, the Company was reconstituted in 1672 as the Royal African Company (RAC), with slavery a principal part of its business.[56] While several histories of slavery state that Pepys was himself an investor in the Royal African Company, this appears to be a mistake.[57] Searches of the company's records have not found him listed among the stockholders.[58] The company's perilous finances might have deterred him from investing as, later, might the risks of being seen to use his new post as Secretary for the Admiralty to line his own pockets, for the navy often acted in the RAC's interests. Royal Navy ships went out on company business, with Pepys facilitating – but apparently not to improve his own dividends.[59]

Despite the nation's growing involvement in the slave trade, direct reference to someone as a 'slave' is comparatively rare in late seventeenth-century English records. Enslaved Black people were often described using job titles that also covered white workers: they were 'servants' or worked as someone's 'boy' (meaning footboy or junior worker).[60] A 'boy' in this sense might be a child or a man in his twenties – Pepys described his 25-year-old white servant Tom Edwards as his 'boy'.[61] When people of colour were working in these roles, Pepys and others frequently used racialized descriptions, referring to them as a 'black boy', 'blackmore-maid', or as a householder's 'black', 'negro', or 'blackmore'.[62] Historians have examined how, despite the social reality of slavery and its expansion in mid-seventeenth-century England, there was no legal framework to enforce slavery on English soil – the first significant court case towards this came in 1677.[63] In legal forums and in general commentary, the idea of enslaving Christians was far more controversial than enslaving 'infidels'. There was a widespread belief (more belief than practice) that the baptism of enslaved people meant their manumission.[64] In this context, the references to Black people's lives found in legal documents, parish records, letters, and diaries can be far from clear about whether someone was enslaved or free, and the assumptions of those making the records (who were very rarely the Black people themselves) can be difficult to deduce.

Slavery in Naval Correspondence and the Diary

Sometimes, however, there is no such ambiguity about enslavement. It is in Pepys's professional correspondence from the 1670s and 1680s that his ownership of enslaved people is made explicit, since this is where their sale and transportation were discussed with naval officers. In April 1675, Lieutenant John Howe offered Pepys 'a small Neager boy'. Howe apologized for not providing 'something better worth your acceptance, hoping he is so well seasoned to endure the cold weather as to live in England'. Pepys was offended, not because he disapproved of slavery, nor because the child was an inadequate present, but because the boy was too obvious a bribe: Howe wanted a captaincy. Pepys wrote back reprovingly (and for the admiralty record) to explain that he had already arranged for Howe's promotion before receiving his offer. Howe was contrite and grateful. There is no sign of whether the small boy was delivered to Pepys as a sign of Howe's 'thankfulnesse'.[65] Later in the 1670s, when living in Westminster, Pepys certainly had one enslaved boy or young man working for him. This youth was handed over to Pepys's colleague Captain John Wyborne, just prior to Wyborne's departure for the Mediterranean in early 1680. Pepys asked Wyborne to arrange for the sale of 'my Black-Boy' as a favour, which he duly did for twenty-five pistoles during the voyage. Pepys thanked him: 'I am much oblig'd to you for the Bargain you have made for mee, & if I may choose, could bee well contented you would at your returne from Spaine buy mee a little good sherry with the proceed of it & a little good Chocolaty against winter.'[66] To Pepys, this boy was one form of luxury good traded for others.

These two boys appear briefly in Pepys's records at the point they were to be traded; the same is true of another young Black man who worked for Pepys in Westminster in the 1680s. He is referred to by Pepys only as 'my Negroe' and his brutal treatment is described in an admiralty letter book preserved in the Pepys Library. In September 1688, Pepys wrote to Captain Edward Stanley, on board the *Foresight*, to apologize for the abrupt arrival of this young man, who had been taken to the ship on the initiative of his housekeeper and a waterman. He also gave instructions:

> Now the end of my troubling you with him is shortly this, that being come to such a degree in Roguery[,] Such as Lying, pilfering, drinking, takeing Tobacco in his bed, & being otherwise mischeivous beyond the power of good or bad Words whipping or Fetters to reforme him, Soe as to render himselfe at length dangerous to be longer continued in a Sober Family, I found it necessary to ridd my selfe of him, & doe take the liberty of sending him aboard you, to be kept to hard Meat, till you can dispose of him in Some Plantacion as <a> Rogue & to invest the proceed of him (his Charge & Entertainment [i.e. maintenance] first deducted) in whatever you please, praying you in the mean time that you'l comit it to some body to keep a Strict Hand & Eye upon him, Suitable to the Cautions I have before given you of him.[67]

Lying, pilfering, drinking, and posing a fire hazard were all behaviours that Pepys had encountered in his young white servants – a whipping or the sack being his harshest responses.[68] The punishments he gave this young Black man for non-violent misdeeds had already gone beyond that. 'Fetters' had apparently been tried. Pepys did not just want the young man transported to a plantation: he ordered him kept *en route* to poor rations, to be confined, and to be labelled as 'a Rogue' – which was likely to make him a target for further persecution on his sale. This vindictive plan was disrupted by the Revolution of 1688, for Stanley's ship was diverted from its original voyage to await William's invasion fleet off the coast.[69] There would be no sea fight. What became of the young man is unknown.

I have quoted Pepys's 1688 letter at some length because it shows a side of him missing from his popular reputation and because the most widely available account of it, written by Bryant in 1938, has distortions. Those distortions have had consequences. For Bryant, this was a mildly amusing affair of a frustrated Pepys, an overzealous housekeeper, and (in his words) 'poor Sambo' the 'troublesome black buck'.[70] 'Sambo' was Bryant's "humorous" racist elaboration of the letter. However, 'Sambo' was also a name given to Black men and boys by English enslavers. As this letter from Pepys's professional correspondence was not in print, Bryant's racist joke has understandably been taken for the young man's name by later historians.[71] Bryant's sympathy with Pepys added to the indignity heaped on this young man, and further obscured his history.

Despite – or rather because of – its flaws, Bryant's treatment of enslaved people in his biographies remains useful as a warning about the hazards of identifying closely with Pepys's viewpoint. When Bryant discussed Pepys's sale of a boy via Wyborne, the point was to demonstrate Pepys's isolation when he was temporarily forced from office: 'He was no longer a housekeeper [i.e. householder] now; even his black boy had been sold for him by kind Captain Wyborne.'[72] Having earlier seen how seventeenth-century uses of 'kind' can mask abuse, here is a twentieth-century instance. Suffice to say, if identification with Pepys's viewpoint extends to adopting Pepys's view of a child as a piece of property and to regarding an act of slave trading as simply 'kind', that identification is pernicious. It is certainly very far from acting to 'quicken [the reader's] perception of humanity', as Bryant had argued was the effect of Pepys's diary.[73]

In that diary, Pepys was highly attuned to matters of status. Since owning enslaved people was a status symbol, this interest shaped many of his references to people of colour in 1660s London.[74] One such reference makes it clear that he had no qualms in this period about treating Black people as commodities: the attitudes seen in his 1670s letters were not post-diary developments. In 1665 he visited the 'very pleasant' home of the goldsmith Sir Robert Vyner. Vyner escorted him around the house and grounds, pointing out the decorations, marble doorframes, and marble chimney:

> He showed me a black boy that he had that died of a consumption; and being dead, he caused him to be dried in a Oven, and there lies entire in a box.
> By and by to dinner, [...]

As Kim Hall remarks, Pepys refers to this young man as if he were another of Vyner's expensive items.[75] The presence of a young Black man's corpse on display in the house was apparently remarkable, but not shocking. As ever, Pepys moved quickly on to his next experience.

Elsewhere, amid busy entries, he observed Black servants attending on colleagues and other neighbours. Working in Seething Lane were Jack (in Sir William Penn's household), Mingo (in Sir William Batten's), and 'a blackmore and blackmore-maid' who lived in the household of the wine merchant William Batelier and his sister Susan.[76] We can infer from the casualness of Pepys's occasional mentions that Jack, Mingo, and the Bateliers' servants were present much more often than he noted, and that Black people would also have been working, unmentioned, in nearby households, such as that of John Buckworth, an official in the Royal African Company.[77]

While Pepys's references to people of colour are often brief, more can be drawn out by comparing them with his allusions to other servants. Towards the end of the diary, on 5 April 1669, he noted that he had Doll (short for Dorothy), working for him and that she was Black. In his words, 'for a cook maid we have, ever since **Bridget** went, used a black **moore** of Mr **Batelier's (Doll)** who dresses our meat mighty well and we mightily pleased with her' (Figure 8.1).[78] Doll may be identical with the 'blackmore-maid' in the Bateliers' household whom Pepys had previously seen at a party – if that was the case she had also been doubling as a waiting maid. Pepys's reference to Doll on 5 April in some respects followed his standard pattern of announcing the arrival of a new cookmaid or chambermaid. Normally, he noted the woman's previous employer or recommender and, slightly less often, gave her name and/or commented on her appearance ('a good pretty mayd', 'a very tall mayd').[79] Here Pepys foregrounded Doll's race. Having a Black person working in his own household was apparently a first. His emphasis on her race included writing 'moore' in longhand, instead of – as might be expected – using the simple shorthand word-symbol for 'more'.[80]

Pepys does not state whether Doll was free or enslaved. His silence on this point does tell us one thing: he had not purchased or been gifted Doll, so he was not her "owner". Given the diary's role in assessing his social status, his owning his first slave certainly would have been worth a mention, being both a significant financial transaction and a mark of rank which demonstrated his equality with colleagues such as Penn. Pepys's comment allows for the possibility that Doll was a free woman, formerly of Batelier's household and recruited in the usual way. Batelier had previously recommended two other female servants to him.[81] However more likely is Susan Amussen's suggestion that Doll was enslaved and that her services were loaned to Pepys.[82] This seems probable as Pepys does not here employ his usual verb 'recommend', or a cognate, to describe Batelier's involvement; instead the phrase 'used a black moore [...] of Mr Batelier's' could mean that Doll remained Batelier's property.[83] In this entry, Pepys's commendation of Doll's skills was a way of registering his debt to Batelier, rather than simple praise of her. Taking personal ownership of people, it seems, was something that Pepys worked his way towards by gradations that barely registered: he benefited from enslaved labour by loan; and then later acquired enslaved people, whether by gift or purchase.

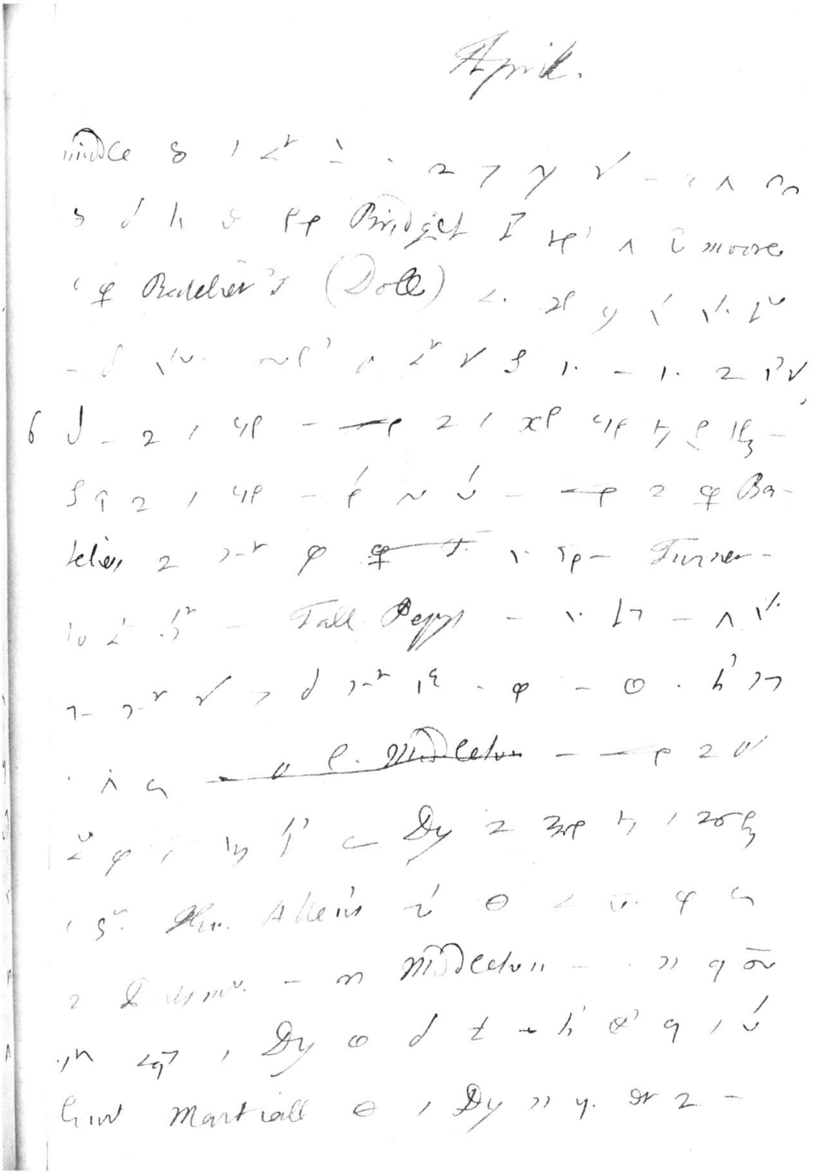

Reading against the Grain

Figure 8.1 Diary of Samuel Pepys, 5 and 6 April 1669. PL 1841. Pepys's reference to Doll begins towards the end of the second line.

This trade for him was not solely financial: when he wanted to dispose of a Black worker, he did so as part of an exchange of favours or patronage.

'Mingo'

While Doll appears only fleetingly in Pepys's journal, and has so far proved untraceable in other records, Pepys gave more attention to a young man named Mingo. 'Mingo' has only one name in the diary and in other documents before 1668. His was a name used in West Africa but also one often given to Black men and boys by enslavers.[84] Mingo worked as a personal servant to Pepys's colleague Sir William Batten for most of the 1660s. 'Servant' was how Batten described Mingo's role. In the early 1660s, when Pepys first met Mingo, that was almost certainly a synonym for slave.[85] By the end of the decade, however, Mingo was free.

Just as Pepys's role as an enslaver grew by gradations, Mingo's path from an enslaved child to a freed young man was not a matter of one simple, conclusive shift. He is first mentioned by Pepys on Valentine's Day 1661, when (by his own later estimation) he was about sixteen. By this point he was well established in Batten's household, as well as quick witted and confident enough to joke with the gentleman next door over a Valentine Day's custom. In one tradition, the first person of the opposite sex that you saw on 14 February became your valentine. Pepys wrote:

> **Valentine's Day.** Up **earely** and to **Sir W. Battens**. But would not go in till I had asked whether they that opened the **doore** was a man or a woman. And **Mingo,** who was there, answered "a **Woman**" which with his **tone** made me **laugh**.[86]

(See Figure 8.2). The longhand in this entry emphasizes Mingo's 'tone', which was presumably either "manly" or a deliberately bad female impersonation. As the amount of longhand makes the episode more easily locatable, it rather suggests this was an anecdote being saved for future use and enjoyment. A couple of months later, Pepys provided a clue as to how Mingo had come to work for Batten. In April 1661, Pepys and the Battens visited the home of Phineas Pett, the master shipwright at Chatham. Pett presented Lady Batten with a parrot which 'knew Mingo as soon as it saw him, having bred formerly in the house with them'. Here we have to resort to a parrot as a witness, but this elliptical reference raises the possibility that Mingo worked in the 1650s for the Pett family, who had long been involved in shipbuilding.[87]

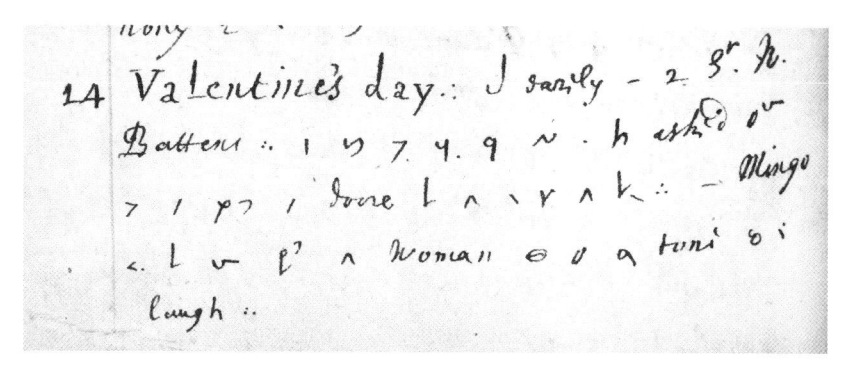

Figure 8.2 Diary of Samuel Pepys, 14 February 1661. PL 1836.

By the middle of the 1660s, if not before, Mingo's status as enslaved had become less clear cut. Tracing Black people in Restoration London, Simon Newman observes that some individuals who appear in parish records 'were probably enslaved, others were free, and many more were in a liminal state between these categories, bound to serve a particular person and living much as an employed English servant might live, yet perhaps believing themselves vulnerable to being sent or taken back to a colony where enslaved status might easily be reimposed upon them'.[88] Mingo seems to have been in a similar kind of 'liminal state' in 1665. In July of that plague year, Batten made a will. He gave 'my servante Mingoe a Negroe That now dwelleth with mee' £10, along with 'the Custody and keeping of my Light houses Att Harwich, and the somme of Twenty pounds a yeare of lawfull money of England dureing the Terme of his naturall life for his paines therein'. Batten's lighthouses were not tall buildings on rocks, but navigation beacons that guided ships into Harwich harbour; one was on the shore and the other on the town's gatehouse. Batten had a royal patent permitting him and his heirs to erect the lights and turn a profit by charging fees to shipping.[89] Minding the beacons was a responsible, if laborious, job in the town (although one that Mingo could have recruited others to assist with). Twenty pounds a year was no small income: it was five times the wages of a well-paid cookmaid.[90] This dual bequest looks like an attempt to give Mingo options, along with the protection of ongoing patronage – if he wanted it. The importance of the job, together with the continued link to Batten's family that came with it, would have provided some defence against the very real risk of re-enslavement via kidnapping. The proffer of a post funded via ships' dues, was also, I suspect, a sign that Batten recognized that neither his family nor his finances could be otherwise trusted to support Mingo: both disintegrated on his death. His wife immediately fell out with her adult stepchildren, the estate was found to be heavily in debt, and lawsuits began.[91]

Whatever Batten's benign intentions, the effects were limited. Habib writes of this will:

> It is instructive to ask what exactly Batten's bequest does to change the ruling conditions of Mingoe's life. It gives him material security but does not affect his discursive marking as a once racialized and enslaved individual. Those markings are the fixed limits within which Mingoe will have to live his subsequent life, no matter how materially secured. Given only a catchy nickname with tropical allusions, Mingoe remains an exotic pet, albeit one with useful skills. [. . .] Contrariwise, what Batten's bequest does do is advertise *his* human largesse and nobility, and by doing so elides his complicity in the inhumanity of the slaving practice itself.[92]

Another thing that Batten's will did do – at least once it was proved after Batten's death – was provide legal documentation that signalled Mingo was not enslaved and which could potentially be used to counter anyone who attempted to deny his freedom. Batten's descriptions of him as 'my servante' and 'a Negroe' left it unclear as to whether Batten regarded him as free at the time of writing, but bequeathing Mingo money and the right to a post with an income indicated he should be treated as free by the family after Batten's death. Between July 1665 and October 1667, when Batten died, Mingo remained in Batten's service. His own sense of his position may have been disturbingly unclear. If he was unpaid, the same was often true of other young people working in local households ('parish' children sent into service and apprentices, among others).[93] A document existed which implied he was free, or would be freed at some unspecified time. The power was with Batten to decide exactly how Mingo should be treated, and presumably the ambiguity suited Batten.

For a long time, the diary entries and Batten's will were all that could be discovered of Mingo's life. It has been suggested that he became the first Black lighthouse keeper.[94] He had other ideas about his future. After Batten's death, Mingo took steps to put his freedom on a more secure footing. In early 1668, the register of St Katharine by the Tower recorded: 'William a Blackmore bapt and sirnamed Mingo about 23 yeares of age bapt Isay William the 19th of January'.[95] It's a brief record, but one which Mingo himself must have had some agency in creating and which provides much information. The record confirms he had certainly been enslaved as a child – otherwise adult baptism would not have been necessary. His baptism now incontrovertibly recognized him as part of the Christian community and (by establishing that he was not an 'infidel') offered some protection against being forced back into slavery.[96] Baptismal entries do not usually involve declaring which part of a person's name was the surname: this one did, because William Mingo wanted it in the official record that 'Mingo' was no longer to be treated as his first (and only) name.[97] Sometime prior to January 1668, he had evidently begun using 'William' – presumably in honour of Sir William Batten – and he now put another name on record 'Isay'. This is a rare name: it may have been chosen to acknowledge a friend or godparent, or because it was a name he had before he was 'Mingo'.[98] The statement that he was 'about 23' is noteworthy. Age was often recorded approximately in parish records, yet some thought must have gone into this particular declaration. It would have been apparent to those around him that, having been forced from his birth family, he could not know his age with any certainty. Twenty-three may well have been his best guess, but it was also a smart one. It was in his interests to be at least twenty-one, the age of full adulthood. Being known as 'about 23' served a purpose: it was high enough over twenty-one to be safe and vague enough to be credible. Also significant, and surprising, is that this ceremony did not take place at St Olave Hart Street, the parish where William Mingo had lived for at least seven years. Instead the ceremony was at St Katharine's, a neighbouring church. There is no obvious reason for this, but the answer may lie in the circumstances of the Batten household. Batten's family had left Seething Lane by mid-December 1667 and were struggling to pay off his debts.[99] At this time, William Mingo may have moved down the road, where there were cheap lodgings to be had in a maritime district, and then elected to be baptized in this community. He may have worried, too, that the financially stricken Battens would be tempted not to treat him as a legatee of the estate, but as one of its assets. Baptism at St Katharine's, rather than St Olave's, may have been expedient.

Isay William Mingo had not, however, removed himself entirely from St Olave's parish. Nor had he taken up the role at Harwich – at least not in any way that required his continual presence there. Instead, he found a patron in Batten's successor as Surveyor of the Navy, Thomas Middleton, who now occupied Batten's lodgings at the Navy Office. In November 1669, Middleton and Mingo were both at Chatham dockyard when a creditor turned up at the Navy Office, threatening legal action against Mingo for a £2 10s debt. Such suits could end in imprisonment. The Navy Board passed the news to Middleton, who reported that 'William Mingoe' was 'content to pay the mony when he commeth to London'. In the meantime, Middleton said he would cover the debt, conveying that, to him, it was a small sum. The complainant was told to drop his suit.[100] William Mingo was evidently struggling to manage his finances: his £10 inheritance may well not have materialized, since Batten's affairs were a mess. Whatever he told Middleton about his debt must have been persuasive, because Middleton made light of it to the other Board members. Middleton could afford to be casually generous to William Mingo for he was a wealthy man: he owned multiple sugar plantations and the enslaved people who worked on them.[101]

While serving Batten, William Mingo had learned a good deal about how the navy worked, and he had been putting that knowledge to use as a free man. Within two years, the Navy Board was again gearing up for war with the Dutch. In the spring of 1672, the *Dover* frigate sailed with the English fleet in search of the enemy. On board was a sailor named 'William Mingo', rated as an able seaman (a position above an 'ordinary' seaman).[102] This meant he had skills normally earned through years on ships or, alternatively, that he had an additional role on board, or had sway with naval patrons to help him to this rating.[103] The manifestations of Navy Board patronage on the *Dover* make it likely that this sailor was the same William Mingo who was known to the Navy Board. The ship's officers included the purser Samuel Martin and the chaplain Jeremiah Wells. Both men owed their positions to Samuel Pepys's influence, thanks to his relationships with their wives: Samuel Martin was the husband of Betty Martin, while Jeremiah Wells had married Deb Willet. Pepys introduced the two men when he helped Wells to his post on the ship.[104] Soon the *Dover* began to see action. On 20 May, in rough seas and dense fog, the two fleets drew close and, after a minor skirmish, the *Dover* towed away a damaged sloop.[105] That day, William Mingo died. This was briefly marked in the pay book with the notation 'DD', for 'Discharged Dead'.[106] If this was indeed William Mingo, erstwhile of the Navy Office, he was by his own count twenty-seven, the same age as Samuel Pepys in the year he began his diary. He had spent most of his life, enslaved and free, working for the navy.

Through Pepys's diary, a will, a baptismal record, and brief references in naval documents, we can trace Isay William Mingo's transition from an enslaved child with a 'pet name' to a free man of three names, established in naval networks. For at least part of the 1660s, his status as free or enslaved was, on paper and perhaps in practice, ambiguous. His life was recorded by others, including the man next door. More than any other surviving document, Pepys's diary preserved William Mingo's actions and personality, but the account of him given there simultaneously shows the diary's limitations. Pepys's scrutiny of social status did not extend to enslavement, and his interest in Mingo did not extend to mentioning him after Batten's death. Quarrels among the Batten household and the Batten estate's financial problems were what concerned him.[107] For all the valuable information that the diary provides on the lives of Black people in London, it is as much a record of Pepys's disregard as his curiosity.

Reading the Diary

Reading Pepys's diary against the grain means being alert to its subtexts, euphemisms, and silences, and to the individuals whose lives were mentioned, however briefly, in his pages. These were people whose experiences of gendered and racialized inequality and violence were profoundly different. Yet in approaching their lives through Pepys's diary, there are some common obstacles. Pepys's language obscures the power dynamics and is sometimes deliberately obfuscating; previous writing focused on Pepys can hinder as much as help; and prejudice has discouraged attention to these experiences. It is possible to be struck by Pepys's frankness and his detail, while also acknowledging that he is often far from explicit, and probing why that is. Adopting this inquisitive approach may mean the diary loses some (though not all) of its traditional comedy, but the rewards are a deeper appreciation of what it holds.

Closely reading the diary in this way reveals truths that otherwise escape notice. For example, Pepys only recorded that he had 'nuper ... saepe' ('lately ... often') been molesting Susan at the point he decided that this behaviour was becoming too risky to continue. If we miss two words in this polyglot (easily done if an edition offers no translation) we miss a pattern of abuse. Notably, Pepys's secrecy – his polyglot and the extra encoding in some passages – is only part of what continues to protect his actions from scrutiny. At least as significant have been his mitigating language ('touch', 'tumble'), his presentation of sexual encounters as inconsequential, and readers' enjoyment in sharing his perspective. It takes effort to avoid galloping on to the next part of the day with him, and to pause long enough to recognize that a 'Mrs' was also a 'child'. It is not easy to register that a 'touch' was an act of sexual violence, nor that what seems opportunistic shows signs of being calculated.

By reading attentively, however, we can appreciate others' planning and discern their agency in surviving records. Other people who appear in the diary's pages – male and female, free and enslaved – were no fools when it came to defensive ambiguity and guarding information. Elizabeth Pepys's 'cunning' in managing her husband and other men emerges from the pages of the diary in ways that her husband did not fully register. Isay William Mingo had little control over the brief accounts of his life but, like Samuel Pepys, he knew how to turn an institutional record to his advantage. In the diary and other sources, we can see William Mingo working patronage networks – networks in which 'black boys' were treated as property to be exchanged and displayed. Remarkably he managed to establish himself as a participant, not property, in those networks without antagonizing naval officials. It must have been a hazardous process of which there are only traces in the surviving records (a joke well received, a debt satisfactorily explained). Enslaved people who tested the constraints put on them risked brutal responses. Pepys's cruelty to the young Black man who worked for him in the 1680s is an example, and he no doubt intended it to serve as a warning to others. Today, if we feel we know Pepys well from his diary, it may serve as a different kind of warning.

Even taken alone, Pepys's diary contains sufficient cautions that his account is best treated with (at the very least) a degree of scepticism. If we follow Pepys in characterizing cruelty and exploitation as kindness or playfulness – if we see him as merely naughty – we are either misled by him or accept his view. Instead, reading the diary can help us to test our own assumptions and to be cautious about easy categorizations. Recognizing whose views are being discounted, where abuse goes unacknowledged, or when benevolence is the kind face of oppression are insights that have uses beyond reading seventeenth-century history. If we can recognize such phenomena in historical sources, and understand what makes perceiving them difficult, then we are likely to be better placed to identify and counter them in ourselves and in our everyday lives. This is not among the benefits to posterity that Pepys foresaw for his library. Yet it follows from pursuing methods that his library scheme encouraged: comparing personal with naval papers, and attending not just to Samuel Pepys, but to 'the Populace of England' who did not leave their own records.[108] In this sense, it is not reading against the grain at all.

Afterword

From the first publication of Pepys's diary, readers have imagined how he would have reacted to it and to his new fame. In 1825, one reviewer wished Pepys could 'be made aware of the publicity that has been given to his secret thoughts, petty weaknesses, and trifling adventures' – and imagined his dismay.[1] If Pepys were surveying the situation in 2025, a verdict beginning with his habitual comment 'But strange to see . . . ' might be the least of it. The knowledge that Samuel Pepys kept 'a diary which was later published and is still read today' has been deemed important information for living in the UK (a development which might surprise most UK citizens almost as much as it might surprise Pepys). This is according to government ministers, who have made it one of the facts that migrants taking the 'Life in the UK test' to gain permanent residency should memorize.[2] The diary is a text that students across the world now read to learn about English history and culture: there are Japanese introductions to Pepys and the Latham and Matthews edition has recently appeared in German.[3] Within England, a good deal of Pepys's continued fame stems from the fact that his diary has unofficially been a staple of the country's National Curriculum for decades. The government-approved curriculum gives the Great Fire as an example of a nationally significant 'event beyond living memory' that primary school children should learn about.[4] For teachers working with six- and seven-year-olds, the diary has become a go-to source for explaining how we can find out about events that happened before everyone started using mobile phones to film disasters. Pepys's diary is therefore used to introduce thousands of primary school children to history each year. Just as children's magazines did in the 1870s, snatches of the diary are used to bring emotions to history and make it memorable, with Pepys's burying his parmesan cheese in his garden being particularly famous.

Pepys's presence in primary schools has helped to reinforce his diary's status as a gateway drug for enticing the wider public to consume history.

Include the diary in your museum exhibition or your historical novel, and it will help draw an audience. The diary's reputation for providing unofficial, illicit history is, of course, part of this. Novelists still creatively explore the diary's narratives – Deb Willet, Elizabeth Bagwell, and Elizabeth Knepp have starred in recent historical fictions.[5] Elizabeth Pepys's viewpoint continues to be rediscovered as a counter to her husband's. In 2017, this included a theatre production, inspired by social media, which offered Elizabeth's and Deb's perspectives through interpretive dance.[6]

Of the many uses that Pepys anticipated for his diary in the writing, it is safe to say inspiring twenty-first-century dance was not one. His journal of social striving, gossip, health, politics, spending, pleasures, and 'strange' things was, however, written with an eye to the future. Most immediately, his diary entries marshalled the recent past to offer a sense of control and reassurance in the present. Part of that reassurance came from making provision for a future when such information would be deployed defensively, retold for enjoyment, or privately relished by him. Clear, neat shorthand and the navigational aids provided by his longhand brought order to his days and provided for himself as a future reader. Decades later, the diary became part of his scheme to benefit future generations and preserve his memory, as one of many records of himself, his contemporaries, and his society. Pepys's diary belonged in his library because, in memorializing him and his times, the library was the diary writ large. Pepys's skills in record management allowed his private journal to survive, not just by astutely setting the conditions to preserve his library collections intact, but by mitigating the risks of letting highly personal documents survive him. When, as Leigh Hunt put it, Pepys made the strange decision to leave his diary 'to the wonder, the amusement, and not very probable respect, of the coming generations', he had taken steps to make that respect more probable.[7] The most sensitive passages were warded by shorthand, polyglot and additional enciphering, by the conditions that required the diary to be read within his impressive library, and by the library guardians motivated to protect his reputation. Pepys calculated that his college would better protect his library in the long term than his family – a calculation that (along with much of his other planning) proved accurate.

Pepys's diary is often not quite what it appears to be. It is known as the work of a singular writer recording his time but, in the forms we read it, it represents the work of many people over more than three hundred years: executors, transcribers, editors, typists, lawyers, printers, and publishers among them. While aristocrats and established scholars have played prominent roles, there have – from Ann Jackson onwards – been no less vital contributors to the diary's survival and circulation whose efforts have received less credit. Decisions made by these groups have collectively determined the diary texts. Early twentieth-century commentators cautioned that conflating 'Pepys' with 'Pepys's diary' risked ignoring Pepys's life beyond the diary. It also risks ignoring the ways that the diary texts have been shaped by other contributors, and by their values and technologies. Pepys was not his diary and Pepys's diary made legible via longhand, typescript, printed pages, or HTML is no straightforward reproduction of what he wrote in the 1660s. Whether readers are interested in Pepys himself or in what his diary can otherwise tell us, it pays to register these distinctions.

Across the nineteenth and the twentieth centuries, making Pepys's diary public simultaneously entailed determining how to limit access to its contents – whether by censorship, cost, or strategic editorial silences. This was for the protection of Pepys, of the text's producers, and sometimes of his readers. Producers' decisions concerning obscenity laws and propriety determined what could be safely published, while copyright law had a major influence on who could purchase the latest, fullest editions. A high price served as a proxy for class and education, marking newly expanded editions as reading material for gentlemen and scholars, and the older tasteful abridgements as best suited to everyone else. Drawing readers to the diary involved a fair amount of misinformation and mythmaking: the diary was in a cipher; its writer never intended it to be read by others; it was arduously decoded without a manual; *this* was the only 'genuine and complete Edition', and so on.[8] Rumours of what remained unpublished were leaked by word of mouth and manuscript. When editions left readers unsatiated, fictions were invented to supply their need for more. For all the traditional emphasis on Pepys's artlessness and frankness, it is craft and craftiness – by Pepys and by others – that are the dominant features in the diary's creation and its publishing history.

Contradictions were seen as characteristic of the diary from its first appearance, although they were usually described as characteristics of the writer. Pepys showed 'sagacity and cunning' combined with 'puerility and folly'; he was both a 'man of business' and a 'man of pleasure'; he did great things, but was oddly preoccupied with little ones.[9] Beyond the diary texts, popular representations of Pepys stressed his love of pleasure, gossip, and scandal. These traits – already seen as defining features of Charles II's court – helped raise Pepys as a figurehead for the Restoration, just as much as his vivid descriptions of the plague and Great Fire. His continued appearances in the periodical press, along with the availability of inexpensive editions in the late Victorian period, made him a widely recognizable representative of the Restoration. By the start of the twentieth century his ordinariness and his role as everyman began to feature more heavily in discussion: a move linked to efforts to market the diary to larger readerships and to the availability of more of Pepys's domestic life in expanded editions. Most of the commentators hailing Pepys as a representative of all humanity did happen to have certain traits in common with him (being middle-ranking, white, English-speaking men) which presumably made them less hesitant about universalizing those traits. Pepys's much noted oddness was now seen as compatible with ordinariness because it suited notions of the English as charmingly eccentric. Few people were minded to scrutinize whether famous attributes that had been established during the first half of the nineteenth century (such as his amusing fixation with pretty women) held up in relation to the later expanded editions, especially if the social attitudes that supported these interpretations had changed little. Almost all the diary was in print by 1900, but the new details had been published incrementally, were expensive, and prompted no dramatic re-evaluation of the diary or its author. Despite calls for wider attention to Pepys's life and archives, naval business continued to play second fiddle to naughtiness. Pepys's multifaceted self-presentation in his diary, and his changing social status within it, mean that over decades he has remained adaptable to whichever versions of ordinariness, greatness, and Englishness best suit the times.

At moments of national or international crisis – world wars and a pandemic – the diary has become particularly valued. For some readers, the journal and its adaptations offer escapism, a way of retreating from a dull or difficult present. Encounters with the diary and its adaptations in times of disaster can bring historical parallels to the fore and reduce the sense of historical distance in ways that are often experienced as psychologically reassuring: individuals and societies survive trauma, and they have done so although – or perhaps because – not everyone behaved impeccably. The diary has encouraged readers to imagine the present and themselves historically, that is, with a long-term gaze as if looking from the past or from the future. In parodies, this takes the form of adopting a Pepysian view of the present – estranging the familiar for comic effect, while highlighting behaviour that seems enduring. For diarists, such a historicized perspective can make mundane routines or fleeting experiences worthy of note: Pepys's example implies a future readership, sympathetically and historically interested in their concerns, as they are in Pepys's. Diary writing becomes history writing.

The texts of Pepys's diary have had a transformative effect on history but, at least initially, this had very little to do with changing readers' understanding of Restoration events and their causes. On that score, it was seen as a disappointment: in 1825 the 'historical importance' of Pepys's *Memoirs* was doubtful, and its literary qualities even more suspect.[10] It did not seem to significantly impact the established narrative of high politics and great men, nor did it offer elegant prose. What it did do was get readers of the edition and the surrounding press coverage talking about the Restoration and historical value. Over the decades, the diary's contributions to history came via helping to transform the experiences, lives, and genres that were deemed history – and enthusing readers and audiences in the process. As noted, it inspired diarists to think of their writing as history. The *Memoirs* and its successors provoked influential essayists to reflect on historiographical practice. Simultaneously, the diary texts provided historians with the kind of intriguing material needed to expand their field to encompass the domestic, the mundane, and 'the people'. These are functions it continues to perform today, when we are far more ready to acknowledge that political history involves social history, and that social history is political. Pepys and his diary have a tradition of prompting debate about what history is for and who it centres – the kind of debate which, in 2025, manifests as a 'culture war'. A hundred years ago, the task was to unite the 'apparently inconsistent characters' of Pepys as an 'amorous buffoon' and a great Secretary of the Admiralty.[11] In the twenty-first century we have to decide how to deal with an energetic, gregarious writer who was also a sexual predator and an enslaver. While it may be tempting to treat these as contradictory attributes, they were not: the traits that make Pepys engaging as a diarist (his energy, his gregariousness, and his networking talents, for example) frequently assisted his rise to power and his ruthless exploitation of others. They also facilitated his collecting, and thus the wider record of his times that he created through his carefully selected library. In leaving this legacy, he was binding his history up with others' and – while clearly putting himself to the fore – ultimately leaving posterity to judge what and who deserved attention.

Pepys's journal is provocative as history, and likewise as literature. On publication, it was discussed alongside dramatic comedy and Scott's novels – its portrayal of character, its detail, its plots, and its appeal to the imagination all seemed to warrant such comparisons. The diary texts inspired satires, fictions, and dramas, many of which were contributions to ongoing historical debates and some of which (like Freeman's parodies) were themselves claimed as valuable historical records. By the twentieth century, the diary's cultural prominence and the vividness of certain famous passages had made it difficult to argue that it was not great literature: if language this evocative ranked at the bottom of the scale of literary esteem then, as Robert Louis Stevenson implied, there was something wrong with the scale.[12] Later, even Pepys's '"curious" passages' that raised 'an image of a lewd nature' began to look defensible on the grounds of literary merit.[13] Literary value, like historical value, was changing in ways that favoured Pepys, and his diary's success helped affirm that change. The diary was, and has remained, a popularizing influence on history and literature because it expanded what those elite categories encompassed, and because it prompted readers to become writers – of annotations, of diaries, of fiction – and to expand those categories themselves.

Pepys left his diary for 'the benefitt of Posterity' and we are now allowed to read the whole 'for the public good'.[14] So what might the diary's future hold? I have been arguing that we can better appreciate the diary by considering it as a manuscript and scrutinizing Pepys's use of shorthand. Greater use of imaging technology would allow for broadening access to the manuscript's contents, while preserving it in accordance with Pepys's conditions. Online texts will clearly be crucial in the diary's future, whether these are manuscript reproductions, revived two-centuries-old editions, or fresh transcriptions. Electronic texts enable the diary to be examined in new ways. What Georgian reviewers called Pepys's 'artless narrative of his feelings and doings and connexions, in his progress from obscurity to considerable wealth and power' is now pithily described by digital humanities researchers as 'complex data'.[15] Much reading and analysis of Pepys's journal may in future be done via artificial intelligence. Well-designed programs can discern patterns in, for example, language or social networks that would otherwise be difficult to detect or prove. Computer analysis can also range across vast and complex sources (diaries, court reports, parish records) to pull together traces of people's lives. On the literary side, AI has (predictably) already been used to write diary parodies, although chatbots have some way to go to catch up on human beings in either quality or quantity in that vein. Responses to the diary can quickly look antiquated, and this paragraph will no doubt do so more than most. Nonetheless, by understanding how readers before us have reacted to Pepys's journal, we can decide which trends we want to avoid repeating, and which trends we might creatively want to continue.

Over two centuries, Pepys's diary has taken many forms and readers have continued to form peculiar relationships with it, to argue about it, attack it, and reap its benefits. Pepys was famously curious, and his readers have frequently sought to go beyond his curiosity – to find out or imagine more than he recorded about himself and his contemporaries. The strange history of Pepys's diary started, of course, with Samuel Pepys, but it reaches out to encompass the histories of others, and it ends with his readers who, through their responses, make his history their own.

Acknowledgements

In this book, I discuss how 'Acknowledgements' often can't do justice to the contributions that go into a publication. This is a prime example.

I'm extremely grateful for the help I've had on this project in terms of expertise from people who contributed knowledge, read drafts, and/or answered my random questions. Thank you to David Clark, Sarah Knight, Victoria Stewart, Phil Shaw, Felicity James, Mary Ann Lund, Ben Parsons, Cathleen Waters, Takako Kato, Rick Nance, Natasha Simonova, William Pettigrew, Roey Sweet, Jacqui Stanford, Jamie Gemell, Tim Somers, Guy de la Bédoyère, Anna Fargher, and Pippa Goodhart.

Jane Hughes (the Pepys Librarian) and Catherine Sutherland (the Special Collections Librarian at Magdalene) both provided expertise and suggested leads for understanding the diary's history. I learned a great deal about how Pepys's diary features in school teaching and in museums today through working with the Learning Team at the Museum of London and their colleagues – thank you especially to Laura Thomson-Turnage, James Harrod, and Charlotte Storey. Knowledge and help also came from archivists at the BBC Written Archives Centre and the BBC Photo Library; from Simon Taylor at the Keep, and Andy Wright at the Cumbria Archive Centre.

Judith and Steve Loveman have done pretty much all of the above (read drafts, provided expertise, answered my random queries, and, above all, provided moral support). They've done so for everything I've managed to write, this thing included. Thank you.

This work was supported by the Arts and Humanities Research Council [grant number AH/W003651/1]. The University of Leicester also supported this project, including a period of study leave.

A. H. Hill Estate granted permission to quote from Benny Hill's lyrics.

Extracts from *The Diary of Samuel Pepys* edited by Robert Latham and William Matthews are reproduced by permission of Peters Fraser &

Dunlop (www.petersfraserdunlop.com) on behalf of The Estate of Robert Latham.

Elements from Chapters 3 and 8 were previously published in my article 'Women and the History of Samuel Pepys's Diary', *Historical Journal*, 65 (2022), 1221–43. Reprinted with the permission of Cambridge University Press.

Notes

Introduction

1. The diary contained seditious libels and evidence of corruption which would have greatly interested the MPs investigating Pepys's work and his politics in the later 1660s and after. On financial malfeasance, see Mark Knights, 'Pepys and Corruption', *Parliamentary History*, 33:1 (2014), 19–35.
2. William Matthews, 'The Diary: A Neglected Genre', *Sewanee Review*, 85:2 (1977), 286–300 (p. 286); Magdalene, D/G/56(A) (enclosure), 'Opinion of Mr Gerald Gardiner Q.C.', 1 Mar. 1960, p. 3; Braybrooke (1825), I, vi, 232n; Bright, I, viii; Wheatley, I, xxiii; Magdalene, Pepys Library Reference Collection, 'Buffet', no. 48, G. H. Bickers to Francis Turner, 14 Feb. 1936.
3. [Leigh Hunt], Review of *The Life, Journal, and Correspondence of Samuel Pepys* transcribed by John Smith, *Edinburgh Review*, no. 149, Oct. 1841, 105–27 (p. 108). For the diary as 'strange' compare, for example, R[obert] L[ouis] S[tevenson], 'Samuel Pepys', *Cornhill Magazine*, July 1881, 31–46 (p. 32); Edwin Beresford Chancellor, *St Paul's Cathedral* (London: Dent, 1925), p. 174.
4. J. R. Tanner, *Samuel Pepys and the Royal Navy* (Cambridge: Cambridge University Press, 1920), p. 11; Gamaliel Bradford, *The Soul of Samuel Pepys* (Boston, MA: Houghton Mifflin; Cambridge: Riverside, 1924), pp. x–xi.
5. Commentators' discussion of Pepys has more often been framed in terms of his 'Englishness' than his 'Britishness', or else the two treated as interchangeable.
6. Kate Loveman, 'Women and the History of Samuel Pepys's Diary', *Historical Journal*, 65:5 (2022), 1221–43 (pp. 1235–7).
7. LM Diary, I, 265, 280 (13 Oct. and 1 Nov. 1660).
8. LM Diary, IV, 121 (2 May 1663).
9. LM Diary, I, 144 (17 May 1660).
10. LM Diary, II, 87 (23 Apr. 1661).
11. LM Diary, IV, 209 (1 July 1663). Geoffrey Robertson, *Obscenity: An Account of Censorship Laws and their Enforcement in England and Wales* (London: Weidenfeld and Nicolson, 1979), pp. 21–3.

12. LM Diary, IV, 37–8, 48 (8 and 17 Feb. 1663).
13. LM Diary, IV, 270 (10 Aug. 1663).
14. LM Diary, VI, 285 (1 Nov. 1665).
15. LM Diary, VI, 233, 256 (20 Sept. and 7 Oct. 1665).
16. LM Diary, VI, 210.
17. LM Diary, VI, 342 (31 Dec. 1665).
18. LM Diary, VII, 267, 271–2.
19. LM Diary, VII 274, 286 (4 and 14 Sept. 1666).
20. LM Diary, VII, 277, 278–9, 280 (5, 6, and 7 Sept. 1666).
21. LM Diary, VII, 277 (5 Sept. 1666).
22. 'The Great Fire of London: During the Fire', ThePlayhouseOnline, youtube.com, www.youtube.com/watch?v=weEveQ4nz4g; Robin Jarvis, *The Alchymist's Cat* (London: Simon and Schuster, 1991); Anna Fargher, *The Fire Cats of London* (London: Macmillan, 2022) – email from author, 9.1.24.
23. LM Diary, VIII, 264 (13 June 1667).
24. For example, LM Diary, II, 180 (18 Sept. 1661); VIII, 585 (22 Dec. 1667).
25. LM Diary, IX, 20 (12 Jan. 1668).
26. LM Diary, IX, 337. For what is going on with this language choice, see Chapter 2, 'Deeper Secrets', pp. 41–2 and 'Other Readers?', pp. 44–5.
27. LM Diary, IX, 353 (6 Nov. 1668).
28. LM Diary, IX, 565.
29. See *Pepys's Later Diaries*, ed. by C. S. Knighton (Stroud: Sutton, 2004); 'Pepys's Brooke House Journal', in *Samuel Pepys and the Second Dutch War*, transcribed by William Matthews and Charles Knighton, ed. by Robert Latham, Naval Records Society 133 (Aldershot: Scolar Press, 1995), pp. 334–435.
30. Loveman, 'Samuel Pepys and Deb Willet after the Diary,' *Historical Journal*, 49:3 (2006), 893–901; TNA, PROB 1/9, Will of Samuel Pepys (1703), codicil, 12 May 1703.
31. C. S. Knighton, *Pepys and the Navy* (Stroud: Sutton, 2003), pp. 146–7.
32. Tanner, *Samuel Pepys and the Royal Navy*, pp. 16–17, 34–5, 70–3; J. D. Davies, *Kings of the Sea: Charles II, James II and the Royal Navy* (Barnsley: Seaforth, 2017), pp. 140–9; J. D. Davies, 'Introduction' to Samuel Pepys, *Memoires of the Royal Navy 1690* (Barnsley: Seaforth; Annapolis, MD: Naval Institute Press, 2010), pp. ix–xi.
33. PROB 1/9, Will of Samuel Pepys, codicil, 12 May 1703, 'The Scheame [. . .] relating to the Completion & Settlement of my Library'.
34. Richard Ollard, *Pepys: A Biography* (London: Sinclair-Stevenson, 1974, repr. 1991), p. 44; Claire Tomalin, *Samuel Pepys: The Unequalled Self*, 2nd edn (London, Penguin: 2012).
35. Braybrooke 1825, I, vii; Braybrooke 1848, I, vi–vii.

36. [Horace Stebbing Roscoe St John], Review of Braybrooke 1848 vols I and II, *Gentleman's Magazine*, Feb. 1849, p. 162. Attribution from Emily Lorraine de Montluzin, *Attributions of Authorship in the Gentleman's Magazine 1731–1868: An Electronic Union List*, www.bsuva.org/bsuva/gm2/browse/GM1849.html.
37. Mark Salber Phillips, *On Historical Distance* (New Haven, CT: Yale University Press, 2013), pp. 187–8.
38. On the history of work on diaries, see Stuart Sherman, *Telling Time: Clocks, Diaries and English Diurnal Form, 1660–1785* (Chicago: University of Chicago Press, 1996), pp. 14–19; Rebecca Steinitz, *Time, Space, and Gender in the Nineteenth-Century British Diary* (New York: Palgrave Macmillan, 2011), pp. 2–3.
39. For example, Harry Berger, Jr, 'The Pepys Show: Ghost-Writing and Documentary Desire in "The Diary"', *ELH*, 65:3 (1998), 557–91; Faramerz Dabhoiwala, 'The Pattern of Sexual Immorality in Seventeenth- and Eighteenth-Century London', in *Londinopolis: Essays in the Cultural and Social History of Early Modern London*, ed. by Paul Griffiths and Mark S. R. Jenner (Manchester: Manchester University Press, 2000), pp. 86–106.
40. Arthur Ponsonby, *English Diaries* (London: Methuen, 1923), pp. 35, 82; Matthews, 'The Diary', pp. 299–300.
41. Jerome de Groot, *Consuming History: Historians and Heritage in Contemporary Popular Culture*, 2nd edn (London: Routledge, 2016), pp. 38–9, 42.
42. Phillips, *On Historical Distance*, pp. 3, 4, 143–4.
43. [Peter Cunningham], Review of Braybrooke 1848 vol. II, *The Athenaeum*, 8 July 1848, p. 669; Wilbur C. Abbott, 'The Serious Pepys', *Yale Review*, 3:3 (1914), 551–75 (pp. 560, 561); 'Peter Easton (PHE)', comment on entry for 31 May 1669, Pepysdiary.com, www.pepysdiary.com/diary/1669/05/31/#c463972 (3 June 2012).
44. In the 'Everyman's Library' series: *The Diary of Samuel Pepys, Selected from the Complete Diary (XI vols) edited by Robert Latham and William Matthews*, ed. by Kate Loveman (Knopf: New York, 2018).
45. PROB 1/9, Will of Samuel Pepys (1703), codicil, 12 May 1703.
46. 'Household word' is Bright's phrase (Bright, I, viii).

1 Writing the Diary

1. LM Diary, I, 1–2; PL 1836, Diary, 1 Jan. 1660.
2. [William Stevenson], Review of Braybrooke 1825, *Westminster Review*, vol. 4, Oct. 1825, 408–56 (p. 409); [Robert Louis Stevenson], 'Samuel Pepys', pp. 34–5.
3. [Walter Scott], Review of Braybrooke 1825, *Quarterly Review*, 33:66, Mar. 1826, 281–314 (p. 283); LM Diary, I, cvii.

4. For example, Francis Barker, *The Tremulous Private Body: Essays on Subjection* (London: Methuen, 1984), pp. 3–9; James Grantham Turner, 'Pepys and the Private Parts of Monarchy', in *Culture and Society in the Stuart Restoration*, ed. by Gerald MacLean (Cambridge: Cambridge University Press, 1995), pp. 95–110 (pp. 96, 98); and, on this divide, Aaron Kunin, 'Other Hands in Pepys's Diary', *MLQ*, 65:2 (2004), 195–219 (pp.195–200).

5. For example, Braybrooke 1825, I, vii; [Cunningham], *The Athenaeum*, 8 July 1848, p. 669; Henry B. Wheatley, *Samuel Pepys and the World He Lived In* (London: Bickers and Son, 1880), p. 16.

6. UCLA, Matthews Papers, 509, Box 8, Folder 1, draft of 'Composition and Literary Art', pp. 13–14, compare LM Diary, I, cvii. See also [Stevenson], 'Samuel Pepys', p. 36; Bradford, *Soul of Samuel Pepys*, p. 20.

7. For example, [Cunningham], *The Athenaeum*, 8 July 1848, p. 669; contrast LM Diary, I, cvii.

8. See William Matthews's analysis in LM Diary, I, c–cii and Mark S. Dawson, 'Histories and Texts: Refiguring the Diary of Samuel Pepys', *Historical Journal*, 43:2 (2000), 407–31 (pp. 415–17).

9. LM Diary, I, 243 (11 Sept. 1660); II, 73 (12 Apr. 1661); VII, 421 (25 Dec. 1666): VIII, 162 (10 Apr. 1667).

10. Thomas Rugg, *The Diurnal of Thomas Rugg, 1659–1661*, ed. by William L. Sachse (London: Royal Historical Society, 1961), p. 1; Mark Goldie, *Roger Morrice and the Puritan Whigs: The Entring Book, 1677–1691* (Woodbridge: Boydell Press, 2016); *The Diary of John Evelyn*, ed. by E. S. De Beer, 6 vols (Oxford: Clarendon Press, 1955), I, 84.

11. J[ohn] B[eadle], *The Journal or Diary of a Thankful Christian* (London, 1656); Effie Botonaki, 'Seventeenth-Century Englishwomen's Spiritual Diaries: Self-Examination, Covenanting, and Account Keeping', *Sixteenth Century Journal*, 30:1 (1999), 3–21; Alan Stewart, *The Oxford History of Life-Writing*, II: *Early Modern* (Oxford: Oxford University Press, 2018), pp. 142–6; Elspeth Findlay, 'Ralph Thoresby the Diarist: The Late Seventeenth-Century Pious Diary and its Demise', *Seventeenth Century*, 17:1 (2002), 108–30 (pp. 109–11).

12. *The Travels of Peter Mundy in Europe and Asia, 1608–1667*, I, ed. by Richard Carnac Temple (Cambridge: Hakluyt Society, 1907) lvii, 3; V, ed. by Richard Carnac Temple and Lavinia Mary Anstey (Ashgate: Farnham, 2010), 98, 155–7.

13. *The Journal of Edward Mountagu, First Earl of Sandwich*, ed. by R. C. Anderson (London: Naval Records Society, 1929) pp. 4, 28, 29.

14. F. R. Harris, *The Life of Edward Mountagu* (London: John Murray, 1912) I, 90 n. 2.

15. Mapperton House, Dorset, Journals of Edward Mountagu, first Earl of Sandwich, 10 vols, II, 4; VIII, 545, 548.

16. 1 January was the start of a new year by one way of counting (25 March was the other).
17. Rugg, *Diurnal*, pp. xiii–xiv, p. 1. *Mercurius Politicus* was the name of a newsbook.
18. Tomalin, *Samuel Pepys*, p. 77.
19. LM Diary I, 126, 131 (4 and 8 May 1660). See Kate Loveman, 'Pepys in Print, 1660–1703', *Oxford Handbooks Online* (2015, rev. 2018), www.academic.oup.com/edited-volume/43514/chapter/364250822.
20. For example, LM Diary, VI, 66–7 (26 Mar. 1665); VII, 426 (31 Dec. 1666).
21. LM Diary, III, 134 (9 July 1662).
22. Beadle, *The Journal or Diary*, pp. 10–11. See Findlay, 'Ralph Thoresby', pp. 108–30.
23. J. B. Williams, *Memoirs of the Life and Character of Mrs Sarah Savage*, 4th edn (London, 1829), p. x.
24. Botonaki, 'Spiritual Diaries', pp. 14–16; Adam Smyth, *Autobiography in Early Modern England* (Cambridge: Cambridge University Press, 2010), pp. 114–20.
25. London Archives, CLC/521/MS00204, Journal of Nehemiah Wallington, pp. 35, 36, 38.
26. LM Diary, IV, 149–50 (21 May 1663); VII, 63 (1 and 2 Mar. 1666).
27. LM Diary, VII, 69 (9 Mar. 1666). Prudence: LM Diary, III, 294 (26 Dec. 1662); IV, 262 (4 Aug. 1663); VII, 421 (25 Dec. 1666); VIII, 579 (13 Dec. 1667).
28. LM Diary, III, 245 (31 Oct. 1662); VI, 20 (23 Jan. 1665).
29. Adam Smyth, 'Money, Accounting, and Life-Writing, 1600–1700: Balancing a Life', in *A History of English Autobiography*, ed. by Adam Smyth (Cambridge: Cambridge University Press, 2016), pp. 86–99 (p. 86).
30. LM Diary, IV, 343 (21 Oct. 1663).
31. LM Diary, IV, 93 (3 Apr. 1663). On bribery, see Knights, 'Pepys and Corruption'.
32. Braybrooke 1825, I, vii.
33. *The Diary of Samuel Pepys*, ed. by Loveman, p. 588 (9 June 1668) (passage misprinted in LM Diary).
34. LM Diary, I, xcviii–ciii; On the influence of finance on the diary see also Smyth, 'Money', pp. 87–9.
35. For example, LM Diary, I, 152 (22 May 1660); VI, 270, 337 (16 Oct. and 22 Dec. 1665).
36. LM Diary, I, xli–xlii, xlv–xlviii. For the contents of the manuscript volumes, see the listing in this book's Bibliography.
37. Sherman, *Telling Time*, p. 35.
38. For example, Pepys recorded his purchase of Shakespeare's plays (probably the third folio) in 1664 but his only mention of reading anything in it that year

is memorizing a *Hamlet* soliloquy months later. LM Diary, V, 198 (7 July 1664); V, 320 (13 Nov. 1664).
39. LM Diary, VI, 152 (9 July 1665).
40. Dawson, 'Histories and Texts', p. 422.
41. LM Diary, IV, 427 (20 Dec. 1663).
42. TNA, PROB 11/316/294, Will of Benjamin Scott (proved 1665).
43. LM Diary, IV, 324, 327, 332, 333 (4–13 Oct 1663).
44. LM Diary, IX, 99–100 (2 Mar. 1668).
45. Greenwich, National Maritime Museum, Caird Library, LBK-8, Letterbook of the Official Correspondence of Samuel Pepys, pp. 549–50, 604–7.
46. LM Diary VII, 331–2 (19 Oct. 1666).
47. 'Pepys's Particular Defence', in *Samuel Pepys and the Second Dutch War*, p. 326.
48. LM Diary, V, 233 (5 Aug. 1664); VII, 235 (5 Aug. 1666).
49. LM Diary VI, 181 (3 Aug. 1665).
50. LM Diary, IX, 564.
51. See Chapter 4, 'The Noble Editor', p. 73.
52. Evelyn, *Diary*, III, 278, 281–3. De Beer's edition preserves Evelyn's abbreviations, which I have sometimes expanded in square brackets for clarity. De Beer's italics indicate underlining in Evelyn's manuscript.
53. LM Diary, II, 83–5.
54. Evelyn, *Diary*, III, 281; De Beer's notes track Evelyn's debt to the newsbook's report.
55. LM Diary, II, 82 n. 7 (21 Apr. 1661).
56. Evelyn, *Diary*, I, 46, 74–5, 83–5.
57. LM Diary, II, 87. 'Foxed' means drunk.
58. LM Diary, II, 88.

2 Shorthand and Secrecy

1. Braybrooke 1825, I, title page, vii; *The Age*, 22 May 1825, p. 1; Bright, I, title page.
2. LM Diary, IX, 564–5 (31 May 1669).
3. Magdalene, L/76/1(1), Matthews Papers, Latham to R.L. Glanville, 8 Nov. 1970 (sender's copy). See Chapter 4, 'The Noble Editor', p. 71 and Chapter 5, 'Wheatley's Edition (1893–1899)', p. 88.
4. LM Diary, I, xlviii–lvi. Confusion in commentaries includes the belief that shorthand cannot be used for names or foreign words and that therefore most of Pepys's sexual passages are easily identified and read; and that shorthand is less phonetic than longhand (it can be a closer reflection of pronunciation than longhand spellings). For example, Kunin, 'Other Hands', p. 206; Berger, 'Pepys Show', p. 576.

5. Letter of 8/18 Oct. 1641, in *Comenius in England*, ed. by Robert Fitzgibbon Young (London: Oxford University Press, 1932), p. 65. On familiarity with shorthand methods see Kelly Minot McCay, '"All the World Writes Short Hand": The Phenomenon of Shorthand in Seventeenth-Century England', *Book History*, 24:1 (2021), 1–36.
6. LM Diary, VIII, 207 (9 May 1668); William Matthews, 'Introduction' to Shelton's *A Tutor to Tachygraphy* (Los Angeles: William Andrews Clark Memorial Library, University of California, 1970), p. ii.
7. Edmond Willis, *An Abbreviation of Writing by Character* ([London], 1618), fol. A3r.
8. The Pepys Library contains two manuals on Shelton's tachygraphy from 1671 (the version for Latin) and 1691 (English). These are too late to be the original copy Pepys used to learn, although he did retain the 1642 supplement *A Tutor to Tachygraphy*. Shelton's title pages declared tachygraphy was 'Approved by both unyversities', e.g. *Tachygraphy* (London, 1641, Wing S3074). *Tachygraphy* was printed at Cambridge in the 1640s and 1650s.
9. Thomas Shelton, *A Tutor to Tachygraphy* (London, 1642; Wing S3088), pp. 1–2.
10. Sara Heller Mendelson, 'Stuart Women's Diaries and Occasional Memoirs', in *Women in English Society 1500–1800*, ed. by Mary Prior (London: Methuen, 1985, repr. Routledge, 1991), pp. 181–201 (pp. 183–4); Stewart, *Oxford History of Life-Writing*, pp. 256–9.
11. Kunin, 'Other Hands', p. 206; Martin K. Foys and Whitney Anne Trettien, 'Vanishing Transliteracies in *Beowulf* and Samuel Pepys's Diary', in *Textual Cultures: Cultural Texts*, ed. by Orietta Da Rold and Elaine Treharne, Essays and Studies 63 (Cambridge: Boydell & Brewer, 2010), pp. 75–120 (p. 106).
12. LM Diary, I, 30, 115 (26 Jan. and 24 Apr. 1660).
13. Pepys's study had a key and was also where he kept his money: LM Diary, VIII, 279 (19 June 1667).
14. 'Wife' (without the incriminating 'my') is occasionally in longhand (PL 1836, Diary, 14 Feb. 1661).
15. Pepys's symbol for home was the letters 'om'.
16. *Tachygraphy* (1641, S3074), p. 1.
17. *Tachygraphy* (1641, S3074), p. 30.
18. *Tachygraphy* (1641, S3074), 'The Table' (of words).
19. PL 1839, Diary, 2 Sept. 1666.
20. LM Diary, VII, 267–8.
21. LM Diary, I, liii–liv, lv–lxi, lxvii. Robert Latham, 'Pepys and his Editors', *Journal of the Royal Society of Arts*, 132: 5334 (1984), 390–400 (p. 393); UCLA, Matthews Papers, Box 8, folder 1, 'Proposals for Text-Method' (p. 3 outlines

22. Bright, IV, 65–6.
23. Kunin, 'Other Hands', p. 216; See also Foys and Trettien, 'Vanishing Transliteracies', p. 108.
24. LM Diary, I, ciii–cv.
25. *Tachygraphy* (1641, S3074), p. 28. Guy de la Bédoyère, an experienced Shelton-writer, confirms this point: *The Confessions of Samuel Pepys* (Abacus 2025).
26. LM Diary, I, xliv–xlv.
27. LM Diary, IV, 270 (19 Aug. 1663).
28. LM Diary, I, xxviii.
29. Thomas Traherne's shorthand marginalia are examples (BL, MS Add 63054, Commentaries of Heaven, fol. 32v).
30. LM Diary, IV, 317 (24 Sept. 1663); V, 17 (16 Jan. 1664); VII, 142 (3 June 1666).
31. LM Diary, VIII, 244–5 (31 May 1667, notes by Matthews) and 255–6 (9 June 1668). 'Garbling' is Latham and Matthews's term.
32. PL 1841, Diary, 30 May 1668; LM Diary, IX, 218.
33. LM Diary, I, lxi; Turner, 'Pepys and the Private Parts', pp. 96–8.
34. Magdalene, PSL 2.2 4 2a, Bright's interleaved copy of Braybrooke 1854, II (note on 21 Feb. 1665); Bright, II, viii.
35. PL 1836, Diary, 23 Apr. 1661.
36. PL 1841, Diary, 25 Oct. 1668. The intermediate stage (ungarbled but with the polyglot) is 'imbracing the girl con my hand sub su coats and endeed I was with my main in her cony'. Pepys's addition of a letter can sometimes mean the vowel position of the next symbol is unclear.
37. PL 1841, Diary, 25 Oct. 1668, 'Deb' is named in longhand and (following some more circumspect shorthand references to her as 'the girl') again during events on 1 and 3 November, when he also notes she is his 'sacrifice'. She is 'Willet' (longhand) on 5 and 6 Nov.
38. PL 1841, Diary, 31 May 1669.
39. It seems, however, to have been disguised enough to baffle Bright who generally managed to deal with Pepys's 'dummy letters'. In his transcript, he rendered 'Deleb' as 'harlots'. This phrase did not make it into Bright's edition. Magdalene, PSL 2.2.4.4a, 31 May 1669.
40. LM Diary, V, 91, 92 (19 and 20 Mar. 1664); VII, 111–12 (28 Apr. 1666).
41. LM Diary, VII, 282 (8 Sept. 1666); VIII, 264, 276–7 (13 and 18 June 1667); IX, 466–7 (4 Mar. 1669).
42. LM Diary, II, 242 (31 Dec. 1661); V, 178 (13 June 1664); IX, 26 (16 Jan. 1668).
43. LM Diary, IX, 361, 366–7 (13 and 18 Nov. 1668). See Chapter 8, 'Girls and Women', pp. 156–7.

3 Saving the Diary

1. F. Sidgwick, 'General Introduction' to *Bibliotheca Pepysiana: A Descriptive Catalogue of the Library of Samuel Pepys*, pt. 2 (London: Sidgwick & Jackson, 1914), p. xviii. TNA, PROB 1/9, Will of Samuel Pepys, codicil 12 May 1703, and 'Scheame'.
2. *A Hue & Cry after P. and H. and Plain Truth* [London, 1679], especially pp. 2, 4.
3. LM Diary, III, 54 (30 Mar. 1662) and n.1.
4. Pepys to Arthur Charlett, 4 Aug. 1694, in *Letters and the Second Diary of Samuel Pepys*, ed. by R. G. Howarth (London: Dent, 1932), p. 244.
5. Pepys to Thomas Gale, 15 Sept. 1692, in *Private Correspondence and Miscellaneous Papers of Samuel Pepys, 1679–1703*, ed. by J. R. Tanner, 2 vols (New York: Harcourt Brace [1926]), I, 60.
6. J. D. Davies, 'Introduction' to Pepys's *Memoires 1690*, pp. vii; Loveman, 'Pepys in Print', p. 11; John Ehrman, *The Navy in the War of William III, 1689–1697* (Cambridge: Cambridge University Press, 1953), pp. 203–4.
7. For instance, *The Secret History of the Reigns of K. Charles II and K. James II* ([London], 1690), pp. 24–5.
8. Kate Loveman, *Reading Fictions: Deception in English Literary and Political Culture, 1660–1740* (Aldershot: Ashgate, 2008), pp. 110–22; Rebecca Bullard, *The Politics of Disclosure, 1674–1725: Secret History Narratives* (London: Pickering & Chatto, 2009), pp. 1–26, 45–53.
9. He enjoyed an early *chronique scandaleuse* (LM Diary, VII, 114 (1 May 1666)), retaining a later edition (PL 90) and the English translation of Procopius's *Secret History of the Court of the Emperor Justinian* (London, 1674; PL 873).
10. Davies, 'Introduction', to Pepys's *Memoires 1690*, pp. viii, xv.
11. Loveman, 'Pepys in Print', pp. 10–11.
12. Bodl., MS Rawlinson A.194, fol. 39r, Pepys to Henry Shere, 14 Aug. 1679, and fol. 86v, Pepys to James Houblon, 14 Oct. 1679. Sender's copies.
13. Samuel Pepys, *Memoires relating to the State of the Royal Navy of England* (London, 1690); translation from Cicero, *Tusculan Disputations*, trans. J. E. King (Cambridge, MA: Harvard University Press, 1927), p. 531.
14. Pepys, *Memoires of the Royal Navy*, p. 209. See Chapter 2, 'Other Readers?', p. 46.
15. BL, R.P. 694, Box 10, 941B, 'Notes – from my Conference this Day with Mrs D[awson]'; BL R.P. 550, Box 8, 941B, George Hickes to Pepys, 9 Dec. 1701. These drafts and letters were not preserved as part of the Pepys Library.
16. William Prynne, *A Breviate of the Life of William Laud* (London, 1644; PL 2136(1)); Thomas Fuller, *The Church-History of Britain* (London, 1656; PL 2437), Book II, p. 218. Pepys often read the *Church-History* during the 1660s.

17. Michel-Rolph Trouillot, *Silencing the Past: Power and the Production of History* (Boston, MA: Beacon Press, 1995), p. 52.
18. See advice from William Coventry, LM Diary, VIII, 15 (16 Jan. 1667).
19. LM Diary, V, 31 (30 Jan.), 360 (31 Dec. 1664). Pepys to Gale, 13 Sept. 1692, in *Private Correspondence*, ed. by Tanner, I, 60.
20. LM Diary, V, 91 (19 Mar. 1664). For example, Bodl., MS Rawlinson A.182, fols. 290, 342, 348, 353.
21. Alan Stewart discusses it as evidence for Pepys's concern for his posterity. *Oxford History of Life Writing*, p. 269.
22. LM Diary, III, 257–8 (13 Nov. 1662).
23. PL 1837, Diary, 9 Jan. 1663.
24. Pepys habitually wrote 'joyn' in both shorthand and longhand; the emphasis by using longhand here may not be intentional, but it fits the sense.
25. LM Diary, IX, 267, 286, 289, 291, 292, 304, 338, 358–9 (24 July; 23, 27, 28, 29 Aug.; 11 Sept.; 26 Oct.; 12 Nov. 1668). PL 2242, 'Papers Conteyning my Addresse to his Royall Highnesse [...] With his Royal Highness's Proceedings upon the Same and their Result'.
26. LM Diary, IX, 547–8 (8 May 1669); PL 2242, 'Papers Conteyning my Addresse to his Royall Highnesse'.
27. TNA, ADM 7/827, 'Duke of York's Orders and Instructions', fols. 54r–74v; Carlisle, Cumbria Archive Centre, DLONS/L/13/7/2/15, Book of Copy of Admiralty Papers.
28. LM Diary, IX, 335, 337–9 (23 and 25–6 Oct. 1668).
29. 'Mr Pepys on the Conditions of a Private Library', in *Private Correspondence*, ed. by Tanner, II, 247–8, compare BL, MS Add. 78680, Evelyn Papers DXIII, item 17.
30. Appendix Classica, 'Contents', pp. 10, 207–23. Pepys to Charlett, 4 Aug. 1694, in *Letters*, ed. by Howarth pp. 244–5.
31. Appendix Classica, pp. 81–107, 125–144B.
32. BL, MS Add. 78680, item 17, fol. 2r 'The Conditions of a Private Library'.
33. On Paul Lorrain and John Jackson's roles in cataloguing see, Kate Loveman, 'Hans Sloane, Samuel Pepys, and the Evidence of a Lost Pepys Library Catalogue', *Electronic British Library Journal* (2021), Article 8, pp. 4–5.
34. Appendix Classica, pp. 276, 299.
35. LM Diary, IX, 277 (10 Aug. 1668).
36. *The Pepys Ballads*, ed. by W. G. Day, 5 vols (Cambridge: Brewer, 1987), Facsimile I, verso of title page.
37. On the growth of this interest see Rosemary Sweet, 'Antiquarian Transformations in Historical Scholarship: The History of Domesticity from Joseph Strutt to Thomas Wright', in *Revisiting the Polite and Commercial*

People, ed. by Elaine Chalus and Perry Gauci (Oxford: Oxford University Press, 2019), pp. 153–70.

38. For more on this point, see Kate Loveman, *Samuel Pepys and his Books: Reading, Newsgathering, and Sociability, 1660–1703* (Oxford: Oxford University Press, 2015), pp. 245–6, 263–74.
39. Appendix Classica, p. 161. In the 'Miscellany' (PL 2874): 'A Journal of What Passed between the Commissioners of Accounts and Myself' (1670) pp. 385–504. In 'Book of Mornamont' (PL 2881): 'A Journal of the Principal Passages relating to the Commitment of Sir Anthony Deane and Mr Pepys', pp. 45–77 and PL 2882, 'A Journal [. . .] of All Passages relating to the Information Given me by Harris and James' (1680), pp. 1189–235.
40. Appendix Classica, p. 163.
41. Paul Lorrain to Pepys, 12 Oct. 1700, in *Private Correspondence*, ed. by Tanner, II, 89.
42. Appendix Classica, p. 10. Thomas Shelton's *Tachy-graphia* (London, 1671; PL 402(1)), *A Tutor to Tachygraphy* (London, 1642; PL 402(11)); *Tachygraphy* (London, 1691; PL 860(10)).
43. Appendix Classica, p. 164.
44. TNA, PROB 1/9, Will of Samuel Pepys, 'Scheame'.
45. PROB 1/9, 'Scheame'. Henry B. Wheatley, *Pepysiana* (London: Bell and Sons, 1899), pp. 33–4.
46. PROB 1/9, codicil, 12 May 1703.
47. PL 1836, Diary, 23 April 1661; PL 1839, Diary, 2 Sept. 1666.
48. Fuller, *Church-History*, Book XI, p. 218. See also Loveman, 'Pepys in Print', pp. 16–17.
49. *Private Correspondence*, ed. by Tanner, II, 315.
50. Magdalene, A/41/1, Indenture between Ann Jackson [. . .] and the Master and Fellows, 1 June 1724.
51. Magdalene, A/41/1, Indenture.
52. Wheatley, *Pepysiana*, p. 34; M. E. J. Hughes, *The Pepys Library and the Historic Collections of Magdalene College Cambridge* (London: Scala, 2015), p. 23.
53. Christian Gabriel Fischer, 'Herrn Nathanael Jacob Gerlachs Erste [. . .] Reise', in Albert Predeek, 'Bibliotheksbesuche eines gelehrten Reisenden im Anfange des 18. Jahrhunderts', *Zentralblatt für Bibliothekswesen*, 45 (1928), 221–65 (p. 246). Translated from German and Latin.
54. LM Diary, VIII, 264 (13 June 1667).

4 First Publication

1. Peter David Looker, 'Performing Pepys: Publication and Reception of the *Diary* in the Early Nineteenth Century' (unpublished PhD thesis, Australian National University, Canberra, 1996), pp. 11, 16; Steinitz, *Time, Space, and Gender*, pp. 120, 122.

2. David Hume, *The History of Great Britain*, II (London, 1757), 371–2, 434; Oliver Goldsmith, *The History of England from the Earliest Times*, 4 vols (Dublin, 1771), III, 257–8, 263, IV, 3–4; John Bigland, *The History of England* (London, 1813), II, 396–7; James Granger, *A Biographical History of England*, 5th edn (London, 1824), IV, 120–1, 127.
3. Early nineteenth-century editions of *Hudibras* included ones with illustrations by Hogarth (1810), by Rowlandson (1810) and with new notes (1819).
4. C. H. Firth, 'The Development of the Study of Seventeenth-century History', *Transactions of the Royal Historical Society*, 7 (1913), 25–48 (p. 41); Looker, 'Performing Pepys', pp. 95–6, 97–8; Steinitz, *Time, Space, and Gender*, p. 3.
5. [Anthony Hamilton], *Memoirs of the Life of Count de Grammont* (London, 1714), title page, pp. 1–2. Compare Hamilton, *Memoirs of the Count of Grammont* [ed. by Walter Scott] (London: 1811) vol. I, p. 1.
6. *A Supplement to the Great Historical [...] Dictionary [...] by Jer[emy] Collier [...] With A Continuation from the Year 1688 [...] By Another Hand* (London, 1705), fol. b3v, 'Preface' to the *Continuation*, fols. A2r, G1v–G2r. The author (like Hewer) was familiar with Pepys's early life, details of his will, and how he wanted to be remembered.
7. [John Barrow], Review of Phillip Patten's *The Natural Defence of an Insular Empire*, *Quarterly Review*, Nov. 1810, pp. 326–7.
8. Thomas Percy, *Reliques of Ancient English Poetry* (London, 1765), I, xi; [David Dalrymple], *An Account of the Preservation of King Charles II* (Glasgow, 1766). See also LM Diary, I, lxxiii–iv.
9. James Granger, *A Biographical History of England* (London, 1769), vol. II, pt 2, 530–2.
10. *Private Journal and Literary Remains of John Byrom*, ed. by Richard Parkinson, vol. I, pt 1 (Manchester, 1854), 301–2; Timothy Underhill, 'John Byrom and Shorthand in Early Eighteenth-century Cambridge', *Transactions of the Cambridge Bibliographical Society*, 15 (2013), 229–77 (p. 235).
11. Thomas Frognall Dibdin, *Bibliomania, or Book Madness* (London, 1811), pp. 421–2. On the restrictions, see Chapter 3, 'The Library', pp. 59–60.
12. Foys and Trettien, 'Vanishing Transliteracies', pp. 113–15.
13. Dibdin, *Bibliomania*, p. 422.
14. *A Later Pepys: The Correspondence of Sir William Weller Pepys*, ed. by Alice C. C. Gaussen, 2 vols (London: Bodley Head, 1904), II, 52, 64.
15. Sir Nathaniel Wraxall to Sir William Weller Pepys, 13 Aug. 1821, in *A Later Pepys*, ed. by Gaussen, II, 56. Wraxall quotes Weller Pepys's words on possible publication of the diary, eight months before John Smith finished his transcript.
16. See Chapter 3, 'Best Laid Plans', p. 62.

17. Foys and Trettien, 'Vanishing Literacies', p. 113.
18. LM Diary, I, 253. *A Later Pepys*, ed. by Gaussen, II, 64; [Charles Taylor], 'History and View of the Tea Trade', *Literary Panorama*, June 1807, p. 569.
19. Markman Ellis, *The Coffee House: A Cultural History* (London: Weidenfeld & Nicolson, 2004), pp. 209–10.
20. *Monthly Repository*, 20, Sept. 1825, p. 522; [Joseph Snow], *Gentleman's Magazine*, Sept. 1825, p. 235; *New Monthly Magazine*, 14 (1825), p. 101 (published by Colburn).
21. Magdalene, L/71/PLB/75, William Wyndham Grenville to George Neville, 21 Aug. 1818 and 13 Dec. 1818.
22. John Smith to the editor, *Illustrated London News*, 27 Mar. 1858, p. 311, and 17 Apr. 1858, p. 394; Henry Gunning, *Reminiscences of the University, Town, and County of Cambridge*, 2nd edn (London: Bell, 1855), I, 311–12.
23. *Illustrated London News*: Smith to the editor, 27 Mar. 1858, p. 311, and 17 Apr. 1858, p. 394; Ralph Neville Grenville to the editor, 10 Apr. 1858, p. 366.
24. LM Diary, I, lxxvi–lxxvii, xc. Foys and Trettien note the popularity of this story about Smith's efforts and were sceptical of it: they were right to be so ('Vanishing Literacies', pp. 112, 115).
25. 'Heaven' next appeared on 1 May 1660 and, for the eating house, on 30 Aug. 1660, showing Smith had not yet worked on these entries when he wrote the note. Smith refers to the Worcester manuscript in a note on the entry for 23 May 1660. Magdalene, PSL, 2.1.1, John Smith's transcription titled 'The Private Journal of Samuel Pepys, Esquire'. *Catalogue of the Pepys Library, Facsimile of Pepys's Catalogue*, ed. by David McKitterick, VII.i, 'Alphabet', p. 8.
26. Smith to the editor, *Literary Gazette*, 12 Dec. 1840, p. 798; Smith to the editor, *Illustrated London News*, 27 Mar. 1858, p. 311, and 17 Apr. 1858, p. 394; Braybrooke 1825, I, title page, xi.
27. Sources he consulted for January 1660 included Bulstrode Whitelocke's *Memorials*, Johnson's *Dictionary*, and the Commons' Journal (PSL 2.1.1, fol. 29v, fol. 32v).
28. PSL 2.1.15, Smith explains his use of 'obj' at the entry for 16 Jan. 1664, describing it as a response to Pepys's 'strange mixture of French, Latin and English words'. The passage in question, however, predates the polyglot and just uses French and English.
29. For example, Pepys's visit to Mrs Bagwell, 20 Feb. 1665, PSL. 2.1.20, fol. 85r.
30. PSL, 2.1.50, fol. 973r.
31. For example, *Literary Gazette*, 25 June 1825, p. 407; *Monthly Repository*, 20, Aug. 1825, p. 449. Braybrooke to the editor, *Notes and Queries*, series 1, 212 (1853), p. 502.
32. PSL 2.1.29, fol. 818v.

33. Steinitz, *Time, Space, and Gender*, pp. 123–4; [Snow], *Gentleman's Magazine*, Sept. 1825, p. 233; [Francis Jeffrey], *Edinburgh Review*, 43:85, Nov. 1825, p. 34. Looker also notes reviewers' attention to Pepys's "unmanly" interest in clothing, and points out that Braybrooke's abridgement served to highlight such passages ('Performing Pepys', pp. 264–9).
34. Braybrooke 1825, I, vii.
35. Braybrooke 1825, I, vii, xxx, xxxiv. For the duke's letter and Pepys's *Memoires* (1690), see Chapter 3.
36. Looker, 'Performing Pepys', pp. 186–92.
37. Braybrooke, 1825, I, vi–vii.
38. Braybrooke 1825, II, 149 (26 Oct. 1667), 270 (23 Oct. 1668).
39. Braybrooke 1825, I, vii.
40. 15 May 1660: PSL 2.1.2, fol. 251r; Braybrooke 1825, I, 45.
41. *Literary Gazette*, 21 May 1825, p. 336.
42. *Monthly Repository*, 20, Aug. 1825, p. 449.
43. On Colburn's repute see John Sutherland and Veronica Melnyk, *Rogue Publisher, The 'Prince of Puffers': The Life and Works of the Publisher Henry Colburn* (Brighton: EER, 2018), pp. 66–9.
44. *Literary Gazette*, 2 July 1825, p. 423. The *Gazette*'s coverage appears to be the work of the editor, William Jerdan, with Colburn supplying information.
45. *The Times*, 27 June 1825, p. 2; [William Stevenson], *Westminster Review*, Oct. 1825, p. 408; Gunning, *Reminiscences*, II, 314–15.
46. For example: *The Times*, 27 June 1825, p. 2; [Snow], *Gentleman's Magazine*, Sept. 1825, pp. 233, 235 and Oct. 1825, p. 339; [?Albany Fonblanque], *The Examiner*, 26 Sept. 1825, p. 607; *Monthly Repository*, 20, Nov. 1825, p. 675; *Edinburgh Review*, Nov. 1825, pp. 30, 44–6; *New Monthly Magazine*, 14 (1825), p. 104.
47. *Literary Gazette*, 18 June 1825, pp. 385, 387.
48. Bedfordshire Archives, L30/11/330/174, Harriet Yorke to Amabel Hume-Campbell, Countess de Grey, 6 Aug. [1825]. My thanks to Natasha Simonova for alerting me to this source and supplying information.
49. *The Examiner*, 26 Sept. 1825, p. 607.
50. Mark Salber Phillips, *Society and Sentiment: Genres of Historical Writing 1740–1820* (Princeton, NJ: Princeton University Press, 2000), especially pp. 55–6, 152, 295.
51. Looker, 'Performing Pepys', pp. 124, 296. 'Trifling occurrences' is Braybrooke's phrase (Braybrooke 1825, I, vi).
52. Steinitz, *Time, Space, and Gender*, p. 120; see also Phillips, *Society*, pp. 266–7, 300–4.
53. Braybrooke 1825, I, 232. *Literary Gazette*, 9 July 1825, pp. 441–2.

54. *Westminster Review*, Oct. 1825, p. 410.
55. [Walter Scott], *Quarterly Review*, Mar. 1826, pp. 283, 287–8.
56. *Quarterly Review*, Mar. 1826, pp. 309–13.
57. *Quarterly Review*, Mar. 1826, pp. 296–7, 298, 300.
58. *Literary Gazette*, 18 June 1825, p. 385, compare *The Examiner*, 26 Sept. 1825, p. 607 and *Quarterly Review*, Mar. 1826, p. 289.
59. *Gentleman's Magazine*, Sept. 1825, p. 234; *Edinburgh Review*, Nov. 1825, p. 37.
60. Steinitz, *Time, Space, and Gender*, p. 119, citing *Quarterly Review*, Mar. 1826, p. 304.
61. *Edinburgh Review*, Nov. 1825, p. 40; *Westminster Review*, Oct. 1825, p. 455.
62. Bedfordshire Archives, L30/11/330/174.
63. *Literary Gazette*, 9 July 1825, p. 440.
64. *Gentleman's Magazine*, Sept. 1825, pp. 233, 234.
65. *Edinburgh Review*, Nov. 1825, pp. 24–5, 40.
66. *The Examiner*, 26 Sept. 1825, pp. 607, 609.
67. *Westminster Review*, Oct. 1825, pp. 410, 414. Looker, 'Performing Pepys' (p. 260) and Phillips, *Society* (pp. 302–3) remark that the sense of the *Memoirs*' relevance in this review relies on seeing human nature as unchanging.
68. *Westminster Review*, Oct. 1825, p. 455.
69. Looker, 'Performing Pepys', pp. 270–9; Steinitz, *Time, Space, and Gender*, pp. 120–1.
70. George Otto Trevelyan, *The Life and Letters of Lord Macaulay*, 2 vols (London: Longman Green, 1876), II, 418.
71. Trevelyan, *Life and Letters of Macaulay*, I, 184.
72. [Macaulay], Review of *The Romance of History* by Henry Neele ('History'), *Edinburgh Review*, no. 94, May 1828, pp. 361–5.
73. Looker, 'Performing Pepys', pp. 273–7.
74. Braybrooke 1825, I, 197, 199 (7 and 17 Feb. 1663). For the episode, see Introduction, 'Scandal', p. 4.
75. [Macaulay], Review of *The Constitutional History of England*, by Henry Hallam, *Edinburgh Review*, no. 95, Sept. 1828, pp. 153, 168–9.
76. Thomas Babington Macaulay, *The History of England from the Accession of James II*, I (London: Longman, 1849), pp. 3, 191; compare Braybrooke 1825, II, 77–8 (21 June 1667).
77. Macaulay, *History*, I, 288, 299, 305, 335–6, 340, 373, 382–3, 409, 418.
78. *Appendix Classica*, p. 299.
79. *Westminster Review*, Oct. 1825, p. 409.
80. J. G. Lockhart, *Memoirs of the Life of Sir Walter Scott, Bart.*, VI (Edinburgh, 1837), 122–3; Scott, *The Journal of Sir Walter Scott*, I (Edinburgh: Douglas, 1890), 218.
81. Trevelyan, *Life and Letters of Macaulay*, II, 243.

5 Victorian Pepys

1. Bright, I, viii.
2. *Sydenham Times*, 14 Sept. 1880, p. [3]; Wheatley, I, lix–lx.
3. Wheatley, I, vi. Proportions from LM Diary, I, lxxxiv, lxxxviii, xciii.
4. [Peter Cunningham], Review of Braybrooke 1848 vol. III, *The Athenaeum*, 9 Sept. 1848, p. 902.
5. *Notes and Queries*, 4th series, vol. 5, 12 Mar. 1870, p. 288. *The Bookseller*, 1 Mar. 1870, p. 286; 3 July 1875, p. 592, and 5 Aug. 1875, p. 674.
6. *Literary Gazette*, 22 Apr. 1848, p. 287.
7. Braybrooke, 1848, I, vi–vii. This was reproduced in the 1854 edition.
8. 23 Apr. 1661: Braybrooke 1825, I, 103, 105; Braybrooke 1848, I, 221, 225; compare LM Diary, II, 84, 87.
9. Bright, I, xiv note 1; II, viii. LM Diary, I, lxxxviii.
10. For example, Magdalene, PSL 2.2.4. 4a, Bright's interleaved copy of Braybrooke 1854, polyglot at 25 Oct. and 13 Nov. 1668.
11. Bright, I, ix.
12. Bell to the editor, *The Academy*, 22 May 1875, p. 533. Magdalene, LN 45, Latimer Neville to Bright, 7 May 1875; Bell on his legal position, June 1875.
13. 'Notes and News', *The Academy*, 10 Apr. 1875, p. 372; 'Notice' by George Bell and Sons, *Publishers' Circular*, 16 Nov. 1875, p. 938.
14. Magdalene, L/71/PLB, Box 3, file 66, Bickers and Son to Latimer Neville and fellows, 23 July 1883 and to Latimer Neville, 13 June 1884.
15. Henry B. Wheatley, 'The Growth of the Fame of Samuel Pepys', in *Occasional Papers Read by Members at Meetings of the Samuel Pepys Club*, ed. by Wheatley (London: Chiswick Press, 1917), pp. 156–73 (p. 163); Wheatley, *Samuel Pepys*, contents.
16. Magdalene, L/71/PLB, Box 3, File 66, J. Patrick to H. Bickers, 10 July 1883; W. Aldis Wright to J. Patrick, 25 Nov. 1884; George Bell and Sons to the Master and Fellows, 27 Mar. 1885; Memorandum Agreement between Latimer Neville and George Bell and Sons, 10. Nov. 1885.
17. Close to publication, Wheatley also had the opportunity to see Smith's transcript, which was given to Magdalene by Braybrooke's relatives. See LM Diary, I, xcii–xciii.
18. Pepys's great fit of the colic was less eruptive: Wheatley, III, 296, 298 (7 and 11 Oct. 1663).
19. Wheatley, VI, 337 (26 May 1667); VII, 79 (10 Aug. 1668).
20. Magdalene, L/7/PLB, Box 3, File 66, Edward Bell to Latimer Neville, 16 Jan. 1895; Neville to Bell and Sons, 31 July 1896. The college had previously benefited from editors donating sums received from publishers. Magdalene College, PSL 1/1/4, D. Pepys Whiteley, 'First Transcript of Pepys [sic] Diary', fol. 68v.
21. Wheatley, I, vii, viii.

22. Wheatley, I, lvii–lix.
23. Review of Bright's vol. I, *The Athenaeum*, 29 Jan. 1876, p. 158.
24. [Hunt], *Edinburgh Review*, Oct. 1841, pp. 107–8.
25. LM Diary, IX, 368.
26. 'Town and Table Talk on Literature', *Illustrated London News*, 20 Mar. 1858, p. 295.
27. Magdalene, LN 45, William Chappell to Latimer Neville, 28 Mar. 1871. Chappell quoted a letter from an unnamed acquaintance of his and Braybrooke's.
28. Braybrooke 1848, IV, 206 (27 Sept 1667); V, 31.
29. Braybrooke 1848, V, 82.
30. Bright, V, 380, 397 (25 Oct and 13 Nov. 1668) compare LM Diary, IX, 337, 361. Compare also, for example, entries for 27 Oct., 12 and 14 Nov., 18–20 Nov. 1668, and 13 Apr. 1669.
31. Other cuts of this nature include removing Pepys's references to being 'troubled for the poor girl' (26 and 27 Oct.) and all the attack on Deb's character on 12 November. Bright, V, 380, 381, 358.
32. [Stevenson], 'Samuel Pepys', p. 46. LM Diary, V, 348 (19 Dec. 1664); Bright, III, 92 (26 Dec. 1664).
33. [Stevenson], 'Samuel Pepys', p. 31.
34. Wheatley, VIII, 131 (25 Oct. 1668).
35. *Notes and Queries*, Review of Wheatley vol. VIII, 8th series, vol. 9, 1 Feb. 1896, p. 99; see also Review of Wheatley, *Quarterly Review*, Jan. 1896, p. 5.
36. Review of Wheatley vol. II, *Saturday Review*, 23 Sept. 1893, p. 359. 'Soi-disant' means 'so-called', 'points' are dots, and 'aposiopeses' are abrupt halts. See also, Charles Whibley's comments in, 'The Real Pepys', *New Review*, 14 (1896), pp. 368–9.
37. Braybrooke 1848, IV, 159 (18 Aug. 1667); *Morning Post*, 1 Feb. 1849, p. 8.
38. *Cheltenham Chronicle and Gloucester Advertiser*, 20 Sept. 1849, p. 4.
39. Braybrooke 1848, III, 170 (17 Mar. 1666).
40. Peter Cunningham, 'The Story of Nell Gwyn', *Gentleman's Magazine*, 35, Feb. 1851, p. 115 and plate; Bright, III, 423; Wheatley, I, frontispiece.
41. William Carpenter, Jr, 'Charles II, in Holland, before the Restoration' (16 May 1660), *The Exhibition of the Royal Academy 1848* (London, 1848), p. 26; a picture on the same scene was in the 1858 exhibition. H. O'Neil, 'An Incident in the Plague of London' (3 Mar. 1665), *The Exhibition of the Royal Academy of Arts 1875* (London, 1875), p. 49 – and another on the same topic in 1898.
42. Braybrooke 1848, III, 383 (23 Jan. 1667). Augustus Egg, 'Pepys' Introduction to Nell Gwynne', *The Exhibition of the Royal Academy of Arts 1851* (London, 1851) p. 23; *Illustrated London News*, 17 May 1851, p. 46.

43. Braybrooke 1848, III, 157 (15 Feb. 1666); Alfred Elmore, 'A Subject from Pepys' Diary', *The Exhibition of the Royal Academy of Arts 1852* (London, 1852), p. 15. *The Examiner*, 15 May 1852, p. 311; *Illustrated London News*, 26 June 1852, p. 504. *The Art-Journal*, 1 July 1866, after p. 204.
44. 'Miscellaneous Notices', *New Monthly Magazine*, 87, Sept. 1849, p. 130. 'Racy' was in use in the senses 'invigorating' and 'characteristically lively', but the use here has implications of a sense the *OED* first records in 1901: 'daring ... risqué'. *Oxford English Dictionary*, s.v. 'racy (*adj.1*),' December 2023, doi.org/10.1093/OED/1159893694.
45. Dudley Costello, 'An Evening with Knipp', *New Monthly Magazine*, 87, Oct. 1849, 206–26 (pp. 220, 225, 226). Compare Braybrooke 1848, III, 142–4 (6 and 7 Jan. 1666).
46. For example, Braybrooke's note on Pepys's motivation on 6 Aug. 1666 (III, 252), compare Costello, p. 216.
47. *The Sun*, 3 Oct. 1849, [p. 3].
48. Bright, I, viii. Bright mistakenly attributed the column to Thackeray.
49. *Punch*, 16 (1849), p. 114.
50. Jane Goodall, 'Reverse Ethnology in *Punch*', *Popular Entertainment Studies*, 2:1 (2011), 5–21 (p. 7).
51. *Punch*, 17 (1849), p. 112.
52. Richard Doyle and Percival Leigh, *Manners and Cvstoms of ye Englyshe [...] to which be Added Some Extracts from Mr Pips hys Diary* (London: Bradbury & Evans [1849]), preface.
53. *The Diary of Samuel Pepys Esq., while an Undergraduate at Cambridge*, 2nd edn (Cambridge: Palmer, 1866); [Emma Buller], *Fragments of Mr. Pips his Diary during a Tour in the Western Provinces, September 1670* ([privately printed, c.1850]); *Monmouthshire Merlin*, 27 Oct. 1849, p. 3; 'Mr Pips his Diary', *Sydney Morning Herald*, 11 Aug. 1855, p. 8.
54. *Biographical and Descriptive Sketches of the Distinguished Characters [...] of Madame Tussaud and Sons* (London: privately printed, 1851).
55. Patrick A. Dunae, 'Penny Dreadfuls: Late Nineteenth-Century Boys' Literature and Crime', *Victorian Studies*, 22:2 (1979), 133–50 (p. 136).
56. Peter Yeandle, *Citizenship, Nation, Empire: The Politics of History Teaching in England, 1870–1930* (Manchester: Manchester University Press, 2015), especially p. 25, ch. 1.
57. For example, *Stories from English History*, Cassell's Historical Course for English Schools (London: Cassell, 1884), pp. 128, 134–7; Charlotte M. Yonge, *English History Reading Book, Part I* (London: National Society's Depository [1881]) pp. 75–8.

58. *The School Board Readers, Standard VI* (London: Griffin, 1872), pp. ii, 15–20; Charlotte M. Yonge, *English History Reading Book*, part 5 (London: National Society's Depository [1883]), preface, p. 192.
59. *Stories from English History*, p. 137. Christopher Banham, '"England and America against the World": Empire and the USA in Edwin J. Brett's *Boys of England*, 1866–99', *Victorian Periodicals Review*, 40:2 (2007), 151–71 (p. 153).
60. John Finnemore, *Famous Englishmen, Book II: Cromwell to Roberts* (London: Black, 1902), pp. 27, 29–30.
61. 'T.B.', 'The Great Fire of London', *Juvenile Companion and Sunday-School Hive*, 24, 1 Apr. 1871, pp. 85–7.
62. Banham, '"England and America against the World"', p. 151.
63. *Boys of England*, 20, 6 Oct. 1876, p. 304.
64. 'Mr Pips hys Diary' had been the title of parody when it was published as a book in 1849.
65. Elinor Glyn, *Romantic Adventure Being the Autobiography of Elinor Glyn* (London: Nicholson and Watson, 1936), pp. 22–3. Glyn's comments indicate she was reading Pepys in the early 1870s, before Bright's edition was out. She was, at this time, Elinor Sutherland.
66. [Stevenson], 'Samuel Pepys', p. 41.
67. Wilbur C. Abbott, 'The Serious Pepys', *Yale Review*, 3:3 (1914), 551–75 (pp. 558, 560, 564).
68. Abbott, 'The Serious Pepys', pp. 566, 567. Abbott designated this figure 'the social Pepys' in a passage added to the essay in the second edition of his collection *Conflicts with Oblivion* (Cambridge, MA: Harvard University Press, 1935), p. 30.
69. Abbott, 'The Serious Pepys' (1914), pp. 555, 566, 568.
70. Wheatley, 'Growth of the Fame', pp. 162, 172, 173.

6 War and the Diary

1. Samuel and Elizabeth appeared in, for example, Louis N. Parker's hit *Mavourneen: A Comedy in Three Acts* (1916) and Clifford Bax's *Mr Pepys: A Ballad Opera* (1926). Bax's opera was broadcast on BBC radio the same year. 'Mr Pepys', 23 Apr. 1926, in 'Bournemouth Programmes', 16 Apr. 1926, *Radio Times*, p.162 https://genome.ch.bbc.co.uk/page/96cb0d35c54441b789674777fd2fb6c7.
2. Player's Cigarette cards, set of '50 Dandies' (1932); London & North Eastern Railway, 'Passengers of the Past' campaign, 'Pepys', by Austin Cooper (1929). Other brands included Schweppes tonic in 1937 and Castell's, which brought out a range of diaries under its Pepys brand (e.g. the 'St Paul's Diary' for 1948).

3. Percy Lubbock, *Samuel Pepys* (New York: Scribner's Sons, 1909), p. 2; E. Hallam Moorhouse, *Samuel Pepys: Administrator, Observer, Gossip* (London: Chapman and Hall, 1909), p. 13; Bradford, *Soul of Samuel Pepys*, pp. 4–5.
4. Looker, 'Performing Pepys', pp. 309–12; Lubbock, *Samuel Pepys*, p. 4; *The Diary of Samuel Pepys: Selections*, ed. by N. V. Meeres (London: Macmillan, 1913), p. v; Moorhouse, *Samuel Pepys*, p. 3; Bradford, *Soul of Samuel Pepys*, p. 4.
5. *Everybody's Pepys*, ed. by O. F. Morshead, illustrated by Ernest H. Shepard (London: Bell and Sons, 1926). For example, Lubbock, *Samuel Pepys*, p. 4; Bradford, *Soul of Samuel Pepys*, pp. 3–4.
6. 'Pop culture (n.)', *Oxford English Dictionary*, September 2023, doi.org/10.1093/OED/5473513726.
7. 'Pepys and Black-Out', *The Scotsman*, 22 Jan. 1942, p. 4.
8. *Juvenile Companion and Sunday-School Hive*, 24, 1 April 1871, p. 86. See Chapter 5, 'Education and Miseducation', pp. 101–2.
9. O. F. Morshead, 'Introduction', *Everybody's Pepys*, p. xii. Morshead was Magdalene's Pepys librarian.
10. Emma Beatrice Brunner, *My Wife, Poor Wretch: Uncensored Episodes Not in the Diary of Samuel Pepys* (New York: Stokes, 1928); E. Barrington [Elizabeth Louisa Moresby], *The Great Romantic, Being an Interpretation of Mr. Saml Pepys and Elizabeth his Wife* (London: Cassell, 1933); and F. D. Ponsonby Senior's *The Diary of Mrs Pepys* (1934).
11. *The Diary of Elizabeth Pepys* "edited by" Dale Spender (London: Grafton, 1991); Sara George, *The Journal of Mrs Pepys* (London: Review, 1998). Liza Picard's history *Restoration London* (London: Weidenfeld & Nicolson, 1997) began life as research for a diary of Elizabeth Pepys (Benjamin Buchan, 'Liza Picard Obituary', *The Guardian*, 22 June 2022, www.theguardian.com/books/2022/jun/10/liza-picard-obituary).
12. For the tongs episode and Costello see Chapter 5, 'Suppressed Passages', p. 92, and 'Imagining Pepys: Pictures, Fiction, Parody', pp. 94, 98–9. Instances of Elizabeth in drama include Parker, *Mavourneen*, pp. 137–41; Angela Bartie, Linda Fleming, Mark Freeman, Tom Hulme, Alex Hutton and Paul Readman, 'The Hinchingbroke Pageant' (1912) www.historicalpageants.ac.uk/pageants/1094/ at *The Redress of the Past: Historical Pageants in Britain* database.
13. Bradford, *Soul of Samuel Pepys*, pp. 200–1; Meeres, *Diary of Samuel Pepys*, p. vi.
14. E[sther] Hallam Moorhouse, author of *Samuel Pepys: Administrator, Observer, Gossip* (1909) is one exception.
15. Brunner, *My Wife, Poor Wretch*, pp. 3, 159, 255, 256, 259.

16. First published as E. Barrington, 'A Portion of the Diurnal of Mrs Eliz[th] Pepys', *The Atlantic*, April 1921, 440–8. Republished as 'The Diurnal of Mrs Eliz[th] Pepys', in Barrington, *The Ladies! A Shining Constellation of Wit and Beauty* (Boston, MA: Atlantic Monthly Press, 1922), pp. 1–21.
17. For example, Barrington, *The Great Romantic*, p. 176–7. Compare LM Diary, VI, 158–9 (15 and 16 July 1665).
18. The name change for Betty Becke signals the departure from history, but may well have had an additional motive: at the time of writing Elizabeth Moresby's married name was Beck, making her a Betty Beck.
19. *The Great Romantic*, p. 125.
20. 'Diurnal of Mrs Eliz[th] Pepys' (1921), pp. 447–8; *The Great Romantic*, pp. 299–301, 308, 317–18.
21. Stevenson, 'Samuel Pepys', p. 46; Barrington, *The Great Romantic*, pp. 315, 316.
22. Arthur Bryant, *Samuel Pepys: The Man in the Making* (Cambridge: Cambridge University Press, 1933), pp. 28, 239, 284.
23. Bryant, *Man in the Making* (1933), pp. xii–xiii; *Samuel Pepys: The Years of Peril*, new edn (London: Collins, 1948), p. xii; *Samuel Pepys: The Saviour of the Navy*, new edn (London: Collins, 1949), p.[i]. Wheatley, 'Growth of the Fame', p. 162.
24. On Bryant's sales see, Julia Stapleton, *Sir Arthur Bryant and National History in Twentieth-Century Britain* (Lanham, MD: Lexington, 2005), p. 88; Reba N. Soffer, *History, Historians, and Conservatism in Britain and America: From the Great War to Thatcher and Reagan* (Oxford: Oxford University Press, 2008), p. 128.
25. *Samuel Pepys: The Man in the Making*, new edn (London: Collins, 1947), pp. [i–ii].
26. *Man in the Making* (1933), pp. 265–74.
27. On this issue see letters from Bryant to Edwin Chappell, 1932–3, described by Richard M. Ford Ltd at www.abebooks.co.uk/paper-collectibles/Sir-Arthur-Bryant-defends-against-attack/30303237606/bd [accessed 4.5.24]; Stapleton, *Sir Arthur Bryant*, pp. 86–7.
28. Bryant, *Man in the Making* (1947), xi–xii. The phrase 'father of the Civil Service' for Pepys seems to have originated with Bryant.
29. Bryant, *Samuel Pepys: The Saviour of the Navy* (Cambridge: Cambridge University Press, 1938), p. 304. Compare, *Man in the Making* (1933), pp. 2, 344.
30. Stapleton, *Sir Arthur Bryant*, pp. 89–91; Soffer, *History*, p. 128.
31. Stapleton, *Sir Arthur Bryant*, pp. 134, 141–59; Soffer, *History*, pp. 132–3.
32. Bryant, *Man in the Making* (1947), pp. xi, xii.

33. Stapleton describes Bryant's disillusionment with the Labour government elected in 1945 (*Sir Arthur Bryant*, pp. 212–14).
34. *Sam Pepys Joins the Navy*, dir. Francis A. Searle (Ministry of Information, 1941), Imperial War Museum, www.iwm.org.uk/collections/item/object/1060019999.
35. Ministry of Information, Home Intelligence Service Report 16, 18 Apr. 1942, www.moidigital.ac.uk/reports/home-intelligence-reports/home-intelligence-special-report-inf-1-293/idm140465680335680/.
36. Claire Langhamer, 'Who the Hell are Ordinary People? Ordinariness as a Category of Historical Analysis', *Transactions of the RHS*, 28 (2018), 175–95, esp. pp. 176–7, 187–8.
37. Joe Moran, 'Private Lives, Public Histories: The Diary in Twentieth-Century Britain', *Journal of British Studies*, 54:1 (2015), 138–62 (pp. 139, 150).
38. Laura Carter, *Histories of Everyday Life: The Making of Popular Social History in Britain, 1918–1979* (Oxford: Oxford University Press, 2021), pp. 4, 39, 40–3. Publishers' interest in cheap, popular Pepys editions predates the mid twentieth century, however. See Chapter 5.
39. [R. M. Freeman and Robert Augustus Bennett], *A Diary of the Great Warr by Saml Pepys Junr* (London: Lane, 1916; 2nd edn 1917); *A Second Diary of the Great Warr* (London: Lane, 1917), pp. 102, 112, 167; *A Last Diary of the Great War* (London: Lane, 1919).
40. Other titles being *Samuel Pepys Looks at Life* (1931); *Samuel Pepys, Listener* (1931); and *Samuel Pepys and the Minxes* (1939).
41. Preface by Collin Brooks in R. M. Freeman, *Pepys and Wife Go to It* (London: Hale, 1941), p. 5.
42. For example, the bombing raid seen from Selsdon on 15 Aug. 1940, which Pepys junior notes is his closest encounter with a raid yet, was close to Freeman's home. *Pepys and Wife Go to It*, pp. 220–3.
43. LM Diary, VIII, 552–3.
44. LM Diary, VI, 210.
45. [Freeman and Bennett], *Second Diary of the Great Warr*, p. 20.
46. *The Times*, 17 Oct. 1916, p. 4.
47. *TLS*, 764, 7 Sept. 1916, p. 423.
48. 'Introduction', *Pepys and Wife Go to It*, pp. 6–7.
49. Peter Mandler, *The English National Character: The History of an Idea from Edmund Burke to Tony Blair* (New Haven, CT: Yale University Press, 2006), pp. 1–2, 164–5.
50. *TLS*, 7 Sept. 1916, p. 423.
51. *Pepys and Wife Go to It*, pp. 6–7.
52. *Mrs Miles's Diary: The Wartime Journal of a Housewife on the Homefront*, ed. by S. V. Partington (London: Simon & Schuster, 2013), pp. 1–18. Imperial

War Museum, Documents.9485, Private Papers of Mrs C. Miles, 'War Diary', I, 66 (29 Sept. 1939). Volume numbers given here are those from the handlist.
53. Miles, 'War Diary', VII, 53–4 ([16 Jan.] 1942).
54. Mass Observation, File Report 1332, Report on Books and the Public, 1942, p. 175, via Mass Observation Online, www.massobservation.amdigital.co.uk/. 'Biography' shared second place with 'Travels'.
55. Mass Observation, Report on Books, pp. 170–1; Gill Plain, *Literature of the 1940s: War, Postwar and 'Peace'* (Edinburgh: Edinburgh University Press, 2013), ch. 5.
56. Miles, 'War Diary', II, 270 (14 Jan. 1940); VII, 81 (3 Feb. 1942) and 147 ([28] Mar. 1942).
57. 'War Diary', V, 727 (18 Oct. 1940).
58. For historians: 'War Diary', V, 872 (2 Jan. 1941); VII, 76 (31 Jan. 1942). Worries: II, [n. pg.] (19 Dec. 1939); VII, 151 ([1 Apr.] 1942).
59. See Chapter 4, 'The Noble Editor', pp. 72–3.
60. Moran, *Private Lives*, pp. 141, 151. *Wartime Women: An Anthology of Women's Wartime Writing for Mass-Observation, 1937–45*, ed. by Dorothy Sheridan (London: Mandarin, 1991), p. 18.
61. For example, 'War Diary', II, 234 (25 Dec. 1939), on Charles Ricketts's *Self Portrait* (1939), 'His words about the worth-whileness of diary-keeping heartened me. I was feeling this journal was hardly worth writing'; IV, 685–6 (29 Sept. 1940); VII, 35 (5 Jan. 1942).
62. 'War Diary', II, [n. pg.] (19 Dec. 1939).
63. 'War Diary', I, 37 (11 Sept. 1939); II, 289 (23 Jan. 1940).
64. 'War Diary', V, 808 (4 Dec. 1940).
65. 'War Diary', VII, 33–4 (4 Jan. 1942).
66. Alwyn Collinson, 'A New Year's Letter from the Second Great Fire of London', Museum of London, www.museumoflondon.org.uk/discover/blitz-letter-great-fire-1940 [accessed 20 Feb. 2024].
67. 'War Diary', V, 868–70 (30 and 31 Dec. 1940). Compare '1940's Great Fire Circles St Paul with Flames', *News Chronicle*, 31 Dec. 1940, p. 6.
68. 'War Diary', VI, 897 (11 Jan. 1641).
69. LM Diary, VII, 271.
70. Robert Dillon, *History on British Television: Constructing Nation, Nationality and Collective Memory* (Manchester: Manchester University Press, 2010), pp. 36, 50. *BBC Handbook 1959* (London: BBC, 1958), p. 208.
71. A. R. Rawlinson, 'A Letter to Samuel Pepys', *Radio Times*, vol. 138, no. 1790, 28 Feb. 1958, p. 3.
72. Ernest Thomson, 'In the Days of Pepys: The Diary Comes to Life on the Screen', *Children's Newspaper*, 22 Feb. 1958, p. 4.

73. Reading, BBC Written Archives, Microfilm TV Drama Scripts 29/30, *The Diary of Samuel Pepys* (hereafter *DSP*) by A. R. Rawlinson, episode 11, pp. 12, 17; Thomson, 'In the Days of Pepys', p. 4.
74. Reading, BBC Written Archives, R9/7/33, *The Diary of Samuel Pepys*, Audience Research Report: episode 1.
75. 'A Letter to Samuel Pepys', *Radio Times*, 28 Feb. 1958, p. 3.
76. *DSP*, episode 1, p. 8; episode 7, p. 20; episode 13, p. 19.
77. *DSP*, Audience Research Reports: episode 1 and final episode.
78. *DSP*, episode 1, pp. 1–2.
79. *DSP*, episode 9, pp. 8, 12, 26–8; episode 14, pp. 29a–30.
80. *DSP*, Audience Research Report: episode 1.
81. *DSP*, Audience Research Reports: episode 7 and final episode.
82. *DSP*, Audience Research Report: final episode.
83. *DSP*, Audience Research Reports: episode 1 and final episode; Thomson, 'In the Days of Pepys', p. 4.
84. *DSP*, Audience Research Report: final episode. Pepys had an average 12% audience share to Austen's 17%.
85. Reading, BBC Written Archives, R9/7/33, Audience Research Report, *The Benny Hill Show*, 1 Mar. 1958. Hill was able to achieve a 30% audience share.
86. Benny Hill, 'Pepys Diary', Youtube, footage compiled by The Benny Hill Fan Consortium, www.youtube.com/watch?v=82TX_88r3zcNB.
87. Benny Hill, Pepy's [sic] Diary, 1961 recording, on Vinylfun, Youtube www.youtube.com/watch?v=tVWuRYd3-rg; Official Singles Chart, 2 March 1961, www.officialcharts.com/charts/singles-chart/19610302/7501/; 1971 version, The Benny Hill Consortium, Youtube, www.youtube.com/watch?v=7zKb55uh4TI; 1989 lyrics at 'Pepys's Diary', The Benny Hill Show Wikia, www.benny-hill.fandom.com/wiki/Pepy%27s_Diary (song).
88. On English comic stereotypes derived from music hall, see Andy Medhurst, *A National Joke: Popular Comedy and English Cultural Identities* (London: Routledge, 2007), pp. 64–7, 134.
89. Georges Couturier, *L'Honorable Monsieur Pepys* (1943); 'Théatre d'Atelier: L'Honorable Monsieur Pepys', *Aujourd'hui*, 20 Feb. 1943 ('vaudevillesque comédie'); Francis Ambrière, 'La Critique dramatique', *Opéra*, 16 Apr. 1947, p. 5.
90. [Scott], *Quarterly Review*, Mar. 1826, pp. 298, 300.
91. *The Listener*, 13 Mar. 1958, p. 468.

7 'Every Last Obscenity': Complete and Online

1. LM Diary, I, title page.
2. UCLA, Matthews Papers, 509, Box 8, Folder 5, draft 'The Hazards of Transcribing Pepys', Edinburgh (c.1964), p. 11.

3. The most widely published abridgement is *The Shorter Pepys*, ed. by Robert Latham (Bell & Hyman, 1985). It was published in the Penguin Classics series in 1993 and, from 2003, retitled *The Diaries of Samuel Pepys: A Selection*.
4. Majorie Heins, *Not in Front of the Children: "Indecency", Censorship and the Innocence of Youth*, 2nd edn (New Brunswick, NJ: Rutgers University Press, 2007), pp. 27–9, citing (1868), Regina v. Hicklin L.R. 3 Q.B. 360.
5. Magdalene, B/605/p.469/min 36 duplicate, 22 July 1933, Francis Turner, 'Mr Bryant's Life of Pepys'. See also Bryant, *Man in the Making* (1933), pp. xi–xii, 315.
6. Magdalene College, Pepys Library Reference Collection, 'Buffet', no. 48, G. H. Bickers to Francis Turner, 14 Feb. 1936.
7. On prosecutions of literary works see Robertson, *Obscenity*, pp. 35–7.
8. Magdalene, 'Buffet', no. 48, Bickers to Turner, 14 Feb. 1936.
9. J. D. Rolleston, 'Venereal Disease in Pepys's Diary', *British Journal of Venereal Diseases*, 19:4 (1943), 169–73, (p. 170).
10. Indiana University, Kinsey Institute, Alfred Kinsey to Henry Willink, 16 Apr. 1952 and Willink to Kinsey, 1 May 1952, via www.sexandsexuality.amdigital.co.uk/.
11. U.K. Government, Obscene Publications Act 1959, c. 66 section 4(1), www.legislation.gov.uk/ukpga/Eliz2/7-8/66/section/4/enacted.
12. Magdalene, D/G/56(A) (enclosure), 'Opinion of Mr Gerald Gardiner Q.C.', 1 Mar. 1960, pp. 3, 4.
13. Obscene Publications Act 1959, c. 66 section 1(1). Gardiner, 'Opinion', pp. 3 (spelling of 'prurient' silently corrected), 4, 6; compare p. 1.
14. Obscene Publications Act 1959, c. 66 section 1(1).
15. Gardiner, 'Opinion', p. 5.
16. Gillian Freeman, *The Undergrowth of Literature* (London: Panther, 1969), pp. 25–6, 70–1, 111–12.
17. Gardiner, 'Opinion', pp. 5–6.
18. Gardiner, 'Opinion', p. 4.
19. David Nokes, 'Crowning Ceremony', *TLS*, 18 Mar. 1983, p. 263.
20. Magdalene, D/G.56(A), A. W. Ready to J. F. Burnet, 9 Mar. 1960; Burnet to Ready, 31 Oct. 1960.
21. Magdalene, F/CSL/2(f), C. S. Lewis to Henry Willink, 12 June 1960.
22. Magdalene, Arthur Bryant to Francis Turner, 17 Sept. 1960 (no catalogue number).
23. Magdalene, B/610, Governing Body Minute, 20 July 1960; D/G/56(A), J. F. Burnet to A. W. Ready, 31 Oct. 1960.
24. See Chapter 4, 'The Decipherer', pp. 69–70; and Chapter 5, 'Bright's Edition (1875–1879)', pp. 87–8.

25. UCLA, Matthews Papers, 509, Box 14, Folder 4, untitled draft talk to audience at Birkbeck, first in a series [1963], [p. 1].
26. Latham, 'Pepys and his Editors', p. 393.
27. Latham, 'Pepys and his Editors', p. 395.
28. UCLA, Matthews papers, 509, Box 14, Folder 3, Matthews, 'Prior Texts and Editors' (draft for the Introduction to LM Diary), p. 15; compare LM Diary, I, xciv, where Wheatley is 'hardly the best'.
29. LM Diary, I, lv–lxi.
30. UCLA, Matthews Papers, Box 8, Folder 5, draft 'The Hazards of Transcribing Pepys', Edinburgh (c.1964), p. 7.
31. UCLA, Matthews Papers, Box 14, Folder 4, speech on the 'hazards' of transcribing the diary (revised c.1966), p. 8a.
32. Magdalene, L/76/1(1), Latham to R. Glanville, 8 Nov. 1970 (sender's copy).
33. Magdalene, L/76/1(1), Matthews to Glanville, 23 Mar. 1970; Matthews to Walter Hamilton, master of Magdalene, 24 Mar. 1970; Latham to Matthews, 26 Apr. 1970 (sender's copy).
34. Magdalene, L/76/1(1), Latham to R. Glanville, 8 Nov. 1970 (sender's copy).
35. Magdalene, L/76/1(1), Matthews to Dudley V. Durrell, 17 Nov. 1970 (copied to Latham); UCLA, Matthews Papers, Box 8, Folder 5, draft 'The Hazards of Transcribing Pepys', Edinburgh (c.1964), p. 7.
36. Matthews continued to submit work he expected to be published: Magdalene, L/76/1(1), Matthews to Latham, 16 Dec. 1972. After his death in 1975, an agreement was reached to pay royalties to his estate and to Latham. Matthews's arguments may well have been remembered, for the college gave up some of its royalties to seal this agreement. See Eamon Duffy, 'Robert Clifford Latham, 1912–1995', *Proceedings of the British Academy* 166 (2010), 198–211 (p. 210); LM Diary, XI (London: Bell & Hyman, 1983), copyright page.
37. See *Thanks for Typing: Remembering Forgotten Women in History*, ed. by Juliana Dresvina, (London: Bloomsbury Academic, 2021), especially 'Editor's Introduction', pp. 1–8 and Rebecca E. Lyons, 'Thanks for Penguin: Women, Invisible Labour and Publishing in the Mid-Twentieth Century', pp. 50–9 (pp. 55–8).
38. Pryor had done a separate reading of three volumes of typescript against the galleys. For this – not part of her normal role – she had been unpaid. LM Diary, I (London: Bell and Sons: 1970), p. xiv; Magdalene, L/76/1(1), Matthews to Latham, 20 May 1970.
39. LM Diary, I (1970), p. xiv.
40. Magdalene, L/76/1(1), Matthews to R. Glanville, 16 Feb. 1970.
41. LM Diary, I (1970) second title page; Magdalene, L/76/1(1), Latham to Matthews, 1 May 1970 (sender's copy). It would be wrong to see this

situation as Latham disputing women's right to credit while Matthews defended it. Latham was responding to William Matthews's recently citing Lois's work as a reason why he, William, deserved the largest share of the royalties. This – as Latham pointed out – was to claim any work done by her as his own.

42. It won the Wheatley Medal in 1983. In a neat coincidence, Henry B. Wheatley, prior to editing Pepys, was founder of the Index Society. The prize was later named in his honour.
43. LM Diary, XI (1983), title page, p. xv.
44. *A Pepys Anthology*, 'selected and edited by Robert and Linnet Latham' (Unwin Hyman, 1987, repr. London: HarperCollins, 2000).
45. LM Diary, I (1970), p. xiv.
46. Michael Ratcliffe, 'Power and a Pimple', *The Times*, 27 May 1976, p. 10. Compare Nigel Dennis, 'Pepys the Perfect Hypocrite', *Sunday Telegraph*, 8 Aug. 1976, p. 9.
47. For example, Ian W. Archer, 'Social Networks in Restoration London: The Evidence from Samuel Pepys's Diary', in *Communities in Early Modern England*, ed. by Alexandra Shepard and Phil Withington (Manchester: Manchester University Press, 2000), pp. 76–94; Kay Staniland, 'Pepys and his Wardrobe', *Costume*, 37:1 (2003), 41–50; Benjamin Kohlmann, "Men of Sobriety and Buisnes': Pepys, Privacy and Public Duty', *Review of English Studies*, 61 (2009), 553–71; Picard, *Restoration London*; Joseph Roach 'Celebrity Erotics: Pepys, Performance, and Painted Ladies', *Yale Journal of Criticism*, 16:1 (2003), 211–30.
48. See Chapter 8, 'Girls and Women', pp. 156, 158.
49. Under the terms of the 1956 Copyright Act, www.legislation.gov.uk/ukpga/Eliz2/4-5/74/enacted.
50. Pepysdiary.com is Wheatley's text, from an electronic edition originally produced by David Widger for Project Gutenberg. Phil Gyford, 'About the Text', pepysdiary.com, www.pepysdiary.com/about/text/.
51. Wheatley, I, vii.
52. [Virginia Woolf], 'Papers on Pepys', *TLS*, 4 Apr. 1918, p. 161.
53. On 31 May 1669 entry, 'Eric Walla', www.pepysdiary.com/diary/1669/05/31/#c462714 (31 May 2012). Other readers commented similarly: www.pepysdiary.com/diary/1669/05/31/#c464044.
54. See Chapter 6, 'Prime-Time TV', p. 127.
55. Entry of 31 May 1669, 'Betty Birney', www.pepysdiary.com/diary/1669/05/31/#c463090 (1 June 2012) and 'Dan Jones', www.pepysdiary.com/diary/1669/05/31/#c464093 (4 June 2012).
56. Although see Braybrooke 1854, I, 261, note (2 Mar. 1662) and Bright, I, xii–xiii, note.

57. Phil Gyford, 'Why I Turned Pepys' Diary into a Weblog', BBC News, 2 Jan. 2003, http://news.bbc.co.uk/1/hi/uk/2621581.stm.
58. Elizabeth Long, 'Textual Interpretation as Collective Action', *Discourse*, 14:3 (1992), 104–30 (pp. 117–18); David Peplow, *Talk about Books: A Study of Reading Groups* (London: Bloomsbury Academic, 2016), pp. 140–1, 171–3.
59. Comments on entry of 29 Mar. 1667, made 29–31 Mar. 2010 (1st cycle), www.pepysdiary.com/diary/1667/03/29/#c296395.
60. Comments on entry of 29 Mar. 1667, made 30–1 Mar. 2020 (2nd cycle), www.pepysdiary.com/diary/1667/03/29/#c549381.
61. Dorothy Anger, *Other Worlds: Society Seen through Soap Opera* (Peterborough, Ont.: Broadview, 1999), pp. 131–4.
62. Peplow, *Talk about Book*s, pp. 159–61.
63. Comment on 5 Sept 1666 entry, 'Nate', www.pepysdiary.com/diary/1666/09/05/#c285259 (7 Sept. 2009)
64. Comment on 4 Sept. 1666 entry, 'Doug', www.pepysdiary.com/diary/1666/09/04/#c285131 (4 Sept. 2009).
65. LM Diary, VII, 268 (2 Sept. 1666).
66. Gyford, 'Samuel Pepys and the Virus', 25 Mar. 2020, www.pepysdiary.com/news/2020/03/25/14052/
67. @Pepys_Diaries, twitter.com/Pepys_Diaries/status/1240668872757391360?s=20 (19 Mar. 2020), 715 retweets (recorded 16 Oct. 2023). An example of the parody with the attribution to Pepys: @CraigOliver100 (23 Mar. 2020), x.com/CraigOliver100/status/1242174298279862273?s=20, 1,120 retweets (recorded 13 Apr. 2024).
68. LM Diary, VII, 40–1 (12 Feb. 1666). Research from Twitter ("X") records on 16 Oct. 2023: @Crashtestbiker, x.com/Crashtestbiker/status/1243826023386558464?s=20 (28 Mar. 2020); @kirstentelliot replied to another account, pointing out the parallel with the parody passage: x.com/KirstenTElliott/status/1242936088739659776?s=20 (22 Mar. 2020).
69. Comment on 20 Mar. 1666/7 entry, 'Tonyel', www.pepysdiary.com/diary/1667/03/23/#c549340 (24 Mar. 2020).
70. Comment on 11 May 1667 entry, 'Timo', www.pepysdiary.com/diary/1667/05/11/#c549650 (11 May 2020). The reference to 'parish records' of deaths evokes the bills of mortality monitored by Pepys.
71. Comment on 15 Mar. 1666/7 entry, 'San Diego Sarah', www.pepysdiary.com/diary/1667/03/15/#c549273 (15 Mar. 2020) and on 10 June 1665 entry, www.pepysdiary.com/diary/1665/06/10/#c555324 (13 Feb. 2022).
72. See Chapter 4, 'Reading Pepys's *Memoirs*', p. 75; and Chapter 5, 'Suppressed Passages', p. 93.

73. Bright's edition does not mention Wheatley's paid work on it. Smith, Braybrooke, and Wheatley were each married while working on their editions – there is no record of any spousal editorial assistance.
74. There is, however, a simple technique to identify a Georgian or Victorian abridgement. Braybrooke's, Bright's, and Wheatley's Pepys is fond of exclamations; Latham and Matthews's Pepys is far less excitable: if the Pepys in front of you is saying 'But Lord!', rather than 'But Lord' and his wonder is frequently punctuated with '!' you are reading an abridged text.

8 Reading against the Grain

1. Review of Bright vol. I, *The Athenaeum*, 29 Jan. 1876, p. 158; UCLA, Matthews Papers, 509, Box 8, Folder 5, draft 'The Hazards of Transcribing Pepys', Edinburgh (c.1964), p. 11.
2. *The Shorter Pepys*, ed. by Robert Latham (London: Penguin, 1993), p. xix; Wheatley, I, lviii (quoting Lowell); *Diary of Samuel Pepys*, ed. by Loveman, dust jacket flap copy ('surprising frankness'). *The Oxford Encyclopedia of British Literature*, ed. by David Scott Kastan (Oxford: Oxford University Press, 2006), IV, 212; LM Diary I, cx.
3. For example, Trouillot, *Silencing the Past*, especially pp. 26–7; Ann Laura Stoler, *Along the Archival Grain: Epistemic Anxieties and Colonial Common Sense* (Princeton, NJ: Princeton University Press, 2009), pp. 46–51; Frances E. Dolan, *True Relations: Reading, Literature, and Evidence in Seventeenth-Century England* (Philadelphia: University of Pennsylvania Press, 2013), pp. 112–18; Marisa J. Fuentes, *Dispossessed Lives: Enslaved Women, Violence, and the Archive* (Philadelphia: University of Pennsylvania Press, 2016), pp. 1–12, 78.
4. 'Black' (with upper-case letter) is used here for people of the African diaspora.
5. See Chapter 5, 'Imagining Pepys: Pictures, Fiction, Parody', pp. 98–9; and Chapter 6, 'The Great Romantic: Novels', pp. 111–13.
6. Tomalin, *Samuel Pepys*, pp. 236–8, 242–51.
7. Phrase from Nigel Dennis, 'Pepys the Perfect Hypocrite' (review of LM Diary, vol. IX), *Sunday Telegraph*, 8 Aug. 1976, p. 9.
8. For example, J. A. Rogers, *Nature Knows No Color-Line*, 3rd edn (New York, NY: Helga M. Rogers, 1952), p. 165; Folarin Shyllon, *Black People in Britain, 1555–1833* (London: Oxford University Press, 1977), p. 10–11; Imtiaz Habib, *Black Lives in the English Archives, 1500–1677: Imprints of the Invisible* (Aldershot: Ashgate, 2008, repr. London: Routledge, 2016), pp. 179–81, 222–4; Simon P. Newman, *Freedom Seekers: Escaping from Slavery in Restoration*

9. See Chapter 5, 'Reputations', pp. 104–6, 107; and Chapter 6, 'A Great Englishman: Biographies', pp. 114–15.
10. LM Diary, IX, 20 (12 Jan. 1668). LM Diary, IV, 9–10 (9 Jan. 1663) – see Chapter 3, 'Controlling Archives', pp. 52–3. LM Diary, VI, 46–7 (28 Feb. 1665).
11. Tomalin, *Samuel Pepys*, p. 204.
12. LM Diary, V, 14 (12 Jan. 1664); 24 (21 Jan.), 61 (22 Feb.), 145–6 (11 May), 151 (15 May).
13. PL 1841, Diary, 10 Nov. 1668.
14. LM Diary, IX, 369 (20 Nov. 1668).
15. LM Diary, IX, 210–11 (24 May 1668).
16. LM Diary, III, 206 (27 Sept. 1662), compare 210 (30 Sept. 1662). Tomalin, *Samuel Pepys*, p. 161.
17. LM Diary, IX, 404 (31 Dec. 1668); IV, 158 (26 May 1663).
18. Braybrooke 1825, I, vii.
19. On the interest in Mrs Knepp, see Costello's 'An Evening with Knipp' (1849), discussed in Chapter 5, 'Imagining Pepys: Pictures, Fiction, Parody', pp. 98–9.
20. For example, Wheatley, IV, 357–8 (20 and 21 Feb. 1664/5); V, 40 (6 Aug. 1665), 153 (23 Nov. 1665), 189 (5 Jan. 1666).
21. See Chapter 7, 'The Public Good', p. 136. An exception is the word 'moher' (Spanish: mujer), meaning wife/woman, which appears in the edition's glossary, e.g. LM Diary, I, 343.
22. For example, LM Diary, XI, 'Bagwell, –, wife of William', 'Udall (Huedell), Frances'.
23. Robert Nye, 'Samuel Pepys: An Angel with Tatty Wings', *The Scotsman*, 14 Nov. 1970, p. 3; Peter Lewis, 'The Bedtime Story that Made Mrs Pepys See Red', *Daily Mail*, 12 Aug. 1976, p. 7; Ratcliffe, 'Power and a Pimple', p. 10.
24. LM Diary, IX, 366 (18 Nov. 1668).
25. E. Pearlman, 'Pepys and Lady Castlemaine', *Restoration*, 7 (1983), 43–53, (p. 43), quoting John Harold Wilson and Richard Ollard.
26. For example, John Vance, 'Pepys, Lady Castlemaine and the Restoration Frame of Mind: A Rejoinder [to Pearlman],' *Restoration*, 9 (1985), 31–6, (p. 32); Berger, 'Pepys Show', p. 564; *Restoration Literature: An Anthology*, ed. by Paul Hammond (Oxford: Oxford University Press, 2002), p. 265; Tomalin, *Samuel Pepys*, pp. 207, 269; Ian Mortimer, *A Time Traveller's Guide to Restoration Britain* (London: Bodley Head, 2017), p. 111; and in my own work, 'Samuel Pepys and Deb Willet', p. 893.

27. For example, Timothy Meldrum, *Domestic Service and Gender, 1660–1750: Life and Work in the London Household* (Harlow: Pearson Education, 2000), p. 109; Bernard Capp, *When Gossips Meet: Women, Family, and Neighbourhood in Early Modern England* (Oxford: Oxford University Press, 2003), pp. 141–2, 158–9.

28. Meldrum, *Domestic Service*, p. 109 and n. 82. LM Diary, XI, for example, 'Mercer, Mary', 'Willet, Deb'.

29. LM Diary, IV, 282, 283–4 (20 and 21 Aug. 1663), 438 (31 Dec. 1663); V, 55 (21 Feb. 1664); VI, 70 (29 Mar. 1665); VII, 108 (23 Apr. 1666). On concepts of maturity, see Sarah Toulalan, '"Unripe" Bodies: Children and Sex in Early Modern England', in *Bodies, Sex and Desire from the Renaissance to the Present*, ed. by Kate Fisher and Sarah Toulalan (Houndmills: Palgrave Macmillan, 2011), pp. 131–50 (pp. 134, 136–7); Toulalan, '"Is He a Licentious Lewd Sort of a Person?": Constructing the Child Rapist in Early Modern England', *Journal of the History of Sexuality*, 23 (2014), 21–52 (pp. 30–1, 33).

30. LM Diary, VI, 185 (6 Aug. 1665).

31. LM Diary, VII, 4–5 (5 Jan. 1666); VIII, 114 (15 Mar. 1667). Tooker is a 'child' at VI, 262 (11 Oct. 1665) and VII, 50 (20 Feb. 1666). Uses of 'little' include VI, 278, 284 (25 and 31 Oct. 1665). For combing see also IX, 277 (10 Aug. 1668).

32. LM Diary, VIII, 158–9, 224, 456. 'Touch' is used in equivalent passages in English, e.g., IX, 55 (6 Feb. 1668).

33. Mary R. Block, 'For the Repressing of the Most Wicked and Felonious Rapes and Ravishments of Women: Rape Law in England, 1660–1800', in *Interpreting Sexual Violence, 1660–1800*, ed. by Anne Greenfield (London: Routledge, 2016), pp. 23–33 (pp. 26–7).

34. LM Diary, VIII, p. 323. An episode also discussed in Laura Gowing, 'Women in the World of Pepys', in *Samuel Pepys: Plague, Fire, Revolution*, ed. by Margarette Lincoln (London: Thames and Hudson, 2015), pp. 73–9 (p. 76).

35. Faramerz Dabhoiwala, *The Origins of Sex: A History of the First Sexual Revolution* (London: Allen Lane, 2012), pp. 147–8; Garthine Walker, 'Rereading Rape and Sexual Violence in Early Modern England', *Gender & History*, 10:1 (1998), 1–25 (p. 6); Laura Gowing, *Common Bodies: Women, Touch and Power in Seventeenth-Century England* (New Haven, CT: Yale University Press, 2003), p. 100.

36. LM Diary, VII, 153 (7 June 1666), 319 (12 Oct. 1666).

37. LM Diary, VIII, 255–6, 318 (9 June and 3 July 1667).

38. Ratcliffe, 'Power and a Pimple', p. 10. Dabhoiwala discusses Pepys's predations but stops short of considering his acts as potential rapes (*Origins of Sex*, pp. 146–7). Geoffrey Pimm is prepared to consider that Pepys committed rape and his book's promotional material uses the term

'rapist'. However, the tone and depth of this consideration is conveyed by Pimm's comments that the woman concerned 'did not come quietly' and that Pepys records 'resorting to rape when the lady became completely intractable' (*The Dark Side of Samuel Pepys: Society's First Sex Offender* (Barnsley: Pen & Sword, 2017), pp. 106, 152). There are additional problems with Pimm's analysis: it is often confused when glossing Pepys's language (including both polyglot and Pepys's English, such as relating pronouns to the right person), e.g., pp. 80–1, 99, 110–11, 130–1. While it indicates it employs the Latham and Matthews edition (p. x), it repeatedly uses what appears to be Wheatley's text, e.g., pp. 103 (15 Nov. 1664), 112–13 (11 Feb. 1667).

39. Block, 'Repressing of the Most Wicked', pp. 23–33, especially p. 31; Garthine Walker, 'Rape, Acquittal and Culpability in Popular Crime Reports in England, c.1670–c.1750', *Past & Present*, 220 (2013), 115–42 (pp. 125 n. 39, 128–30, 134).
40. Gowing, *Common Bodies*, p. 101.
41. TNA, PROB 11/443/275, Will of William Bagwell (proved 1698); PROB 11/466/77, Will of Elizabeth Bagwell (proved 1702). Guy de la Bédoyère has recently confirmed this identification via a baptism record for Elizabeth Bagwell's son, John, on 20 July 1673 at St Mary, Chatham. Medway Archives, P85/1/4.
42. LM Diary, IV, 222, 266 (9 July and 7 Aug. 1663); V, 313, 322 (3 and 15 Nov. 1664).
43. LM Diary, V, 351 (20 Dec. 1664).
44. LM Diary, VI, 39–40 (20 and 21 Feb. 1665).
45. For example, John Trapp, *A Commentary or Exposition upon the XII Minor Prophets* (London, 1654), p. 42; *A Lamentable Ballad of the Tragical End of a Gallant Lord, and a Vertuous Lady* ([London, ?1658–1664]). Chester City Record Office, MF 86/125, examination taken 5 Aug. 1668, qu. in Walker, 'Rereading rape', p. 10; trial of William Woodbridge, 7 Dec. 1681 (t16811207-1), *Old Bailey Proceedings Online*, version 9.0, www.oldbaileyonline.org.
46. LM Diary, VI, 20, 35.
47. On vow interpretation see, in 1664, LM Diary, V, 2–3 (2 Jan.), 33 (1 Feb.), 230 (2 Aug.), 232 (4 Aug.), 236 (8 Aug.), 240 (13 Aug.).
48. LM Diary, VI, 158 (15 July 1665).
49. For example, Lawrence Stone, *The Family, Sex and Marriage in England 1500–1800* (London: Weidenfeld and Nicolson, 1977), p. 556; Pearlman, 'Pepys and Lady Castlemaine', p. 44; Nokes, 'Crowning Ceremony', p. 263.
50. Louise Ellison, 'Credibility in Context: Jury Education and Intimate Partner Rape', *International Journal of Evidence and Proof*, 23 (2019), 263–81, especially pp. 270–1; compare Walker, 'Rape, Acquittal and Culpability', p. 135.

51. K. L. Little, *Negroes in Britain: A Study of Race Relations in English Society* (London: Kegan Paul, 1947), p. 166; Rogers, *Nature Knows No Color-Line*, p. 165; James Walvin, *Black and White: The Negro in English Society, 1555–1945* (London: Allen Lane, 1973), p. 10. Little's source was a much earlier essay, 'The Black Man', published in Charles Dickens's journal *All the Year Round* (6 Mar. 1875, p. 490).
52. Habib, *Black Lives*, p. 181.
53. Bryant, *Years of Peril*, pp. 134–5, 140, 336; Bryant, *Saviour of the Navy* (1949), pp. 269–70.
54. On the distribution of London's Black inhabitants see Newman, *Freedom Seekers*, pp. 12–13, 49–50, 62.
55. In the 1660s, Assistants of 'the Company of Royal Adventurers of England trading into Africa' included, for example, Pepys's colleagues William Coventry, George Carteret, Thomas Povey, and William Rider; his business associate George Cocke; and his neighbour John Buckworth. His friend James Pearse worked as a surgeon for the company. TNA, T70/75, Company of Royal Adventurers, Minute Books, 1664–72, fols. 6r, 73r, 77r, 102v.
56. K. G. Davies, *The Royal African Company* (London: Longmans, Green and Co, 1957), pp. 41–5.
57. Such statements do not come with citations that evidence them. The idea that Pepys was a stockholder may have originated with his several references in the diary to the company's business, e.g. LM Diary, IV, 152 (23 May 1663), compare Hugh Thomas, *The Slave Trade: The History of the Atlantic Slave Trade, 1440–1870* (London: Simon & Schuster, 1997), p. 199.
58. Pepys is not listed as a founder member in the Company charters of 1660, 1663, or 1672. I have searched in stock journals, ledgers, and minutes held in the National Archives (T70/75, 76, 77, 100, 185–192, 599, 600) without locating him as an investor. Will Pettigrew's more systematic work for his project *The Register of British Slave Traders* has also found no evidence Pepys invested in the early African companies – I am grateful to him for this information.
59. For an example of Pepys aiding naval and RAC business see Holly Brewer, 'Creating a Common Law of Slavery for England and its New World Empire', *Law and History Review*, 39:4 (2021), 765–834 (pp. 790–1 and note).
60. Newman, *Freedom Seekers*, pp. xii–xiii, 43.
61. LM Diary, IX, 422 (21 Jan. 1669). Lambeth Palace Library, Vicar General Marriage Allegations 1666–1671, MS Film 442, VM I/6, 19 Mar. 1668/9.
62. For example, LM Diary, II, 61 (27 Mar. 1661); III, 95 (30 Mar. 1662); VI, 215 (7 Sept. 1665); IX, 464 (2 Mar. 1669). Habib points out that Pepys's adjectival use of 'black' is routinely understood by critics to mean 'a dark-haired person', whereas it may sometimes mean 'a black person'. *Black Lives*, pp. 179–80.

63. Habib, *Black Lives*, pp. 184–7; Brewer, 'Creating a Common Law', especially pp. 793–5. For further discussion of Brewer's treatment of race and anti-slavery sentiment, see Dana Y. Rabin, 'Slavery, Law, and Race in England and its New World Empire', *Law and History Review*, 40 (2022), 581–90.
64. Walvin, *Black and White*, pp. 64–65, 109–10; Brewer, 'Creating a Common Law', pp. 784, 795; Susan Dwyer Amussen, *Caribbean Exchanges: Slavery and the Transformation of English Society, 1640–1700* (Chapel Hill: University of North Carolina Press, 2007), pp. 114–15, 185–6, 220.
65. Bodl., MS Rawl. A.185, John Howe to Pepys, 30 Apr. 1675, fol. 66r, and 6 May 1675. fol. 70r; PL 2851, Admiralty Letters, IV, 94–5 (copy by an amanuensis). Phillip Emanuel identifies the boy offered by Howe as the boy sold by Wyborne in 1680, but there is no firm evidence to link them. Emanuel, '"[A]s Fast as Ships Return He Will Send Every One a Boy": Enslaved Children as Gifts in the British Atlantic', *Slavery & Abolition*, 44:2 (2023), 334–49 (p. 342). Bryant (*Years of Peril*, p. 140) appears to have wrongly identified the boy offered by Howe with 'Jack', a footman recommended to Pepys by Henry Shere in May 1676. There is no evidence that Jack was Black and the correspondence implies he was an employee, not enslaved. Bodl., MS Rawl. A.181, Henry Shere to Pepys, 25 May 1676, fol. 86r; MS Rawl. A.342, Shere to William Hewer, 27 May 1676, p. 2.
66. Bodl., MS Rawl. A.181, John Wyborne to Pepys, 3 June 1680, fol. 317r. MS Rawl. A.194, Pepys to John Wyborne, 4 Dec. 1679, fol. 115r (copy by amanuensis); Pepys to Wyborne, 15 June 1680, fol. 166v (copy by amanuensis).
67. PL 2861, Admiralty Letters, XIV, Pepys to Capt. Edward Stanley, 11 Sept. 1688, 408–9 (copy by amanuensis).
68. For example, LM Diary, I, 233–4 (29 Aug. 1660); II, 206–7 (2 Nov. 1661); VIII, 126 (23 Mar. 1667).
69. Bodl., MS. Rawl. A.186, 'The present Disposall of all his Majesties Shipps in Sea-Pay', 18 Oct. 1688, fol. 95v.
70. Bryant, *Saviour of the Navy* (1938), pp. 269–70 – and much reprinted. The relevant section of the letter has recently been published in Emanuel, '[A]s Fast as Ships', p. 342.
71. Tomalin, *Samuel Pepys*, pp. 180, 421n; Newman, *Freedom Seekers*, pp. 65–6.
72. Bryant, *The Years of Peril*, p. 336.
73. Bryant, *Man in the Making* (1947), p. xii.
74. On Black servants as status symbols see Kim F. Hall, *Things of Darkness: Economies of Race and Gender in Early Modern England* (Ithaca, NY: Cornell University Press, 1995), ch. 5; Amussen, *Caribbean Exchanges*, 191–217.
75. LM Diary, VI, 214–15 (7 Sept. 1665); Hall, *Things of Darkness*, p. 212, n. 1. Vyner was another of Pepys's associates who held shares in the 'Company of Royal Adventurers of England trading into Africa' (TNA, T/70/75, fol. 12v).

76. LM Diary, II, 61 (27 Mar. 1661); IX, 464 (2 Mar. 1669).
77. Buckworth, living round the corner from Pepys, was active in the Company of Royal Adventurers in the early 1660s and was made deputy governor of the RAC in 1672. TNA, T70/75, fol. 6r; TNA, T70/100, Royal African Company, General Court Minute Book, 1671–8, fol. 28v.
78. PL 1841, Diary.
79. LM Diary, II, 218 (22 Nov. 1661); V, 158–9 (27 May 1664).
80. Shelton, *Tachygraphy* (1641, S3074), 'The Table'.
81. Nell, another cookmaid, and Deb Willet. LM Diary, VIII, 419, 448 (2 and 24 Sept. 1667).
82. Amussen, *Caribbean Exchanges*, pp. 220–1.
83. 'Used' reads here as objectifying language, but in the 1660s that connotation was less strong. Pepys also writes of 'using' a coachman and a clerk, e.g. LM Diary, VIII, 173 (21 Apr. 1667).
84. Jerome S. Handler and JoAnn Jacoby, 'Slave Names and Naming in Barbados, 1650–1830', *William and Mary Quarterly*, 53:4 (1996), 685–728 (p. 699 n. 4).
85. TNA, PROB/11/325/434, Will of Sir William Batten (proved 22 Nov. 1667).
86. PL 1836, Diary, 14 Feb. 1661.
87. Alternatively, it suggests Mingo had been with Batten prior to 1659, when he married his second wife – but this would mean Pett was returning the parrot rather than gifting it. LM Diary, II, 69 (10 Apr. 1661).
88. Newman, *Freedom Seekers*, p. 43.
89. PROB/11/325/434, Will of Batten; W. R. Chaplin, 'The History of Harwich Lights and their Owners', *American Neptune*, 11 (1951), 5–35 (pp. 7–12).
90. LM Diary, IV, 86 (26 Mar. 1663).
91. Batten bequeathed profits in the lighthouse dues to his wife, children, and niece. On the strife: LM Diary, VIII, 476–7 (12 Oct. 1667); TNA, C/8/249/47, Batten vs. Batten (William Batten the grandson and his guardian vs. Elizabeth Batten).
92. Habib, *Black Lives*, pp. 223–4.
93. On service and servitude for young people see Urvashi Chakravarty, *Fictions of Consent: Slavery, Servitude, and Free Service in Early Modern England* (Philadelphia: University of Pennsylvania Press, 2022), pp. 63–7.
94. Chaplin, 'History of Harwich Lights', p. 12; 'Three Black Lightkeepers and their Stories' (31 Aug. 2021, updated 18 July 2024), *The Lighthouse Keeper's Cottage*, www.lighthousekeeperscottage.co.uk/black-lightkeepers-and-their-stories/
95. London Archives, CLC/199/TC/002/MS09659/003, Register of St Katharine by the Tower, fol. 86r.
96. This was better protection before 1686 than after. See Brewer, 'Creating a Common Law', pp. 804–9.

97. This is the only instance of a baptismal entry between 1651–1700 explicitly declaring the surname in the London Archives database *Switching the Lens: Rediscovering Londoners of African, Caribbean, Asian and Indigenous Heritage, 1561 to 1840* [accessed 25.4.24]. Such phrasing remained unusual in the early eighteenth century.
98. The last letter of 'Isay' is not well defined. 'Isaac' is unlikely as it is spelt differently by the register's scribe (Izaack(e)). Isay is a variant of 'Isaiah', meaning 'God is salvation'. There are three records of babies baptized Isay/Isaie in London between 1660 and 1680 (Ancestry.co.uk, accessed 18.4.24).
99. LM Diary, VIII, 582 (19 Dec. 1667).
100. TNA, SP/29/267, fol. 313v, Thomas Middleton to the Navy Commissioners, 19 Nov. 1669. The figure owed is expressed as '50s', with the 's' for shillings blotted.
101. TNA, PROB 11/340/502, Will of Thomas Middleton (proved 16 Dec. 1672).
102. TNA, ADM 33/95, Ships' Pay Books, Dover, 1671–74, 'Begun Wages January the first 1671/2', 6.
103. J. D. Davies, *Gentlemen and Tarpaulins: The Officers and Men of the Restoration Navy* (Oxford: Clarendon Press, 1991), pp. 79–80; J. D. Davies, *Pepys's Navy: Ships, Men and Warfare, 1649–1689* (Barnsley: Seaforth, 2008), pp. 122, 127.
104. Loveman, 'Samuel Pepys and Deb Willet', pp. 896–7. Wells had left the ship by the time William Mingo's death was recorded.
105. TNA, SP 29/309, Silas Taylor to Joseph Williamson, 21 May 1672, fol. 91; 'Journal of John Narborough', in *Journals and Narratives of the Third Dutch War*, ed. by R. C. Anderson (London: Naval Records Society, 1946), pp. 91–3.
106. TNA, ADM 33/95, Ships' Pay Books, Dover, 1671–74, 6.
107. For example, LM Diary, VIII, 476–7, 483 (12 and 17 Oct. 1667); IX, 149–50 (4 Apr. 1668).
108. See Chapter 3, 'The Library', pp. 56–8, and 'Risks and Rewards', p. 63.

Afterword

1. [Stevenson], *Westminster Review*, Oct. 1825, p. 409.
2. *Life in the United Kingdom: A Guide for New Residents*, 3rd edn (Norwich: TSO, 2013), copyright page, p. 35.
3. Akira Usuda, *The Hidden Diary of Mr Pepys* (Iwanami Shoten, 1982); Pepys, *Die Tagebücher 1660–1669*, ed. by Gerd Haffmans and Heiko Arntz (Frankfurt: Haffmans bei Zweitausendeins, 2010).

4. Department for Education, *The National Curriculum in England: History Programmes of Study* (11 Sept. 2013), Key Stage 1.
5. Deborah Swift's *Pleasing Mr Pepys* (Cardiff: Accent, 2017), *A Plague on Mr Pepys* (Cardiff: Accent, 2018), and *Entertaining Mr Pepys* (London: Headline Accent, 2019).
6. *17c*, dir. by Annie-B. Parson, The Big Dance Theater (2017), www.bigdancetheater.org/shows/pepys/. The production toured the US and played in London in 2018.
7. [Hunt], *Edinburgh Review*, Oct. 1841, p. 108.
8. 'Notice' by George Bell and Sons, *Publishers' Circular*, 16 Nov. 1875, p. 938.
9. [Jeffrey], *Edinburgh Review*, Nov. 1825, p. 27; [Scott], *Quarterly Review*, Mar. 1826, p. 309.
10. [Snow], *Gentleman's Magazine*, Sept. 1825, p. 233.
11. Wheatley, 'Growth of the Fame of Samuel Pepys', p. 162; Bryant, *Years of Peril*, p. xii.
12. [Stevenson], 'Samuel Pepys', p. 41.
13. Magdalene, F/CSL/2(f), Lewis to Willink, 12 June 1960; 'Buffet', no. 48, Bickers to Turner, 14 Feb. 1936.
14. TNA, PROB 1/9, Will of Samuel Pepys (1703), codicil, 12 May 1703; Obscene Publications Act 1959, section 4(1).
15. *Monthly Repository*, 20, Aug. 1825, p. 450.

Select Bibliography

Texts of Pepys's Diary

Pepys's Manuscript

PL 1836	1 January 1660 to 30 June 1661
PL 1837	1 July 1661 to 30 June 1663
PL 1838	1 July 1663 to 30 June 1665
PL 1839	1 July 1665 to 28 February 1667
PL 1840	1 March 1667 to 30 April 1668
PL 1841	1 May 1668 to 31 May 1669

Braybrooke, Richard Griffin, third baron, ed., *Diary and Correspondence of Samuel Pepys F.R.S. [...]. The Third Edition, Considerably Enlarged*, 5 vols (London: Henry Colburn, 1848–9)
  Diary and Correspondence of Samuel Pepys, F.R.S. [...]. The Diary Deciphered by Rev. J. Smith [...] the Fourth Edition, Revised and Corrected, 4 vols (London: for Henry Colburn by Hurst and Blackett, 1854)
  Memoirs of Samuel Pepys, Esq. F.R.S. [...] Comprising his Diary from 1659 to 1669, Deciphered by the Rev. John Smith [...] and A Selection from his Private Correspondence, 2 vols (London: Henry Colburn, 1825)
Bright, Mynors, ed., *Diary and Correspondence of Samuel Pepys, Esq., F.R.S.*, 6 vols (London: Bickers and Son, 1875–9)
Latham, Robert, ed., *The Shorter Pepys* (London: Penguin, 1993)
Latham, Robert, and Linnet Latham, eds, *A Pepys Anthology* (Unwin Hyman, 1987, repr. London: HarperCollins, 2000)
Latham, Robert, and William Matthews, eds, *The Diary of Samuel Pepys, A New and Complete Transcription*, 11 vols (first published London: G. Bell and Sons/Bell & Hyman, 1970–83; repr. London: HarperCollins; University of California Press: Berkeley and Los Angeles, 2000)
Loveman, Kate, ed., *The Diary of Samuel Pepys, Selected from the Complete Diary (XI vols) edited by Robert Latham and William Matthews* (Knopf: New York, 2018)
Meeres, N. V. ed., *The Diary of Samuel Pepys: Selections* (London: Macmillan, 1913)
Morshead, O.F., ed., *Everybody's Pepys*, illustrated by Ernest H. Shepard (London: Bell and Sons, 1926)

Pepysdiary.com, run by Phil Gyford, www.pepysdiary.com
Wheatley, Henry B., ed., *The Diary of Samuel Pepys M.A. F.R.S.*, 9 vols (London: Bell & Sons; Cambridge: Deighton Bell, 1893–9)

Manuscripts

BBC Written Archives, Reading
Microfilm TV Drama Scripts 29/30, *The Diary of Samuel Pepys*, by A. R. Rawlinson
R9/7/33, *The Diary of Samuel Pepys*, Audience Research Reports

Bedfordshire Archives, Bedford
L30/11/330/174, Harriet Yorke to Amabel Hume-Campbell, Countess de Grey, 6 Aug. [1825]

Bodleian Libraries, Oxford
MS Rawlinson, Pepys Papers, A.181, A.182, A.185, A.186, A.194

British Library, London
Add. 78680, Evelyn Papers DXIII, item 17
R.P. 550, Box 8, 941B, George Hickes to Samuel Pepys, 9 Dec. 1701
R.P. 694, Box 10, 941B, Samuel Pepys, 'Notes – from my Conference this Day with Mrs D[awson]'

Imperial War Museum, London
Documents.9485, Private Papers of Mrs Constance Miles, 'War Diary', 10 vols

London Archives
CLC/199/TC/002/MS09659/003, Register of Saint Katharine by the Tower
CLC/521/MS00204, Journal of Nehemiah Wallington, 1630–c.1641

Magdalene College, Cambridge
A/41/1, Indenture between Ann Jackson [...] and the Master and Fellows, 1 June 1724
B/605/p.469/min 36 duplicate, 22 July 1933, Francis Turner, 'Mr Bryant's Life of Pepys'
B/610, Governing Body Minute, 20 July 1960
D/G/56(A) Documents and Correspondence relating to the decision to publish a full text of the diary (1960)

F/CSL/2(f), C.S. Lewis to Henry Willink, 12 June 1960
L/71/PLB, Box 3, file 66, Correspondence concerning diary editions from 1868 to 1896
L/71/PLB/75, William Wyndham Grenville to George Neville, 21 Aug. 1818 and 13 Dec. 1818
L/76/1(1), William Matthews Correspondence [with Robert Latham], 1970
LN 45, Correspondence of Latimer Neville regarding the Pepys Library and diary editions in the 1870s and 1880s
Pepys Library Reference Collection, 'Buffet', no. 48, G.H. Bickers to Francis Turner, 14 Feb. 1936
PSL 2.1.1–2.1.54 John Smith, 'The Private Journal of Samuel Pepys, Esquire, Deciphered and Transcribed from the Original MS' (1822)
PSL 2.2.4. 1a–4a Mynors Bright's transcription of Pepys's diary (1875), made in an edition of *Diary and Correspondence of Samuel Pepys*, ed. by Richard Lord Braybrooke, 4th edn 'revised and corrected' (London: Henry Colburn, 1854)

Magdalene College, Cambridge: Pepys Library

PL 2242, 'Papers Conteyning my Addresse to his Royall Highnesse'
PL 2851, Admiralty Letters, IV
PL 2861, Admiralty Letters, XIV

Mapperton House, Dorset

Journals of Edward Mountagu, first Earl of Sandwich, 10 vols

National Archives, Kew, London

PROB 1/9, Will of Samuel Pepys (1703)
PROB/11/325/434, Will of Sir William Batten (1667)
SP/29/267, fols 312–15, Thomas Middleton to the Navy Commissioners, 19 Nov. 1669
T70/75, Company of Royal Adventurers of England Trading into Africa, Minute Books, 1664–72
T70/100, Royal African Company, General Court Minute Book, 1671–8

National Maritime Museum (Caird Library), Greenwich, London

LBK-8, Letterbook of the Official Correspondence of Samuel Pepys

University of California, Los Angeles, Charles E. Young Research Library

William Matthews Papers (1940–74)

Print and Online Sources

Abbott, Wilbur C., 'The Serious Pepys', *Yale Review*, 3:3 (1914), 551–75
    'The Serious Pepys', in *Conflicts with Oblivion*, 2nd edn (Cambridge, MA: Harvard University Press, 1935), 1–30
Amussen, Susan Dwyer, *Caribbean Exchanges: Slavery and the Transformation of English Society, 1640–1700* (Chapel Hill: University of North Carolina Press, 2007)
Archer, Ian W., 'Social Networks in Restoration London: The Evidence from Samuel Pepys's Diary', in *Communities in Early Modern England*, ed. by Alexandra Shepard and Phil Withington (Manchester: Manchester University Press, 2000), pp. 76–94
Banham, Christopher, '"England and America against the World": Empire and the USA in Edwin J. Brett's *Boys of England*, 1866–99', *Victorian Periodicals Review*, 40:2 (2007), 151–71
Barrington, E. [Elizabeth Louisa Moresby], *The Great Romantic, Being an Interpretation of Mr. Saml Pepys and Elizabeth his Wife* (London: Cassell, 1933)
    'A Portion of the Diurnal of Mrs Elizth Pepys', *The Atlantic*, April 1921, 440–8
[Beadle, John], *The Journal or Diary of a Thankful Christian* (London, 1656)
Berger, Harry, Jr, 'The Pepys Show: Ghost-Writing and Documentary Desire in "The Diary"', *ELH*, 65:3 (1998), 557–91
Block, Mary R., 'For the Repressing of the Most Wicked and Felonious Rapes and Ravishments of Women: Rape Law in England, 1660–1800', in *Interpreting Sexual Violence, 1660–1800*, ed. by Anne Greenfield (London: Routledge, 2016), pp. 23–33
Botonaki, Effie, 'Seventeenth-Century Englishwomen's Spiritual Diaries: Self-Examination, Covenanting, and Account Keeping', *Sixteenth Century Journal*, 30:1 (1999), 3–21
Bradford, Gamaliel, *The Soul of Samuel Pepys* (Boston, MA: Houghton Mifflin; Cambridge: Riverside, 1924)
Brewer, Holly, 'Creating a Common Law of Slavery for England and its New World Empire', *Law and History Review*, 39:4 (2021), 765–834
Brunner, Emma Beatrice, *My Wife, Poor Wretch: Uncensored Episodes Not in the Diary of Samuel Pepys* (New York: Stokes, 1928)
Bryant, Arthur, *Samuel Pepys: The Man in the Making* (Cambridge: Cambridge University Press, 1933)
    Samuel Pepys: The Man in the Making, new edn (London: Collins, 1947)
    Samuel Pepys: The Saviour of the Navy (Cambridge: Cambridge University Press, 1938)
    Samuel Pepys: The Saviour of the Navy, new edn (London: Collins, 1949)
    Samuel Pepys: The Years of Peril, new edn (London: Collins, 1948)
Bullard, Rebecca, *The Politics of Disclosure, 1674–1725: Secret History Narratives* (London: Pickering & Chatto, 2009)

Capp, Bernard, *When Gossips Meet: Women, Family, and Neighbourhood in Early Modern England* (Oxford: Oxford University Press, 2003)

Carter, Laura, *Histories of Everyday Life: The Making of Popular Social History in Britain, 1918–1979* (Oxford: Oxford University Press, 2021)

Chakravarty, Urvashi, *Fictions of Consent: Slavery, Servitude, and Free Service in Early Modern England* (Philadelphia: University of Pennsylvania Press, 2022)

Chaplin, W. R., 'The History of Harwich Lights and their Owners', *American Neptune*, 11 (1951), 5–35

'Comic Lives of the English Kings and Queens, no. 33, Charles II', *Boys of England*, 20, 6 Oct. 1876, 304.

Costello, Dudley, 'An Evening with Knipp', *New Monthly Magazine*, 87, Oct. 1849, 206–26

[Cunningham, Peter], Review of *Diary and Correspondence of Samuel Pepys vol. II*, *The Athenaeum*, no. 1080, 8 July 1848, 669–70

Dabhoiwala, Faramerz, *The Origins of Sex: A History of the First Sexual Revolution* (London: Allen Lane, 2012)

—— 'The Pattern of Sexual Immorality in Seventeenth- and Eighteenth-Century London', in *Londinopolis: Essays in the Cultural and Social History of Early Modern London*, ed. by Paul Griffiths and Mark S. R. Jenner (Manchester: Manchester University Press, 2000), pp. 86–106

Davies, J. D., 'Introduction' to Samuel Pepys, *Memoires of the Royal Navy 1690* (Barnsley: Seaforth; Annapolis, MD: Naval Institute Press 2010)

Davies, K. G., *The Royal African Company* (London: Longmans, Green and Co., 1957)

Dawson, Mark S., 'Histories and Texts: Refiguring the Diary of Samuel Pepys', *Historical Journal*, 43:2 (2000), 407–31

De Groot, Jerome, *Consuming History: Historians and Heritage in Contemporary Popular Culture*, 2nd edn (London: Routledge, 2016)

de la Bédoyère, Guy, *The Confessions of Samuel Pepys* (London: Abacus, 2025)

Dibdin, Thomas Frognall, *Bibliomania, or Book Madness* (London, 1811)

Dillon, Robert, *History on British Television: Constructing Nation, Nationality, and Collective Memory* (Manchester: Manchester University Press, 2010)

Dolan, Frances E., *True Relations: Reading, Literature, and Evidence in Seventeenth-Century England* (Philadelphia: University of Pennsylvania Press, 2013)

Doyle, Richard and Percival Leigh, *Manners and Cvstoms of ye Englyshe [...] to which be Added Some Extracts from Mr Pips hys Diary* (London: Bradbury & Evans [1849])

—— 'Mr Pips his Diary / Manners and Cvstoms of ye Englyshe in 1849', beginning *Punch*, 16 (1849), 112

Dresvina, Juliana, ed., *Thanks for Typing: Remembering Forgotten Women in History* (London: Bloomsbury Academic, 2021)

Emanuel, Phillip, '"[A]s Fast as Ships Return He Will Send Every One a Boy": Enslaved Children as Gifts in the British Atlantic', *Slavery & Abolition*, 44:2 (2023), 334–49

Evelyn, John, *The Diary of John Evelyn*, ed. by E.S. De Beer, 6 vols (Oxford: Clarendon Press, 1955)
Findlay, Elspeth, 'Ralph Thoresby the Diarist: The Late Seventeenth-Century Pious Diary and its Demise', *Seventeenth Century*, 17:1 (2002), 108–30
Finnemore, John, *Famous Englishmen, Book* II: *Cromwell to Roberts* (London: Black, 1902)
[?Fonblanque, Albany], Review of *Memoirs of Samuel Pepys*, *The Examiner*, no. 921, 26 Sept. 1825, 607–9
Foys, Martin K., and Whitney Anne Trettien, 'Vanishing Transliteracies in *Beowulf* and Samuel Pepys's Diary', in *Textual Cultures: Cultural Texts*, ed. by Orietta Da Rold and Elaine Treharne, Essays and Studies 63 (Cambridge: Boydell & Brewer, 2010), pp. 75–120
Freeman, R. M., *Pepys and Wife Go to It* (London: Hale, 1941)
[Freeman, R. M. and Robert Augustus Bennett] *A Diary of the Great Warr by Saml Pepys Junr* (London: Lane, 1916; 2nd edn 1917)
A Second Diary of the Great Warr (London: Lane, 1917)
Fuentes, Marisa J., *Dispossessed Lives: Enslaved Women, Violence, and the Archive* (Philadelphia: University of Pennsylvania Press, 2016)
Fuller, Thomas, *The Church-History of Britain* (London, 1656)
Glyn, Elinor, *Romantic Adventure Being the Autobiography of Elinor Glyn* (London: Nicholson and Watson, 1936)
Gowing, Laura, *Common Bodies: Women, Touch and Power in Seventeenth-Century England* (New Haven, CT: Yale University Press, 2003)
'Women in the World of Pepys', in *Samuel Pepys: Plague, Fire, Revolution*, ed. by Margarette Lincoln (London: Thames and Hudson, 2015), pp. 73–9
'The Great Fire of London', *The Juvenile Companion and Sunday-School Hive*, 24, 1 Apr. 1871, 85–7
Gunning, Henry, *Reminiscences of the University, Town, and County of Cambridge*, 2nd edn, 2 vols (London: Bell, 1855)
Habib, Imtiaz, *Black Lives in the English Archives, 1500–1677: Imprints of the Invisible* (Aldershot: Ashgate, 2008, repr. London: Routledge, 2016)
Hall, Kim F., *Things of Darkness: Economies of Race and Gender in Early Modern England* (Ithaca, NY: Cornell University Press, 1995)
[Hamilton, Anthony], *Memoirs of the Life of Count de Grammont* (London, 1714)
Heins, Marjorie, *Not in Front of the Children: "Indecency", Censorship and the Innocence of Youth*, 2nd edn (New Brunswick, NJ: Rutgers University Press, 2007)
Hill, Benny, 'Pepys Diary' (song), *The Benny Hill Show*, BBC (26 Apr. 1958)
Hughes, M. E. J., *The Pepys Library and the Historic Collections of Magdalene College Cambridge* (London: Scala, 2015)
[Hunt, Leigh], Review of *The Life, Journal, and Correspondence of Samuel Pepys* transcribed by John Smith [ed. by John Towill Rutt], *Edinburgh Review*, no. 149, Oct. 1841, 105–27
[Jeffrey, Francis], Review of *Memoirs of Samuel Pepys*, *Edinburgh Review*, vol. 43 no. 85, Nov. 1825, 23–54

Knighton, C. S., *Pepys and the Navy* (Stroud: Sutton, 2003)
Knights, Mark, 'Pepys and Corruption', *Parliamentary History*, 33:1 (2014), 19–35
Kohlmann, Benjamin, '"Men of Sobriety and Buisnes": Pepys, Privacy and Public Duty', *Review of English Studies*, 61 (2009), 553–71
Kunin, Aaron, 'Other Hands in Pepys's Diary', *MLQ*, 65:2 (2004), 195–219
Langhamer, Claire, 'Who the Hell are Ordinary People? Ordinariness as a Category of Historical Analysis', *Transactions of the Royal Historical Society*, 28 (2018), 175–95
Latham, Robert, 'Pepys and his Editors', *Journal of the Royal Society of Arts*, 132: 5334 (1984), 390–400
Looker, Peter David, 'Performing Pepys: Publication and Reception of the *Diary* in the Early Nineteenth Century' (unpublished PhD thesis, Australian National University, Canberra, 1996), http://hdl.handle.net/1885/145880
Loveman, Kate, 'Pepys in Print, 1660–1703', *Oxford Handbooks Online* (2015, rev. 2018), www.academic.oup.com/edited-volume/43514/chapter/364250822
  Reading Fictions: Deception in English Literary and Political Culture, 1660–1740 (Aldershot: Ashgate, 2008)
  'Samuel Pepys and Deb Willet after the Diary,' *Historical Journal*, 49:3 (2006), 893–901
  Samuel Pepys and his Books: Reading, Newsgathering, and Sociability, 1660–1703 (Oxford: Oxford University Press, 2015)
  'Women and the History of Samuel Pepys's Diary', *Historical Journal*, 65:5 (2022), 1221–43
Lubbock, Percy, *Samuel Pepys* (New York: Scribner's Sons, 1909)
Macaulay, Thomas Babington, *History of England from the Accession of James II*, I (London: Longman, 1849)
[Macaulay, Thomas Babington], Review of *The Constitutional History of England* by Henry Hallam, *Edinburgh Review*, vol. 48, no. 95, Sept. 1828, 96–169
  Review of *The Romance of History* by Henry Neele ('History'), *Edinburgh Review*, vol. 47, no. 94, May 1828, 331–67
McCay, Kelly Minot, '"All the World Writes Short Hand": The Phenomenon of Shorthand in Seventeenth-Century England', *Book History*, 24:1 (2021), 1–36
Mandler, Peter, *The English National Character: The History of an Idea from Edmund Burke to Tony Blair* (New Haven, CT: Yale University Press, 2006)
Matthews, William, 'The Diary: A Neglected Genre', *Sewanee Review*, 85:2 (1977), 286–3
  'Introduction' to Shelton's *A Tutor to Tachygraphy*, Augustan Reprint Society 145–6 (Los Angeles: William Andrews Clark Memorial Library, University of California, 1970)
Meldrum, Timothy, *Domestic Service and Gender, 1660–1750: Life and Work in the London Household* (Harlow: Pearson Education, 2000)
Mendelson, Sara Heller, 'Stuart Women's Diaries and Occasional Memoirs', in *Women in English Society 1500–1800*, ed. by Mary Prior (London: Methuen, 1985, repr. Routledge, 1991)

Miles, Constance, *Mrs Miles's Diary: The Wartime Journal of a Housewife on the Homefront*, ed. by S. V. Partington (London: Simon & Schuster, 2013)

Moorhouse, E. Hallam, *Samuel Pepys: Administrator, Observer, Gossip* (London: Chapman and Hall, 1909)

Moran, Joe, 'Private Lives, Public Histories: The Diary in Twentieth-Century Britain', *Journal of British Studies*, 54:1 (2015), 138–62

Newman, Simon P., *Freedom Seekers: Escaping from Slavery in Restoration London* (London: University of London Press, 2022), doi.org/10.14296/202202.978191 2702947

Nokes, David, 'Crowning Ceremony', *TLS*, 18 Mar. 1983, p. 263

Ollard, Richard, *Pepys: A Biography* (London: Sinclair-Stevenson, 1974, repr. 1991)

Pearlman, E., 'Pepys and Lady Castlemaine', *Restoration*, 7 (1983), 43–53

Peplow, David, *Talk about Books: A Study of Reading Groups* (London: Bloomsbury Academic, 2016)

Pepys, Samuel, *Catalogue of the Pepys Library at Magdalene College Cambridge*, VII, *Facsimile of Pepys's Catalogue, Parts i and ii*, ed. by David McKitterick (Cambridge: Brewer, 1991)

— *Letters and the Second Diary of Samuel Pepys*, ed. by R. G. Howarth (London: Dent, 1932)

— *Memoires relating to the State of the Royal Navy of England* (London, 1690)

— *The Pepys Ballads*, ed. by W. G. Day, 5 vols (Cambridge: Brewer, 1987), Facsimile I

— *Pepys's Later Diaries*, ed. by C. S. Knighton (Stroud: Sutton, 2004)

— *Private Correspondence and Miscellaneous Papers of Samuel Pepys, 1679–1703*, ed. by J. R. Tanner, 2 vols (New York: Harcourt Brace [1926])

— *Samuel Pepys and the Second Dutch War*, transcribed by William Matthews and Charles Knighton, ed. by Robert Latham, Naval Records Society 133 (Aldershot: Scolar Press, 1995)

Pepys, William Weller, *A Later Pepys: The Correspondence of Sir William Weller Pepys*, ed. by Alice C. C. Gaussen, 2 vols (London: Bodley Head, 1904)

Phillips, Mark Salber, *On Historical Distance* (New Haven, CT: Yale University Press, 2013)

— *Society and Sentiment: Genres of Historical Writing 1740–1820* (Princeton, NJ: Princeton University Press, 2000)

Picard, Liza, *Restoration London* (London: Weidenfeld and Nicolson, 1997)

Ratcliffe, Michael, 'Power and a Pimple', *The Times*, 27 May 1976, p. 10

Rawlinson, A. R., 'A Letter to Samuel Pepys', *Radio Times*, vol. 138, no. 1790, 28 Feb. 1958

Roach, Joseph, 'Celebrity Erotics: Pepys, Performance, and Painted Ladies', *Yale Journal of Criticism*, 16:1 (2003), 211–30

Robertson, Geoffrey, *Obscenity: An Account of Censorship Laws and their Enforcement in England and Wales* (London: Weidenfeld and Nicolson, 1979)

Rogers, J. A., *Nature Knows No Color-Line*, 3rd edn (New York, NY: Helga M. Rogers, 1952)

Rugg, Thomas, *The Diurnal of Thomas Rugg, 1659–1661*, ed. by William L. Sachse (London: Royal Historical Society, 1961)
Sam Pepys Joins the Navy, dir. Francis A. Searle (Ministry of Information, 1941), Imperial War Museum, www.iwm.org.uk/collections/item/object/1060019999
[Scott, Walter], Review of *Memoirs of Samuel Pepys*, *Quarterly Review*, vol. 33 no. 66, Mar. 1826, 281–314
Shelton, Thomas, *Tachygraphy* (London, 1641)
  Tachygraphy (London, 1691)
  A Tutor to Tachygraphy (London, 1642)
Sherman, Stuart, *Telling Time: Clocks, Diaries and English Diurnal Form, 1660–1785* (Chicago: University of Chicago Press, 1996)
Shyllon, Folarin, *Black People in Britain, 1555–1833* (London: Oxford University Press, 1977)
Smyth, Adam, *Autobiography in Early Modern England* (Cambridge: Cambridge University Press, 2010)
  'Money, Accounting, and Life-Writing, 1600–1700: Balancing a Life', in *A History of English Autobiography*, ed. by Adam Smyth (Cambridge: Cambridge University Press, 2016), pp. 86–99
[Snow, Joseph], Review of *Memoirs of Samuel Pepys*, *Gentleman's Magazine*, vol. 95, Sept. 1825, 233–40
Soffer, Reba N., *History, Historians, and Conservatism in Britain and America: From the Great War to Thatcher and Reagan* (Oxford: Oxford University Press, 2008)
Staniland, Kay, 'Pepys and his Wardrobe', *Costume*, 37:1 (2003), 41–50
Stapleton, Julia, *Sir Arthur Bryant and National History in Twentieth-Century Britain* (Lanham, MD: Lexington, 2005)
Steinitz, Rebecca, *Time, Space, and Gender in the Nineteenth-Century British Diary* (New York: Palgrave Macmillan, 2011)
[Stevenson, Robert Louis], 'Samuel Pepys', *Cornhill Magazine*, July 1881, 31–46
[Stevenson, William], Review of *Memoirs of Samuel Pepys*, *Westminster Review*, vol. 4, Oct. 1825, 408–56
Stewart, Alan, *The Oxford History of Life-Writing*, II: *Early Modern* (Oxford: Oxford University Press, 2018)
Stoler, Ann Laura, *Along the Archival Grain: Epistemic Anxieties and Colonial Common Sense* (Princeton, NJ: Princeton University Press, 2009)
Sweet, Rosemary, 'Antiquarian Transformations in Historical Scholarship: The History of Domesticity from Joseph Strutt to Thomas Wright', in *Revisiting the Polite and Commercial People*, ed. by Elaine Chalus and Perry Gauci (Oxford: Oxford University Press, 2019), pp. 153–70
Tanner, J. R., *Samuel Pepys and the Royal Navy* (Cambridge: Cambridge University Press, 1920)
Thomson, Ernest, 'In the Days of Pepys: The Diary Comes to Life on the Screen', *Children's Newspaper*, 22 Feb. 1958

Tomalin, Claire, *Samuel Pepys: The Unequalled Self*, 2nd edn (London, Penguin: 2012)

Toulalan, Sarah, '"Is He a Licentious Lewd Sort of a Person?": Constructing the Child Rapist in Early Modern England', *Journal of the History of Sexuality*, 23 (2014), 21–52

'"Unripe" Bodies: Children and Sex in Early Modern England', in *Bodies, Sex and Desire from the Renaissance to the Present*, ed. by Kate Fisher and Sarah Toulalan (Houndmills: Palgrave Macmillan, 2011), pp. 131–50

Trevelyan, George Otto, *The Life and Letters of Lord Macaulay*, 2 vols (London: Longman Green, 1876)

Trouillot, Michel-Rolph, *Silencing the Past: Power and the Production of History* (Boston, MA: Beacon Press, 1995)

Turner, James Grantham, 'Pepys and the Private Parts of Monarchy', in *Culture and Society in the Stuart Restoration*, ed. by Gerald MacLean (Cambridge: Cambridge University Press, 1995), pp. 95–110

UK Government, Obscene Publications Act 1959, c. 66, www.legislation.gov.uk/ukpga/Eliz2/7-8/66/contents/enacted

Walker, Garthine, 'Rereading Rape and Sexual Violence in Early Modern England', *Gender & History*, 10:1 (1998), 1–25

'Rape, Acquittal and Culpability in Popular Crime Reports in England, c.1670–c.1750', *Past & Present*, 220 (2013), 115–42

Walvin, James, *Black and White: The Negro in English Society, 1555–1945* (London: Allen Lane, 1973)

Wheatley, Henry B., 'The Growth of the Fame of Samuel Pepys', in *Occasional Papers Read by Members at Meetings of the Samuel Pepys Club*, ed. by Henry B. Wheatley (London: Chiswick Press, 1917), pp. 156–73

Pepysiana (London: Bell and Sons, 1899)

Samuel Pepys and the World He Lived In (London: Bickers and Son, 1880)

Yeandle, Peter, *Citizenship, Nation, Empire: The Politics of History Teaching in England, 1870–1930* (Manchester: Manchester University Press, 2015)

Index

Abbott, Wilbur Cortez, 12, 104–106
acknowledgements, 140–141
advertising, 32, 73–74, 85, 86, 87, 108, 109, 120, 130, 151
Anglesey, Arthur Annesley, 5th Earl of, 62
art, 94–97
Athenaeum, 87, 90, 151
Austen, Jane, 128

Bagwell, Elizabeth, 8, 92, 156, 161–163, 178
Barrow, John, 66
Batelier, William, 167, 168, 174
Batten, William, 167, 170, 171–172, 173, 174
BBC, 125, 126–128, 130
Becke, Betty, 5, 72, 112, 113
Bell (publisher), 87–88, 89, 110, 130, 133, 134, 136, 137, 138, 139–140, 141–142
Bennett, Robert Augustus, 117, 120
Bickers, Guy Henry, 133–134, 135, 149
Bickers and Son (publisher), 87–88, 93, 140
biographies, 79–80, 122
    of Pepys, 108, 110, 111–112, 113–116, 129, 152, 166–167
Birch, Jane, 8, 16, 37, 53, 152
Black people, 14, 152–153, 163–174
    small boy offered to Pepys, 165
    young man enslaved by Pepys (1670s), 165, 167
    young man enslaved by Pepys (1680s), 165–166, 176
    see also Doll (cookmaid); Jack; Mingo, Isay William
Boys of England, 102–103, 104
Braybrooke, Richard Griffin, 3rd Baron, 11, 71, 85, 91
    Diary and Correspondence of Samuel Pepys (1848–9)
        editing and publication of, 13, 84, 86, 87, 91–92
        reception of, 11, 83, 91, 94–100, 104
    Diary and Correspondence of Samuel Pepys (1854), 86, 87, 88

Memoirs of Samuel Pepys (1825)
    editing and publication of, 13, 64, 68–73
    reception of, 64, 73–83, 85–86, 90, 96, 181
    see also Smith, John
Memoirs of Samuel Pepys (1828), 85
Bright, Mynors, *Diary and Correspondence of Samuel Pepys* (1875–9), 13, 33, 42, 84, 86–88, 92–93, 103
Britishness. *See* Englishness and Britishness
Brooks, Collin, 120, 121, 129
Brunner, Elizabeth Beatrice, 112
Bryant, Arthur, 110, 113–116, 118, 121, 127, 129, 132, 136–137, 164, 166–167
Buckworth, John, 168
Butler, Samuel, 65, 74, 105

Castlemaine, Barbara Palmer, Countess of, 4, 72, 74
censorship. *See* diary (Pepys's diary of the 1660s), censorship of; obscene publications, laws on
Charles II, 4–5, 6
    coronation of, 4, 26–30, 42–44, 60, 86
    later reputation of, 49–50, 65, 78, 80, 101, 102–103, 104
children, publications for, 7, 85, 101–103;
    see also readers of Pepys's diary, young
Clarendon, Edward Hyde, 1st Earl of, 65, 105, 128, 131
Colburn, Henry, 66, 73–74, 75, 82, 86
Collier, Jeremy, supplement to his *Great Historical Dictionary*, 66
Company of Royal Adventurers into Africa. *See* Royal African Company
copyright, 84, 85, 87, 88, 138, 140, 143, 179
Costello, Dudley, 98–99, 111
Couturier, Georges, 130
Coventry, William, 34, 46
COVID-19 pandemic, 14, 132, 146–148, 150, 180
Creed, John, 17
Cromwell, Oliver, 3, 101, 104, 108

233

Cunningham, Peter, 12, 94
Cunningham, T., 67

dance, 178
Daniel, Mrs, 8
diaries (genre), 11, 12, 16–17, 18–19, 61, 65–66, 74–75, 117, 122, 123
diarists inspired by Pepys, 82–83, 124–125, 180
diary (Pepys's diary of the 1660s)
   as history, 11, 149, 181
      in the nineteenth century, 64, 72, 74–75, 76–81, 82, 84, 93, 101, 103–106
      in the twentieth century, 115–116, 133, 134–135
   as literature, 11, 71, 76, 78, 82, 101, 104, 105–106, 133, 134–135, 149, 181–182
   catchphrases in, 8, 40, 100, 108, 116
   censorship of, 1, 179
      in the nineteenth century, 70, 72, 75–76, 80, 84–85, 86, 87, 88–89, 91–93, 106, 156
      in the twentieth century, 133, 134–135
      see also obscene publications, laws on
   circulation of unprinted passages, 90–91
   comedy in, 24–25, 26, 29, 76, 78, 89–90, 106–107, 119, 129–130, 162, 163
   composition of, 20–21
   editions of, cheap, 85–86, 93
   editions of, major. *See* Braybrooke, Richard Griffin; Bright, Mynors; Latham and Matthews, *Diary of Samuel Pepys*; Wheatley, Henry
   electronic texts of, 149–150, 182; *see also* pepysdiary.com
   finances and, 19–21, 30
   first passage in print, 67–68
   first plan to publish (c. 1800), 67
   frankness of, 12, 89–90, 111, 112, 144, 151–152, 161, 175, 179
   health and, 24, 30
   longhand in, 32, 35, 39, 41, 42–45, 47, 60–61, 168, 170, 178
   manuscript of, 2, 21, 33, 40–41, 47, 58, 68, 140
   motivations for writing, 16, 17–20, 21–26, 29–30
   Pepys's names for, 16, 58
   Pepys's plans for, 30, 45–46, 48, 53–54, 58–61, 63, 82, 178; *see also* Pepys Library
   pleasure and, 19, 25–26, 29–30, 32, 42
   politics and, 5, 17–18, 51, 76–77, 78–79, 80
   polyglot in, 33, 39, 41–42, 44, 45, 70, 88, 136, 149, 156, 158, 175
   readers. *See* readers of Pepys's diary
   religion and, 18–19, 30, 41
   scandal in, 4–5, 72, 76, 77, 80, 103, 114, 179
   sex and, 16, 26, 33, 41–42, 44–45, 51, 134, 136, 156–160, 161–163, 175; *see also* diary (Pepys's diary of the 1660s), censorship of
   social status and, 23, 30, 168, 174, 180
   see also shorthand
Diary of Samuel Pepys (1958 TV drama), 111, 125–128, 130, 143
Dibdin, Thomas Frognall, 67
Doll (cookmaid), 168, 170
Doyle, Richard, 100
Dryden, John, 105
Dutch War. *See* Second Anglo-Dutch War

Edinburgh Review. See Macaulay, Thomas Babington; Jeffrey, Francis
education, 7, 85, 100–101, 103–104, 106, 177
Edwards, Tom, 165
Egg, Augustus Leopold, 95, 96
Elmore, Alfred, 96–97, 98
Englishness and Britishness, 3, 67, 99–100, 110, 115–116, 120–121, 129, 130, 177, 180
Evelyn, John, 26–27, 28–29, 39, 66, 68, 73, 77, 101, 127, 131
Examiner, 74, 78, 96

Finnemore, John, 101
First World War, 110, 117–118, 119–120, 180
Fischer, Christian Gabriel, 62
Freeman, Robert Massie, 117–121, 129, 130, 146, 181
   Diary of the Great Warr, 117–118, 119–120, 121
   Pepys and Wife Go to It, 118–119, 124
Fuller, Thomas, 51, 61

Gardiner, Gerald, 134–136
Gentleman's Magazine, 11, 94; *see also* Snow, Joseph
George IV, 78
Gibson, Chloe, 125
Glorious Revolution, 10, 49, 64, 166
Glyn, Elinor, 103–104
Grammont, Count of. *See* Hamilton, Anthony
Granger, James, 66–67, 76
Great Fire of London
   in Pepys's diary, 1, 6–7, 8, 26, 37–39, 46, 60
   in reception of the diary, 7, 71, 101–102, 106, 110–111, 112, 115, 124–125, 130, 145–146, 177, 179
Great Plague. *See* plague (1665)
Grenville, Thomas, 68
Grenville, William Wyndham, 1st Baron Grenville, 68, 69, 70
Gwyn, Nell, 74, 95–96

Index

Gyford, Phil, 132, 144, 146; *see also* pepysdiary.com

Hamilton, Anthony, 65–66, 76, 77, 105
Hayls, John, 94, 95, 96, 97
Henry, Sarah, 18–19, 34
Hewer, William (Will), 20, 25, 34, 59, 62, 66, 154, 155
    in fiction, 127
Hill, Benny, 110, 111, 128–129, 157
history
    concepts of, 11, 72, 74–75, 77–78, 79–80, 105–106, 117, 181; *see also* diary (Pepys's diary of the 1660s), as history
    Pepys's concept of, 56–59, 63, 81
Howe, John, 165
Howe, William, 17
Hunt, Leigh, 1, 90, 105, 178

Jack (enslaved to William Penn), 167
Jackson, Ann, 61–62, 178
Jackson, John, 59, 61, 62
James II
    as duke of York, 4, 5, 10, 25, 54, 55, 164
    as king, 10
    reputation of, 49–50, 51, 65, 71–72, 81
Jeffrey, Francis, 64, 76, 77–78, 79
Jonson, Ben, 76
Juvenile Companion and Sunday-School Hive, 101–102, 103, 110

Kinsey, Alfred, 134
Kneller, Godfrey, 94
Knepp, Elizabeth, 6, 8, 42, 95–96, 98–99, 156, 178

Lady Chatterley trial, 131, 134, 136, 137–138
Lane, Betty. *See* Martin, Betty
Lane, Doll, 8, 160
Latham, Eileen, 141
Latham, Linnet, 141
Latham, Robert, 24, 33, 138–142; *see also* Latham and Matthews, *Diary of Samuel Pepys*
Latham and Matthews, *Diary of Samuel Pepys*, 8, 14
    reception of, 11, 141–142, 152, 156–158, 177
    treatment of sex in, 136, 156
    work on, 33, 37–39, 69, 131–132, 138–141, 149
Laud, William, 51, 61
Lawrence, D. H., 131, 134, 137, 149; *see also* Lady Chatterley trial
Leigh, Percival. *See Punch*
Lewis, C. S., 136–137, 149
Leycester, Ralph, 67
life-writing, 16, 19–20, 56, 65, 117, 122–123; *see also* diaries (genre)

Literary Gazette, 73–74, 75, 77
literature, concepts of, 11, 104, 106, 134–135, 182; *see also* diary (Pepys's diary of the 1660s), as literature
Lowell, James Russell, 89–90, 105, 107

Macaulay, Thomas Babington, 64, 75, 79–81, 83
Magdalene College, Cambridge
    custodians of Pepys's diary, 1, 2, 10, 59, 60, 84, 178
    nineteenth-century publication of Pepys's diary, 68, 79, 82, 88, 89
    Pepys attends, 3
    transfer of Pepys's library to, 61–62
    twentieth-century publication of Pepys's diary, 131, 132, 134, 136–138, 139–140, 149
    see also Pepys Library
Martin, Betty, 8, 41, 88–89, 91, 160, 174
Mass Observation, 122, 123
Matthews, Lois, 139, 141
Matthews, William, 16, 20, 33, 42, 138–142; *see also* Latham and Matthews, *Diary of Samuel Pepys*
Middleton, Thomas, 173–174
Miles, Constance, 122–125, 129, 130
Mingo, Isay William, 164, 167, 170–174, 175–176
Mitchell, Betty, 8
Mountagu, Edward, 1st Earl of Sandwich, 3–4, 5, 72, 73, 114, 127, 154–155, 164
    journal of, 17, 26
Mountagu, Edward, Viscount Hinchingbrooke, 154
Mountagu, Jemimah, Countess of Sandwich, 112
Mundy, Peter, 17
music hall, 129

Nabokov, Vladimir, 131, 136, 149
Navy Board, 5, 24–25, 54, 173
Neville, George, 68, 71, 85
Neville, Latimer, 85, 87, 89
New Monthly Magazine, 97–98
newsbooks, 17, 18, 28, 29
Newton, Isaac, 34
novels, historical, 78, 79, 82, 97–99, 111–113, 129, 178, 181; *see also* secret histories

obscene publications, laws on, 4, 131, 132–133, 134–138, 149, 179
ordinariness, 80, 108, 117, 121, 180

paintings. *See* art
pandemic. *See* COVID-19 pandemic
parody, 99–100, 102, 103, 106, 117–121, 129, 146, 150, 180, 182
Payne, Nell, 8

Penn, William, 18, 24, 167, 168
Pepys, Elizabeth, 3, 72, 114, 142, 152, 153–155, 175
　death of, 9, 88
　"diaries" of, 110, 111, 112, 113
　drama about, 111, 126, 178
　fiction about, 98–99, 111–113, 118–119, 152
　marriage of, 7–8, 90, 92–93, 153–155
　papers of, 52–53, 153
　pictures of, 95–97
　potential reader of husband's diary, 35, 44
　rage of, 8, 92, 94, 98–99
Pepys, John (Samuel's brother), 45–46, 52
Pepys, John (Samuel's father), 3
Pepys, Lucas, 67
Pepys, Margaret, 3
Pepys, Samuel
　account of Charles II's escape after Worcester, 66, 69
　Catholicism and, 10, 49, 71
　corruption and, 9–10, 20, 24–25, 49, 51, 66, 71, 77, 78, 113, 114–115, 165
　enslaver, 9, 153, 163–164, 165–167, 168–170, 176, 181
　everyman, 110, 120, 125, 180
　follower of fashion, 5–6, 20, 71, 74, 76, 100, 101
　historian, 46, 50–51, 56, 63, 81
　Jacobite, 10, 49, 50, 51, 71, 81
　library, his. *See* Pepys Library
　life of, 3–10
　Memoires relating to the State of the Royal Navy, 50–51, 71, 81
　memorial to, 88, 89
　naval career of, 5, 7, 9–10, 20, 54–55
　naval papers of, 25, 54–55, 56, 58, 163, 165–166, 176
　naval reputation of, 66, 81, 89, 105–106, 114, 116, 127, 129, 181
　other diaries of, 9, 58, 81
　pictures of, 94–97, 103, 116, 126, 127
　pronunciation of, 2, 84, 102
　record-keeping and, 16, 20–21, 23–24, 50, 51, 52–55, 60, 63, 178
　representative of the English. *See* Englishness and Britishness
　representative of the Restoration, 2, 13, 100, 103, 104–105, 106, 179–180
　servants of, 8, 26, 32, 35, 72, 152, 158, 164, 166, 168; *see also* Birch, Jane; Hewer, William; Willet, Deborah
　sex life of, 7–9, 41–42, 152, 155–163; *see also* diary (Pepys's diary of the 1660s), sex and
　sexual abuser, rapist, 8, 9, 156–163, 175, 181
　will of (1703), 10, 21, 48, 59–60, 61–62, 67, 68, 82, 140; *see also* diary (Pepys's diary of the 1660s)
Pepys, Tom, 45–46, 52
Pepys, William Weller, 67
Pepys Club, 107
Pepys Library
　after Pepys's death, 2, 16, 21, 61–62, 66–67, 68, 69–70, 81, 82, 85, 140, 166, 176
　during Pepys's life, 10, 13, 48, 53–60, 63, 178, 181
　Pepys's plans for, 59–60
pepysdiary.com, 12, 14, 132, 143–148, 150
Percy, Thomas, 66
Pett, Phineas, 170
plague (1665)
　in Pepys's diary, 1, 5–6, 26
　in reception of the diary, 74, 95, 101, 106, 112, 115, 119, 125, 128, 146–148, 179
pornography, 135–136
Punch, 99–100, 103, 117, 120

Radio Times, 117, 125
rape, legal treatment of, 159, 160–161, 162–163; *see also* Pepys, Samuel, sexual abuser, rapist
Rawlinson, Arthur, 125, 127
readers of Pepys's diary, 2, 12, 180–182
　before first publication, 67, 68–69, 71
　early nineteenth century (*Memoirs*), 73–82, 177
　later nineteenth century, 83, 89–90, 92–93, 97–98, 104–106
　twentieth century, 122–125, 130, 132, 136–137, 156–158
　twenty-first century, 143–149, 150
　young, 100, 101–104, 106, 177–178
Restoration period
　Georgian views of, 64, 65–66, 76–77, 78–79, 80
　twentieth-century views of, 110–111, 115–116, 125, 156
　twenty-first-century views of, 144
　Victorian views of, 81, 101–103, 104–105, 106, 179
　see also Charles II
Revolution of 1688–9. *See* Glorious Revolution
Royal African Company, 164, 168
Rugg, Thomas, 17, 18

Sallis, Peter, 126, 128
Sam Pepys Joins the Navy, 116, 121
Sandwich, Earl of. *See* Mountagu, Edward, 1st Earl of Sandwich
Savage, Sarah. *See* Henry, Sarah
scandal. *See* diary (Pepys's diary of the 1660s), scandal in
Scott, Judith, 23

Scott, Walter, 64, 75–76, 77, 78, 82, 93, 105, 130, 149
  novels of, 78, 79, 181
Second Anglo-Dutch War (1665–7), 5, 46, 111, 114, 115
  Chatham, Dutch raid on, 7, 46, 101
Second World War, 110–111, 115–117, 118–119, 120–125, 129–130, 145, 150, 180
secret histories, 50, 51, 78–79, 82, 113
Sedley, Charles, 4, 75
Seething Lane, 5, 6, 23, 125, 167, 173
sex. *See* diary (Pepys's diary of the 1660s), sex and; Pepys, Samuel, sex life of; Pepys, Samuel, sexual abuser, rapist
Shakespeare, William, 74
Shelton, Thomas, 34–35, 36–37, 40, 58, 69–70, 82, 87; *see also* shorthand
Shepard, Ernest H., 110
shorthand, 2, 13, 32–45, 47, 49, 53, 178
  copyright and, 87, 140
  editors'/transcribers' handling of, 39
    Braybrooke, Richard Griffin, 3rd Baron, 33, 71
    Bright, Mynors, 32–33, 39, 42, 87
    Callendar, Hugh, 88
    Cunningham, T., 67
    Grenville, William Wyndham, 1st Baron Grenville, 68, 69
    Latham and Matthews, 33, 37–39, 138–139
    Smith, John, 68–70, 82
    Wheatley, Henry, 33, 138
  extra protections and, 33, 41–42, 44–45, 178
  identification of Pepys's system, 69–70, 87
  images of, 38, 43, 45, 169, 171
  in England, 33–34
  influence on Pepys's prose, 40, 47
  manuals, 34, 36, 56, 58, 60, 67, 69–70
  Pepys's notes in, 20–21
  Shelton's *Tachygraphy* (Pepys's system), 34–38
Skinner, Mary, 9
slavery, 9, 163–167, 168–172, 174, 175–176; *see also* Pepys, Samuel, enslaver
Smith, John, 68–71, 73, 74, 81, 82, 85, 87, 91, 139
Snow, Joseph, 76, 77
soap opera, 128, 145
social media, 146–147, 150, 178
Stevenson, Robert Louis, 92–93, 104, 105, 113, 149, 182

Stevenson, William, 77, 78–79
Susan (cookmaid), 8, 156, 158–159, 175

tachygraphy. *See* shorthand
Tanner, Joseph Robson, 114
television, 125–129
Third Anglo-Dutch War (1672–4), 174
Tomalin, Claire, 18, 152, 153, 154
Tooker, Frances, 156, 158, 160
Truth (journal), 117
Turner, Francis, 132–133, 137, 138
Twitter (X), 146–147

Udall, Frances, 159–160

Vyner, Robert, 167

Wallington, Nehemiah, 19
Westminster Review. *See* Stevenson, William
Wheatley, Henry
  Diary of Samuel Pepys (1893–9), 13, 33, 84, 88–90, 93, 114, 130, 132, 135, 138, 139, 143
  electronic texts, 132, 142
  Pepys's fame and, 107, 114
  Samuel Pepys and the World He Lived In, 88
  work on Bright's edition, 88
whisky, 108, 109, 119
Wight, William, 154, 155
Willet, Deborah (Deb), 8, 9, 26, 32, 44–45, 47, 55, 154, 174
  in editions and reception of Pepys's diary, 70, 72–73, 86, 88–89, 90, 91–92, 93, 126, 132, 156–157, 178
William III, 10, 49, 115, 166
women
  editorial and publishing work by, 140–141, 149, 178–179
  in Pepys's diary and its reception, 8, 72–73, 152, 155–163; *see also* Pepys, Elizabeth; Willet, Deborah
Woolf, Virginia, 143
Wyborne, John, 165, 167

X. *See* Twitter

Yonge, Charlotte, 101
Yorke, Charles Philip, 77
Yorke, Harriet, 74, 77, 105